T0325479

# Value-Based Management in Government

I Founded in 1807, John Wiley & Sons is the oldest independent publishing company in the United States. With offices in North America, Europe, Asia, and Australia, Wiley is globally committed to developing and marketing print and electronic products and services for our customers' professional and personal knowledge and understanding.

The Wiley Corporate F&A series provides information, tools, and insights to corporate professionals responsible for issues affecting the profitability of their company, from accounting and finance to internal controls and performance management.

# Value-Based Management in Government

## DOUGLAS W. WEBSTER
## AND GARY COKINS

# WILEY

Published by John Wiley & Sons, Inc., Hoboken, New Jersey.
Published simultaneously in Canada.

For general information on our other products and services or for technical support,
please contact our Customer Care Department within the United States at (800)
762–2974, outside the United States at (317) 572–3993, or fax (317) 572–4002.

Wiley publishes in a variety of print and electronic formats and by print-on-demand.
Some material included with standard print versions of this book may not be included
in e-books or in print-on-demand. If this book refers to media such as a CD or DVD
that is not included in the version you purchased, you may download this material
at http://booksupport.wiley.com. For more information about Wiley products, visit
www.wiley.com.

***Library of Congress Cataloging-in-Publication Data is Available:***

ISBN 978-1-119-65867-2 (hardback)
ISBN 978-1-119-66012-5 (ePDF)
ISBN 978-1-119-66016-3 (ePub)

Cover Design: Wiley
Cover Image: © scnhnc052008/Shutterstock

Printed in the United States of America

V10016412_121919

# Contents

# About the Authors

DR. DOUG WEBSTER HAS EXTENSIVE EXPERIENCE BOTH leading and consulting to public sector organizations. He is a past CFO of both the US Department of Labor and the US Department of Education, where he led financial management for organizations with budgets exceeding $60billion. As the Director of Government-to-Government Risk Management for the US Agency for International Development (USAID), he led development and oversight of all risk management worldwide for USAID funding through foreign governments. As a management consultant to over two dozen public sector organizations, he has advised and led projects implementing cost management, performance management, risk management, strategic planning, and organizational realignment. He has also provided management consulting services in a dozen countries and worked in nonconsulting roles in over three dozen countries.

Dr. Webster is also an internationally recognized expert in Enterprise Risk Management (ERM). He convened the very first group of senior federal executives interested in ERM and guided that group in convening the annual Federal ERM Summits beginning in 2008. He then led the transition of that group into the Association for Federal Enterprise Risk Management in 2011. He has guided the development and implementation of ERM at both the USAID and the US Department of Education as a government leader, and has provided ERM consulting services to several federal agencies. He developed and taught a course on ERM for George Washington University, and has served as an adjunct professor in strategic planning, financial management, managerial accounting, engineering economic analysis, and business ethics. He is the coauthor of four books: *Activity Based Costing and Performance* (1994), *Chasing Change: Building Organizational Capacity in a Turbulent Environment* (2009), *Managing Risk and Performance: A Guide for Government Decision Makers* (2014), and *Value-Based Management in Government* (2019).

Dr. Webster is an elected Fellow of the National Academy of Public Administration (NAPA), Director Emeritus at Pentagon Federal Credit Union, and a member of the National Science Foundation Business Operations Advisory Committee. His certifications include Project Management Professional (PMP), Certified Government Financial Manager (CGFM), Certified in the Governance of Enterprise IT (CGEIT), Prosci Organizational Change Management, and the RIMS Certified Risk Management Professional (CRMP) (including federal certification). His degrees include a BS in engineering, MS in systems management, and Doctorate in Business Administration.

**Gary Cokins** is an internationally recognized expert, speaker, and author in enterprise and corporate performance management improvement methods and business analytics. He is the founder of Analytics-Based Performance Management, an advisory firm located in Cary, North Carolina; www.garycokins.com. Gary received a BS degree with honors in industrial engineering/operations research from Cornell University in 1971. and his MBA with honors from Northwestern University's Kellogg School of Management in 1974.

Gary began his career as a strategic planner with FMC's Link-Belt Division and then served as financial controller and operations manager. In 1981 he began his management consulting career first with Deloitte consulting, and then in 1988 with KPMG consulting. In 1988 with KPMG, Gary was trained by Professor Robert S. Kaplan of the Harvard Business School on implementing activity-based cost management (ABC/M) systems. He subsequently wrote several books on ABC/M. In 1992 Gary headed the National Cost Management Consulting Services for Electronic Data Systems (EDS), now part of HP. From 1997 until 2013 Gary was a principal consultant with SAS, a leading provider of business analytics software.

Gary is certified in Production and Inventory Management (CPIM) by the American Production and Inventory Control Society (APICS). He is active on committees with the Institute of Management Accountants (IMA) and served a three-year term in 2016–2018 as the IMA's Executive in Residence. He has served on the ABC advisory board for the International Monetary Fund.

His two most recent books are *Performance Management: Integrating Strategy Execution, Methodologies, Risk, and Analytics*, and *Predictive Business Analytics*. His books are published by John Wiley & Sons.

One interesting honor that few know about Gary is that he is in the Baseball Hall of Fame in Cooperstown, New York, for the "Oldest Computer Baseball Game," the result of his 1970 junior-year operations research game theory course project at Cornell.

# Acknowledgments

I WOULD LIKE TO THANK THOSE COUNTLESS INDIVIDUALS I have had the opportunity to work with and learn from over many years. Whether in my early military career, my subsequent consulting career, or my federal service career, every job and every encounter has influenced who I am today. To allow that learning and collaboration to take place, however, I must acknowledge my wife of 44 years, Connie. She has been by my side every step of the way, put up with late nights and extended time away from home, and all the other elements of life that test one's patience. The emotional support and love she has provided have been every bit as important as the schools I have attended or the jobs I have held. Finally, I would like to thank my co-author, Gary Cokins. I have developed an approach to my interpretation of value-based management that I wanted to share with others. However, had I been waiting on myself to write such a book, it would likely have been years more to reach fruition. Gary saw the value in this message and agreed to team with me to turn a vision into reality. I clearly recognize that without Gary, this book would not have been written for a long time to come – if ever.

Doug Webster
businessdr@aol.com
www.drdougwebster.com

I am forever grateful to my wife, Pam Tower, for tolerating my challenge to balance my work and family life. I would also like to dedicate this book to the late Robert A. Bonsack as a mentor and friend under whom I worked at both Deloitte consulting and Electronic Data Systems (now part of Hewlett Packard). It was a privilege for me to attend two prestigious universities, Cornell University and Northwestern University's Kellogg MBA program, plus gain meaningful experiences with consulting at Deloitte, KPMG, EDS, and SAS. But with privilege comes responsibility, and it is important for me to share what I have learned, some of which is in this book. Finally, I want to thank Doug Webster for co-authoring this book. There are three escalating "ships" – relationship, partnership, and friendship. Doug and I evolved to the third ship – "friendship."

Gary Cokins
gcokins@garycokins.com
garyfarms@aol.com
www.garycokins.com

# Foreword

THE UNITED STATES IS CURRENTLY THE WORLD'S major Superpower from an economic, military, diplomatic, and cultural perspective. However, the United States needs to learn from history and address the major challenges of today and tomorrow if we want to stay great and stand the test of time. For example, the Roman Empire fell for many reasons, including decline in political civility and moral values, fiscal irresponsibility, an overextended military, and an inability to control its borders. Does this sound familiar?

While the United States is currently the longest-standing republic, its current political system is neither representative of nor responsive to the general public. Too many federal elected officials are "career politicians" who are ideologically to the right or left of the "sensible center." In addition, they do not embrace the "problem-solver" mentality that comprises the majority of the American voting population. Current disgust with partisan politics and a lack of progress on a range of large, known, and growing public policy challenges (e.g., growing deficit and debt burdens, impending social insurance program insolvency, immigration reform, deteriorating infrastructure, health-care reform, climate change, and changing national security threats) has caused many Americans to be turned off and tuned out on the daily partisan political battles and current gridlock in DC.

The fact that Congress has passed timely budget and appropriations bills only four times in the past 45 years serves as clear and compelling evidence that Washington is broken and has been for a long time. Furthermore, the fact that over 40 percent of American voters, and growing, do not want to be identified with a particular political party serves to reinforce this disgust with the status quo. Clearly major budget, policy, and political reforms are needed to revitalize our republic, regain the trust of the American people, and restore our stewardship responsibility to current and future generations of Americans.

The authors of this book are well aware that major tax, spending, political, and other reforms will be necessary to create a better future for all Americans. They also understand that irrespective of the future role of governments at all levels they need to operate in a more future-focused, results-oriented, economical, efficient, effective, and sustainable manner. In order to do so, the federal government needs to place much greater focus on "value-based management."

This book provides an extensive overview of value-based management and how it can be applied to improve performance and ensure accountability in government. It properly recognizes that effective leadership and management requires taking some risks to achieve needed innovation and change. However, those risks need to be well understood and properly managed to achieve and sustain the desired outcomes.

This book can be a valuable tool for government leaders and managers who want to "lead by example" in improving the performance and ensuring the accountability of government for the benefit of the American people. The time to do so is now!

Hon. David M. Walker
Former U.S. Comptroller General

# Preface

THERE IS A GROWING IMPATIENCE BY TAXPAYERS, citizens, and governance boards with waste and inefficiency that is leading to demands for evidence of outputs, outcomes, transparency, and accountability. Terms like "doing more with less" and "value for money" are prevalent and aimed at governments at all levels – federal, counties, cities, municipalities, villages, and towns.

A key word in the second term is "value." This book is about how governments can increase the value to their taxpayers, citizens, and all stakeholders. The authors refer to this as "value-based management" (VBM).

Most governments have all the money to do *something*. However, they do *not* have all the money to do *everything*. This means they need to better prioritize and embrace productivity, effectiveness, and efficiency. They need to react. However, the longer they wait, the bigger will be the pain.

 ## HISTORY AND THE AUTHORS' BROADER VIEW OF VBM

The idea that organizations seek to create stakeholder value, and consideration of how that value is increased and ideally maximized, is a relatively recent evolution in management theory and practice. The industrial revolution dates back to the end of the eighteenth century and the age of "Scientific Management" began with the industrial engineering luminaries Frederick Winslow Taylor and Harrington Emerson in the early twentieth century. Yet various approaches for calculating financial value, such as return on investment (ROI), discounted cash flow (DCF), capital asset pricing model (CAPM), and others, did not develop until the twentieth century to advance the discussion of the elements of value. Not until 1986, however, when Alfred Rappaport authored the book, *Creating*

*Shareholder Value,*[1] did the concept of value begin to enter the management lexicon. The first use of the term "value-based management" comes from Jim McTaggart in his 1994 book, *The Value Imperative: Managing for Superior Shareholder Returns.*[2]

While the term "value-based management" has been with us since 1994, universal agreement has never been reached on its meaning. Moreover, the term has largely been used in relation to shareholder and owner value in commercial sector companies. With the dawning of concepts like risk-adjusted return on capital (RAROC) in the 1970s, activity-based costing (ABC) in the 1980s, and enterprise performance management (EPM) methods such as the balanced scorecard in 1992, the stage was set for a broader, more meaningful discussion of what it means to manage value. Unfortunately, VBM has become mired in its history and remains largely focused on financial shareholder value for commercial private sector companies.

This book seeks to present a much broader view of VBM. Understanding the concept of value to support decision making related to every human endeavor expands VBM to a fundamental management concept, not some narrow concept focused on financial management of private sector companies. This broader concept, which seeks to integrate considerations of results to be achieved, resources to be effectively and efficiently consumed, and risks to be appropriately accepted, is a universal management model that applies in every situation. VBM applies from selecting any individual decision at the operating level up to managing the very largest organizations. It is from this vastly broader concept of VBM that we share how any organization – public sector, private sector, or not-for-profit – can better achieve its full potential to create and increase value.

 **SOME THOUGHTS ABOUT "VALUE"**

Value is "in the eye of the beholder." One individual or family will evaluate the value of a particular automobile differently than another individual or family. Parents may have different sets of criteria in determining value, as will the

---

[1] Rappaport, Alfred (1986), *Creating Shareholder Value: The New Standard for Business Performance* (New York Free Press).

[2] McTaggart, James, M. (1994), *The Value Imperative: Managing for Superior Shareholder Returns* (New York: Free Press).

various children of the family. Similarly, organizations evaluate the value of the choices before them. However, while individuals make these decisions to support their self-interests, organizations must make decisions to maximize the value delivered to a much broader and potentially more diverse set of stakeholders.

Stakeholder interests in private sector companies must be considered and balanced as a whole, as many such interests – sometimes in conflict with one another – can be key to the organization's success. For example, shareholders seek a good return on their financial investment; customers seek value for money in the products or services they purchase; regulators seek compliance with laws and regulations; and employees seek competitive compensation, working conditions, and potential for advancement.

However, as diverse as these various stakeholder interests may be, public sector stakeholders in government can be considerably greater in number and even more diverse. Public sector agencies seek to meet citizen and taxpayer expectations, meet the needs of beneficiaries of particular services, comply with guidance from legislative bodies, and respond to many other stakeholder demands. Moreover, stakeholders of a public sector entity can have very divergent interests and expectations, thereby resulting in very different perceptions of what constitutes "value." Just a single government agency at any level (e.g., federal, regional, municipal), for example, may have to deal with multiple funding or oversight committees with very divergent interests and definitions of "value." This makes the articulation of overall value for a government agency's combined portfolio of products and services typically much more challenging in the public sector than in the private sector.

 ## OVERVIEW OF THE BOOK

The book's chapters are organized into eight parts:

**Part One** introduces the subject of VBM. It begins with an essay chapter regarding dissatisfaction by citizens, taxpayers, and stakeholders with their governments. The second chapter describes VBM, including the need to balance what is referred to as the three Rs: risk, results, and resources. The concluding chapter describes the component methods that, like gears in a machine, should ideally be seamlessly integrated.

**Part Two** describes the process of identifying key stakeholders, evaluating what those stakeholders consider to be of "value," and establishing strategic goals and objectives to be pursued in delivering that stakeholder value.

**Part Three** describes the shortcomings of enterprise performance management (EPM) as practiced to date, and how this book proposes an improved role for EPM.

**Part Four** contains three chapters that describe in depth the three Rs with a chapter devoted to each R.

**Part Five** contains six chapters that describe progressive management accounting practices and systems. It includes effective planning and budgeting, plus techniques to quickly implement these systems.

**Part Six** describes the role that information technology (e.g., software and databases) has as an enabler to inform and operationalize VBM.

**Part Seven** describes behavioral change management. Its premise is that resistance to change is human nature. People are comfortable with the status quo. There is need to overcome resistance and gain buy-in from those impacted by the changes required to achieve the full vision of VBM.

**Part Eight** describes the future of VBM that the authors envision with adoption of the VBM methodology and mindset.

 ## BALANCED VBM BUT AN UNBALANCED BOOK

Part Five, involving resource and cost management, is unbalanced in terms of the number of pages in the book compared to the other two Rs in Chapter 6 on risk management and Chapter 7 on results management. This is because author Gary Cokins has substantial experience with management accounting methods and practices, including writing several books and many articles on this subject.

Part Five discusses the full spectrum of management accounting not only for measuring past period consumption of resources and their resulting costs but also the forward-looking future view of budgeting and "what-if" trade-off analysis.

The extensive length of Part Five is intended to educate practitioners (including consultants) on the "how," not just the "why," to design and implement progressive management accounting in organizations. If you are not directly involved with the CFO's department, then the authors suggest that perhaps you read only Chapter 9 of Part Five and share the entire Part Five with accountants whom you care to influence to implement what is covered in this Part.

**CONCLUDING REMARKS**

The authors believe that taxpayers, citizens, and stakeholders will be substantially better and more economically served if governments embrace VBM and implement the methods and technologies that support VBM.

PART ONE

# Value-Based Management in Government Concepts and Components

# CHAPTER ONE

# Challenges and Solutions to Address Dissatisfaction of Citizens and Taxpayers

G OVERNMENT DEPARTMENTS AND AGENCIES at all levels are challenged to improve program and service performance. Public sector agencies are becoming performance-centric and citizen-centric, and their long-term survival depends heavily on agency innovation and the ability to demonstrate value creation.

In the US, the President's Management Council, composed of Agency Deputy Secretaries and led by the Federal Chief Performance Officer of the Office of Management and Budget, is demanding accountability with transparency and demonstrated effectiveness. Agencies not demonstrating results must defend their program missions and budgets. Compliance now means a more stringent assessment of programs and services with fact-based communication of performance. Furthermore, funding support relies on the continual improvement of programs. The bottom line is that funding is tied to clearly demonstrating and articulating results. Agencies that cannot do so face the risk of having their programs reformed, constrained, or even terminated. Agencies also stand to lose their budgets and face negative publicity.

The US federal government is not alone on driving performance. State, county, municipal, and local governments as well as governments of countries throughout the world are responding to an increasing awareness of the need for fiscal spending responsibility and austerity. "More with less" is a common theme.

At the state and local levels, governors, legislatures, and citizens demand that agencies and departments provide transparency of their spending and demonstrate the benefit achieved in relation to government expenses. The same goes for international government agencies. Increasing budget crises with some agencies globally have prompted further scrutiny from lawmakers and the public for agencies to prove the effectiveness of their programs and services. Challenges for leaders now revolve around assessing costs, justifying budget requests, transparently assessing risk, and communicating expected and tangible results in the large context of driving value.

##  THE US'S ACCOUNTABLE GOVERNMENT INITIATIVE

There have been numerous government management improvement initiatives in the United States over the past century, such as the President's Committee on Administrative Management in 1937, the Commission on Organization of the Executive Branch of the Government in 1947 (also known as the Hoover Commission), the Private Sector Survey on Cost Control in 1982 (also known as the Grace Commission), and in 1993 the National Partnership for the Reinvention of Government. In 2001, President George W. Bush originated the President's Management Agenda to make government more "citizen-centered, market based, and results oriented" by focusing on human capital, financial accountability, e-government,[1] competitive sourcing, and budget and performance integration. In 2010 President Obama announced the Accountable Government Initiative to cut waste and make government more open and responsive to the American public. The announcement stated, "When government does not work like it should, it has a real effect on people's lives – on small business owners who need loans, on young people who want to go to college, on the men and women in our Armed Forces who need the best resources when in uniform and deserve the benefits they have earned after they have left." Finally, in 2017, President Trump replaced the Accountable Government Initiative with a revised President's Management Agenda, which "lays out a long-term vision for modernizing the Federal Government in key areas that will improve the ability of

---

[1] E-government, or electronic government, is the use of computers, the internet, and other electronic means to provide public services (see https://en.wikipedia.org/wiki/E-government).

agencies to deliver mission outcomes, provide excellent service, and effectively steward taxpayer dollars on behalf of the American people."

According to the current President's Management Agenda, the "Federal Government has become overly bureaucratic and complex in ways that have prevented agencies from seamlessly transitioning services to meet the needs of the 21st century. Many of these challenges and shortcomings arise from statutory, administrative, management and regulatory practices designed in the past that no longer align to the realities of today."[2] The report goes on to list specific root cause challenges, including:

- Accumulated regulatory burdens
- Structural issues
- Decision-making and processes
- Leadership and culture
- Capabilities and competencies

The long history of management improvement initiatives in the US federal government demonstrates an ongoing recognition of the need for improvement in management practices. The history of such initiatives is a result in part of the changing needs for government management practices in the modern era. However, it also reflects increased insights into how those needs can be better met.

 **FROM PERFORMANCE-BASED MANAGEMENT TO VALUE-BASED MANAGEMENT**

A US government website article[3] states, "The federal government spent over $4 trillion in fiscal year 2018, but according to a Gallup poll, more than 60 percent of Americans are dissatisfied with federal government services. When pressed to explain which services cost too much or why they think Americans don't get what they pay for, there's no clear answer. Instead, a general perception exists, often created by partisan politics and the media."

A way to address this is to develop a uniform and consistent way to assess the cost-benefit trade-offs for each federal program. This is what the authors propose in this book.

---

[2] https://www.whitehouse.gov/wp-content/uploads/2018/03/Presidents-Management-Agenda.pdf, page 4.
[3] https://www.govexec.com/excellence/management-matters/2019/01/agencies-spent-4-trillion-last-year-did-taxpayers-get-what-they-paid/154087/.

The article continues, "There are currently 2,277 domestic assistance programs offered by the federal government, according to the General Services Administration. Federal agencies administer these programs, reporting their cost and performance to the public according to federal management legislation such as the 1990 CFO Act and the 1993 Government Performance and Results Act. While these decades-old laws have gotten us far, they didn't carry us over the finish line of fully-functioning performance-based management. We now have the opportunity to go the rest of the way. ... There is no comprehensive analysis of the 2,277 programs that administration and congressional staff can use to assist with their investment portfolio decisions."

This book proposes to go beyond the article's reference to "performance-based management" to "value-based management" (VBM).

What is needed to determine financial budget amounts for resources among government agency programs is framework like VBM for any government. To address this, like any effort to produce useful reports, one should first identify the users of cost and benefit data and understand how they will use the data. The article cites "There are four key decision-making groups to target with reporting improvements: program managers, senior administration leaders, the legislative body, and the public citizens and taxpayers."

As an example, with its 2006 Federal Funding Accountability and Transparency Act, the US Congress required the Office of Management and Budget (OMB) to create www.USASpending.gov. This website segments financial spending data into 19 budget "function" categories to facilitate a standard way for comparative analysis of similar functions. The result is that it displays a complete spending picture for the federal government.

At the end of each fiscal year, the agencies are instructed to revise their reporting on this website, then various stakeholders can evaluate any agency's overall performance as it relates to the cost of their services.

The article continues: "Merging cost and performance data in a way that significantly alters how Congress and the administration allocates resources and how Americans objectively gauge the performance of their elected officials has been the Holy Grail of performance-based budgeting for decades. It took a huge commitment of resources just to get to this point."

## WHAT DO GOVERNMENTS HOPE TO GAIN FROM VBM?

Six primary benefits for public sector organizations can be realized from implementing modern management methods:

1. Optimizing the use of resources
2. Aligning cross-departmental work activities and priorities with collaboration and increased accountability
3. Linking the budget and planning processes with an executive team's strategy
4. Displaying greater financial visibility and transparency for what outputs cost, and their drivers
5. Incorporating risk as an equal tradeoff consideration with results sought and resources committed
6. Maximizing overall stakeholder value delivered by the organization

The lack of alignment – typically a symptom of silo and bunker mentality – allows various departments to independently pursue their own pet projects rather than the more mission-critical ones to achieve their organization's overarching mission. Among taxpayers and governance boards, there is a growing impatience with waste in government. As previously mentioned, the phrase "more for less" increasingly appears in media editorials about government spending. A variation can be "more with same," meaning maintain the same level of resource spending but produce better and higher results.

Chapter 2 will define and describe VBM. Subsequent chapters will then take a deeper dive into the various components that comprise the VBM framework.

# Generating Value in a World of Uncertainty

ROM THE MOMENT WE enter this world as a baby until the moment we depart, we are constantly faced with choices. Those choices may range from the inconsequential to those having tremendous, life-long impacts. Those impacts can extend from us individually, to those immediately around us, and in some cases to many others around the world. Choices also differ from those that are very simple to make to those that are exceedingly complex and multifaceted. Choices can be focused on high-level, long-term objectives such as the selection of a professional career or interest, a more near-term selection of a university degree or educational program that will enable the choice of professional career, or even more near-term choices such as which classes to take, which professor to sign up with, or how much to study for an upcoming exam.

In all cases, however, individuals seek one general outcome for all choices: to maximize the value of that choice, whether in the short term or the long term. For example, if asked whether a two-seater sports car or an SUV offered greater value, a family needing to transport children to after-school activities might logically view the SUV as offering greater value while the bachelor or bachelorette might choose the sports car as offering greater value. Value as used here does not refer to which costs more. Instead, it is related to the perceived return on investment. Only in cases

9

where resources are unconstrained – a very unlikely scenario in the "real" world in which we live – does value reflect benefits absent consideration of resources consumed.

It is important to note that value is "in the eye of the beholder." One individual or family will evaluate the value of a particular automobile differently than another individual or family. Parents may have different sets of criteria in determining value, as will the various children of the family. Similarly, organizations evaluate the value of the choices before them. However, while individuals make these decisions to support their self-interests, organizations must make decisions to maximize the value delivered to a much broader and potentially more diverse set of stakeholders.

Stakeholder interests in private sector companies must be considered and balanced as a whole, because many – sometimes in conflict with one another – can be key to the organization's success. For example, shareholders seek a good return on their financial investment; customers seek value for money in the products or services they purchase; regulators seek compliance with laws and regulations; and employees seek competitive compensation, good working conditions, and potential for advancement.

However, as diverse as these various stakeholder interests may be, public sector stakeholders in government can be considerably greater in number and even more diverse. Public sector agencies seek to meet citizens and taxpayer expectations, meet the needs of beneficiaries of particular services, comply with guidance from legislative bodies, and respond to many other stakeholder demands. Moreover, stakeholders of a public sector entity can have very divergent interests and expectations, thereby resulting in very different perceptions of what constitutes "value." Just a single government agency at any level (e.g., federal, regional, municipal), for example, may have to deal with multiple funding committees with very divergent interests and definitions of "value." This makes the articulation of overall value for a government agency's combined portfolio of products and services typically much more challenging in the public sector than in the private sector.

The authors reject the statement made by some employees in government who say, "We are not a business." This is shortsighted. It is true that unlike commercial companies, public sector organizations cannot choose their customers and their goal is not to make a profit. But what else is different compared to a commercial company? Just like private sector organizations, government agencies and departments are responsible to attempt to optimize their resources and align them with the policies and strategies of their executive team, all with the purpose of best serving their citizens.

Today, public sector organizations are behaving more like businesses. They are converging with commercial companies in the ways they adopt businesslike improvement methods, such as Six Sigma quality and lean management practices. Many case studies from the private sector cite that using modern management methods has elevated a company's industry rankings and provided increased profits, market share, and customer satisfaction. Government agencies and departments can also expect improved service levels and financial performance.

 ## DEFINING VALUE

We noted that the fundamental management challenge facing any organization is to consistently make decisions that increase, and ideally maximize, organizational stakeholder value. However, while organizations can discuss the importance of generating stakeholder value for achieving success, that discussion will remain largely philosophical until one defines more precisely what is meant by "value." We began this discussion by suggesting that value was a function of both benefits or results achieved and the costs or resources consumed in achieving those benefits. We can define this as Value = Results achieved/Resources consumed.

However, at what point do we calculate benefits and costs? In a world of uncertainty, the projected value at any point in time is subject to change. This is because there is some level of uncertainty at the point in time when any initial decision is made to take action to achieve a future result. We thus need to add to this tradeoff a consideration of risk. Evaluation of stakeholder value therefore becomes a three-way balancing act, as depicted in Figure 2.1.

### Balancing Stakeholder Value

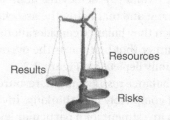

**FIGURE 2.1** Balancing stakeholder value. Source: © Douglas Webster. Used with permission.

All organizations are accustomed to considering the tradeoffs of results to be achieved for a particular level of resources invested. However, too often the analysis leading to a decision stops with a cost-benefit analysis at a point in time. There is no in-depth analysis of the risks faced regarding either the achievement of desired objectives, or the ability to deliver those objectives within the predicted level of resource requirements. Effective management requires that risk not be a minor consideration, or worse yet, a mere afterthought. The element of risk must be analyzed as thoroughly as the elements of results delivered and resources required. Only with a three-way analysis of results, resources, and risks can a decision maker expect to truly understand the options that offer greatest potential value. The importance of risk management will become even more important as we discuss the critical need to operate in a world of constant change.

As was noted, stakeholders define what constitutes value in ways that may be unique to them. However, the criteria for this determination can be generally thought of as a need to balance these three specific considerations. To summarize:

- **Results** as used in this discussion are those outputs and outcomes of any decision. That decision may be to deliver any one of thousands of services provided to citizens and taxpayers, complete projects or transactions required to run an organization, satisfy employee needs, and so on.
- **Resources** are those financial assets, nonfinancial assets (such as facilities and physical assets), time (of employees or others), and other elements of limited availability required to achieve a result.
- **Risks** are the uncertainties associated with achieving the results sought, the ability to achieve those selected results with budgeted resources, or both.

 **MAXIMIZING VALUE**

An organization delivers value by achieving desired results with available resources while recognizing and managing the associated risks. Organizations maximize that value when they balance considerations of results, resources (or costs), and risks in a manner that best meets the overall interests of key stakeholders. This is conceptually depicted in Figure 2.2.

This simple need to balance results sought, resources committed, and risks accepted is certainly not completely new thinking. Investors, for example, seek to maximize a return on investment for a particular level of risk that is deemed acceptable. This is illustrated in Figure 2.3.

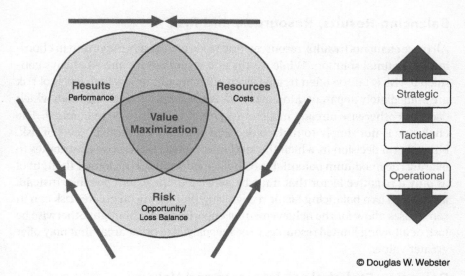

© Douglas W. Webster

**FIGURE 2.2** Maximizing stakeholder value. Source: © Douglas Webster. Used with permission.

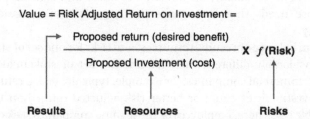

**FIGURE 2.3** Risk-adjusted ROI. Source: © Douglas Webster. Used with permission.

VBM brings the following to the management conversation:

- Results, resources, and risks must all be interactively balanced.
- Stakeholder interests can be diverse and internally in conflict, and maximum value generation requires balancing potential conflicts.
- VBM requires a portfolio management approach across the organization.

## Balancing Results, Resources, and Risk

All three elements (results, resources, and risks) are equally important in choosing the optimal solution. While results and resources are almost always considered, risk is far too often treated as an afterthought unless high levels of risk are immediately apparent. Moreover, risk is not simply a "gate" through which decisions otherwise already made must pass if value is to be maximized. The challenge is not simply to make a decision with an "acceptable" level of risk, but rather a decision in which the level of accepted risk directly contributes to offering the maximum potential stakeholder value. Risk is no longer thought of as only a negative factor that must be avoided to the extent possible. Instead, it is viewed as a balancing factor recognizing that taking on greater risk can in some cases allow for the achievement of opportunities that might otherwise be lost, or allowing limited resources to be redeployed to other areas that may offer greater value.

## Balancing Stakeholder Interests and Values

Achieving maximum stakeholder value requires explicit recognition of the diversity of stakeholder interests typically found in any organization. The goal is not to select a primary stakeholder and focus solely on their definition of value, but to consider all stakeholder needs and determine a balance among those needs that best meets the organization's mission, vision, and strategy.

The ideal balance of results, resources, and risks for one set of stakeholders may be considerably different than for another set of stakeholders. Shareholders of commercial companies, for example, typically seek a return on their financial investment at equal or better risk-adjusted rates than they might have available elsewhere. Employees of those same companies seek competitive compensation, satisfying working conditions, and potential for advancement. Customers seek value for money in the products or services they purchase, and regulators seek compliance with laws and regulations. Moreover, while these generalizations may characterize groups of stakeholders in general, there can be great diversity even among stakeholders of any one particular group.

## A Portfolio Perspective

Portfolio management at the enterprise level in balancing considerations of results, resources, and risks is perhaps the most significant addition of VBM to traditional management practices. The ultimate goal of VBM is not to maximize value for any one particular part of the organization, but rather for the organization as a whole. Organizations must therefore consider their business decisions in making tradeoffs among results, resources, and risks from an overall portfolio perspective.

Managing a portfolio of options to maximize overall stakeholder value is much like an investor seeking to maximize the value of an investment portfolio. An investor may invest in stocks, bonds, real estate, and various other options, and even leave some funds in cash. Such decisions are driven by a desire to manage the overall balance between return on investment and the level of risk reflected in the investment portfolio.

Viewing management tradeoff decisions for the overall organization from a portfolio management perspective of course means that all business units, functions, and other organizational partitions must be considered collectively in the balancing of results, resources, and risks. Seeking to maximize overall organizational value does not mean that subordinate parts of the organization do not consider actions they need to take to maximize value at their level. What it does mean, however, is that they are ready to adjust those decisions, resulting in less value for their particular undertaking or part of the organization, if doing so allows for reallocation of results, resources, or risks for the greater good of the overall organization. VBM thus explicitly recognizes that some programs, organizational units, or individual decisions may face suboptimization at the local level in order to contribute to greater value at the enterprise value. Isolation any one part of the organization from such discussions invalidates the essential portfolio view of VBM.

It might be, for example, that reducing resources to one part of the organization will suboptimize the potential value from that part of the organization, but the redeployment of those resources to another part of the organization increases the overall value of the organization as a whole.

It is critical to note that the need to maximize value applies at any level of the organization. Needless to say, executive levels must consider the strategic consequences of their decisions to balance results, resources, and risks. However, every decision maker at every level of the organization must be motivated to maximize value from their part of the organization. The need to balance results, resources, and risks is not limited to a particular level of the organization – it is in fact an inherent part of any management decision at any organizational level. Moreover, aligning the *entire* organization in pursuit of maximum stakeholder value means that there must also be an integration of requirements and capabilities vertically across the organization. This will be discussed in more detail later in this chapter, but it is important to note that creating a true portfolio management approach across the organization is not something required only of the executive team. It is an enterprise-wide imperative.

 ## BUILDING AN ORGANIZATIONAL STRATEGY TO DELIVER VALUE

Recognizing the critical importance of stakeholder value to any organization is simply a starting point. Delivering that value requires a number of organizational capabilities, competencies, and actions. The first of these is development of a strategy and strategic planning process that recognizes the importance of aligning three considerations: (1) the organization's mission, (2) the products and services delivered by the organization consistent with that mission, and (3) the alignment of diverse stakeholder interests with both the mission and the organization's selected products and services. This three-way tradeoff must balance a variety of considerations that hopefully guide the achievement of maximum organizational value delivery. This interplay of considerations can be depicted as shown in Figure 2.4.

In the private sector, any of these may potentially be the starting point for establishing an organization. As one example, an inventor or innovator may create a product or service that he or she believes will "set the world on fire." They may use this vision of a particular product or service to establish a mission of meeting a particular customer need consistent with certain organizational values, such as social responsibility considerations. Once these are defined at a high level, they may further consider investor needs, regulatory needs, subclasses of customer needs, employee needs, and other stakeholder needs.

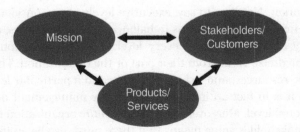

**FIGURE 2.4** Guiding organizational value. Source: © Douglas Webster. Used with permission.

As an alternative example, a group of individuals may decide to go into commercial banking because they perceive a general opportunity with an above-market financial rate of return. They are not necessarily seeking to employ a new product or service, but seek a competitive advantage through lower cost of operations or other means.

It is thus not essential that a strategy first start with mission, stakeholder analysis, or selection of the products and services to be delivered. However, it is required that all three be considered as part of a balancing act that creates a strategy delivering maximum stakeholder value. Once an initial strategy is established, however, the focus on the influencing drivers of revised or updated strategy may shift over time. For example, if an investor envisions a completely new product or service that has the potential to transform society, that product or service may be the starting point for discussions of tradeoffs in defining mission and multiple stakeholder interests. However, once an organization is established to deliver that product or service, with a clearly articulated mission, and while meeting various and potentially conflicting stakeholder interests, those considerations may easily shift over time. If, for example, the product or service remains leading edge after a year or two, but regulators take notice and begin to focus on that product or service with new and unique regulatory oversight, stakeholder interests may take a much larger role in guiding future strategy.

Research indicates that the majority of strategies fail to be executed effectively – a fact that is potentially the cause of increasing involuntary CEO turnover rates and validated by shorter CEO job tenures with commercial companies. One can conclude that developing a great strategy is not the problem; however, executing the strategy is. What is needed is an understanding of the required modern management methods not only to identify a strategy, but also to bring it to fruition. The same goes for government agencies to deliver on their mission and policies.

The need to balance mission, stakeholder interests, and the products and services provided by the organization (as illustrated in Figure 2.2) is not to suggest any particular order of analysis. The interplay between these three factors will be unique to each organization and may certainly shift over time. However, none of the three should ever be totally ignored in any organization seeking to maximize stakeholder value.

It should also be noted at this point that while the above is a general description of factors to be balanced in maximizing stakeholder value, the diversity of those interests is typically greater in the public sector than in the private sector. Key government stakeholders include beneficiaries receiving services from the agency (e.g., citizens), taxpayers who are funding the delivery of services, and legislative bodies that provide the funding needed to run the agency and provide services. Reaching an understanding of key interests from any one stakeholder body can be challenging.

As an example, in the US federal government, a single agency can have multiple legislative committees overseeing operations, prioritizing agency goals, establishing specific program requirements, and providing funding. Each committee can have subcommittees, and all of these legislative bodies can establish different priorities for different parts of the agency. Adding to this great diversity of stakeholder interests, there will typically be great diversity of stakeholder interest even within a single committee dealing with a specific part of an agency. A universal challenge for any decision maker is to understand the diversity of needs in relevant groups of stakeholders, and this challenge is often greater for public sector decision makers than for their private sector counterparts.

 ## BUILDING UPON A STRATEGY

The Cheshire Cat in Lewis Carrol's *Alice in Wonderland* had an exchange with Alice that has long been paraphrased as "if you don't know where you're going, any road will take you there." Knowing where you are headed is certainly the first requirement in undertaking any journey. The strategic planning process establishes strategic goals and objectives that set direction for the organization. However, once you know where you are headed, thought must obviously be given to how you will get there.

This requires translating or decomposing strategic goals of value to stakeholders into operational objectives for the overall organization. These goals and objectives are in turn decomposed and cascaded downward to lower organizational levels that are focused on delivering more specific elements of the higher-level objectives. This can be conceptually represented as shown in Figure 2.5. Whether evaluating the current capabilities of an existing organization or considering the capability requirements of a newly created organization, careful thought must be given to: (1) how higher-level requirements get decomposed and communicated down to lower levels of the organization, and (2) how existing as-is or need-to-be organizational capabilities and capacity are aligned to meet the delegated requirements.

While top-level organizational goals and objectives must be cascaded downward to derive subobjectives to be achieved by lower-level organizational components, it is critical to recognize that the capabilities of every part of the

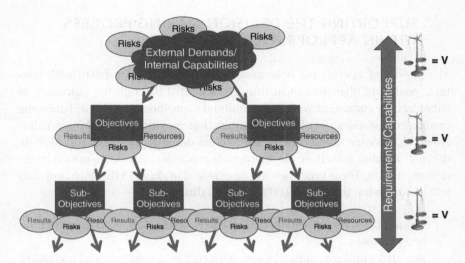

**FIGURE 2.5** Moving from goal setting to execution. Source: © Douglas Webster. Used with permission.

organization, regardless of the organizational level, must be aligned to deliver existing capability to meet those designated goals.

Setting direction for an organization obviously accomplishes little if the organization lacks the capability to deliver on meeting the defined objectives. It is thus a two-way conversation between adjoining levels of organization management to ensure that capabilities at any level of the organization are sufficient and fully leveraged to meet the objectives that are passed down to that organizational level. Through a two-way dialog between adjoining organizational levels, objectives can and should be fine-tuned based on the capabilities of the organization to deliver on those objectives, and organizational capabilities can be fine-tuned based on the objectives that are established for it. Through this iterative process across organizational levels:

- Stakeholder value can be maximized at each level of the organization – and ultimately for the overall organization as a whole – by having managers come together with their direct reports and engaging collaboratively in discussing the balancing of requirements and organizational capabilities.
- Simultaneous balancing is possible of results sought, resources allocated, and risks to be assumed.
- Lower-level objectives can be identified that must be accomplished in order to successfully achieve higher-level objectives.

**SUPPORTING THE DECISION-MAKING PROCESS WITHIN APPROPRIATE LIMITATIONS**

The pursuit of operational objectives derived from and consistent with strategic goals and objectives must thus be facilitated through the cascading of subobjectives consistent with organizational capabilities, and while balancing results, resources, and risks in a manner that maximizes stakeholder value. However, decision makers who seek to accomplish such an approach to decision-making must have the appropriate processes in place supported by the necessary data. These processes will be explored in detail in the book, but they will include what the authors refer to as the three Rs:

- Result objectives management for achieving results of outcomes, outputs, and processes
- Resources and cost management, with cost-informed financial budgeting
- Risk management and the role of Enterprise Risk Management (ERM) to integrate risk considerations across the enterprise

It must also be noted that the need to balance results, resources, and risks is not without some limitations. Decisions should in all cases comply with legal and business ethics considerations. While some individuals may consider such compliance as a risk consideration, the authors believe that compliance with laws and sound business ethics must always be viewed as constraints within which stakeholder value tradeoff decisions are made.

 **PROVIDING REQUIRED DATA FOR APPROPRIATE DECISION-MAKING**

In addition to having the required decision-making processes for maximizing stakeholder value by balancing results, resources, and risks, the relevant data must exist and be collected, validated, distributed, and used as appropriate in the decision-making processes. In many cases this requires appropriate information technology. Depending on the nature of data required for the organization's decision-making processes, organizations can potentially benefit from a multitude of techniques and technologies, including:[1]

---

[1] https://simplicable.com/new/decision-support.

- Decision algorithms: An algorithm is a procedure with a rigorous design. They can be used to make decisions or aid human decision-making.
- Search applications: A tool that searches a large repository of information such as the internet or a corporate knowledge management system.
- Data analysis tools: Tools that support statistical analysis of data sets.
- Reporting tools: Technologies that allow you to design and generate ad hoc or regular reports.
- Data analytics: Analytics is the automated discover of meaning in data. In many cases, analytics software is specific to a particular domain such as the analysis of web traffic data. The benefit of analytics is that users don't have to understand the underlying data and statistical models to obtain useful reports.
- Information visualization: A generic term for technologies that automatically visualize data or support human-driven design of information visuals.
- Data mining: Analysis of large sets of historical data typically using statistical models.

Technology barriers are an impediment to delivering stakeholder value. Causes for this are the lack of systems integration from various software vendors or homegrown legacy systems and from insufficient decision support information despite, in some cases, substantial raw source data. A simple way of describing this condition is that organizations are drowning in data but starving for information. This is one reason that the application of analytics, including leveraging Big Data, for insights on which to take actions is emerging as an important competency for all organizations to achieve.

The role of information technology will be described in Part Seven.

 ## MANAGING THE ORGANIZATIONAL CHANGE

Decisions can be made, but translating those decisions into sustainable actions can be challenging. Evidence abounds that attempted changes internal to organizations have a high risk of failure due to an organization's inability to implement and maintain new direction by the employees and others on whom the change is dependent.

A major obstacle to adopting or successfully implementing organizational improvement initiatives is cultural resistance to change. Another significant obstacle is that internal departments do not share information or collaborate. Combined, these two obstacles imply fear of being held accountable for results.

A third obstacle is when the executive team's policies and strategy are insufficiently communicated to their managers and employees.

While not the focus of this book, the critical importance of organizational behavioral change management in making significant change within any organization will receive further discussion in Part Eight.

##  GOVERNING THE VALUE-BASED MANAGEMENT FRAMEWORK

Pulling all of the above considerations together requires a governing process that ensures the organizational leadership collaborates to guide the organization toward maximizing value. This requires a communications and decision-making process that aligns and coordinates decisions intended to maximize value vertically from the top of the organization to the lowest levels – from the top desk to the desk-top. It also requires a decision-making process that coordinates laterally across the organization in a manner that eliminates silos of self-interest and a willingness to subordinate local interests for the greater organizational good.

For such a governance process to be effective in maximizing organizational value, it must integrate all of the elements of the value-based management (VBM) framework. This includes the governance of selected objectives and subobjectives, as well as the elements of results (performance), resources, and risks that must be balanced to maximize value. These are the three scales in Figure 2.1.

As a result, the financial budgeting process allocating resources, establishment of program performance targets, and the risk management governance process must all link together to ensure decisions made are done so fully recognizing the risk-adjusted cost-benefit of those decisions.

##  PUTTING IT ALL TOGETHER

To summarize the above points, we offer the value-based management model, or the "House of VBM," in Figure 2.6.

Here are the building blocks of the "House of VBM":

- ■ "The Goal" at the top of the house is what government organizations should aspire to: to maximize value for stakeholders.

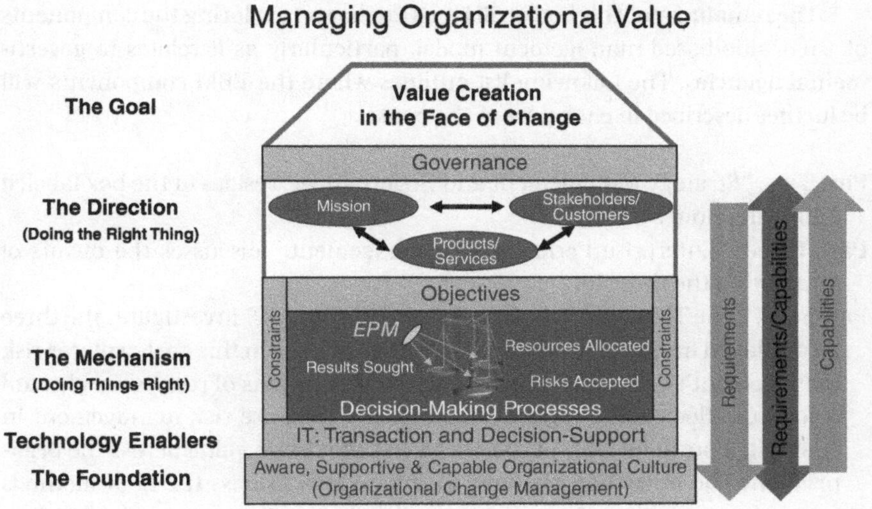

## Managing Organizational Value

**FIGURE 2.6** Managing organizational value. Source: © Douglas W. Webster. Used with permission.

- ■ "The Direction" is from Figure 2.2. It involves governance to oversee and guide the alignment of organizational mission, understanding and balancing of stakeholder needs, and delivery of products and services meeting those stakeholder needs
- ■ "The Mechanism" is from Figure 2.1. It includes the enterprise performance management (EPM) methods in the ellipse in the floor. The EPM methods contribute to the balancing of the three scales in Figure 2.1. The EPM methods, described in the Chapter 3, are continuously interacting to balance and improve the three scales: the three Rs, results, resources, and risks. This is where decision-making occurs.
- ■ "Technology Enablers" involve information technology (IT) that supports the modeling and calculations used by ERM and the EPM methods (including resources and cost management).
- ■ "The Foundation" is recognition that the core of any organization is its culture. Those people must have the understanding, motivation, skills, and abilities to execute and manage the components of the VBM framework. In many cases this will require a cultural shift in the organization.

The remainder of this book will focus further on exploring the components of this value-based management model, particularly as it relates to governmental agencies. The following list outlines where the VBM components will be further described in each part of the book:

Part Two, "Strategy Management and Governance," resides in the box labeled "The Direction".

Part Three, "Enterprise Performance Management," discusses the means of integrating the three Rs.

Part Four, "The Three Rs: Risk, Results, and Resources," investigates the three Rs displayed in "The Mechanism." The first chapter in this part explores risk management's role in helping balance considerations of results sought and resources allocated, along with the role of enterprise risk management in enabling a portfolio view of risk that helps maximize value across the organization. The other two chapters in this section discuss the EPM methods in results management, and managerial accounting practices, including (1) activity-based costing (ABC) to calculate the costs of services and outputs, and (2) capacity-sensitive driver-based budgeting and rolling financial forecasts.

Part Five, "Management Accounting in Government," consists of six chapters. Management accounting provides VBM resource information in the language of money. It explains activity-based costing (ABC) as an effective way to report the costs of outputs, including their per-unit cost. It explores driver-based budgeting and rolling financial forecasts, and concludes by describing how an ABC system can be implemented in weeks, not months, using a rapid prototyping implementation method.

Part Six, "How Information Technology Impacts VBM" – residing in the "Technology Enablers" foundation – will address the role of technology in facilitating the execution of the methods and processes used in results management, resources management, and risk management to maximize stakeholders.

Part Seven, "Influencing Behavior for VBM." As noted above, the Foundation of the VBM framework is a capable, motivated, and empowered workforce. While some organizations may already have a workforce able to execute the VBM framework, most organizations will require changes in that workforce. These changes will include: (1) development of understanding of the framework and implications for individual work activities, (2) motivation to become part of the revised organization and processes, (3) developing competencies in the use of new processes and methods, and (4) becoming a learning and growth organization that constantly seeks improvement in the delivery of value.

Part Eight, "The Future," describes the future of VBM that the authors envision with adoption of the VBM methodology and mindset.

The next two chapters in Part Two will describe strategy management and governance residing in the box labeled "The Direction" in Figure 2.6.

# PART TWO

# Strategy Management and Governance

# CHAPTER THREE

# Strategy Setting and Execution

## Setting and Linking Goals and Capabilities

 **MANAGING CHANGE AS A PREREQUISITE TO MANAGING VALUE**

Imagine for a moment a world without change. That was the basis for the 1993 movie *Groundhog Day*, starring Bill Murray. Every day that the main character awoke was set to become an exact repeat of the preceding day. The only change in that new day would be a direct result of a change that Bill Murray's character introduced. Other than his actions, the actions of everyone and everything around him remained the same day after day.

Putting aside the fact that living such a life might be rather boring, knowing each day how tomorrow's events would unfold would make for much simpler decision-making. The consequences of continuing past actions would be known with certainty. Of course, in the real world, we do not know what events will come with the passing of time, whether that is measured in years, months, or even hours and minutes. The world around us is always changing and is increasingly more volatile, and this of course brings uncertainty in what new challenges we as individuals or organizations will face.

Individuals and organizations both face two general types of change:

1. One is that from the world around us – that source of change that was magically put on hold in the Bill Murray movie. This change in the external environment in which we all live and work, but which is outside of our control and influence, is what has been called first-order change.[1] This is the change that occurs in the world around us external to our organizations, and which drives a need for our organizations to react in order to continue to meet stakeholder needs. We can also call this change "external change," as it is change in the external environment beyond our control.
2. The other type of change is that which we as individuals – as was the case with Bill Murray – or organizations initiate on our own to influence future outcomes. The effort to influence the future may be in reaction to today's environment, or in preparing to be better situated to meet an expected future environment. This change has been called second-order change[2] because it is often driven by the need to respond to first-order external change. We can also call this "internal change," as it occurs within the internal environment over which we have control or strong influence.

We can further differentiate internal change as that which is focused on reacting to today's environment, or change based on expectations of a future environment. In the former case, we will call this "reactive" internal change, because we are "reacting" to the current environment and seek to make changes to improve the effectiveness or efficiency of our actions, or to otherwise more successfully achieve objectives in the current environment. The second type of internal change is change we initiate in order to position ourselves or our organizations to better take advantage of an expected future environment. We will call this change "proactive" internal change, as we are seeking to proactively position ourselves or our organization for success in a future environment. These concepts are pictured in Figure 3.1.

As individuals, we employ both reactive and proactive internal change. For example, we may take actions to perform our work more efficiently or to achieve desired outputs more consistently, not because of external changes, but because of new insights to better meet existing conditions and demands. This is reactive internal change. However, we also employ proactive internal change to meet the needs of an expected future environment. For example, we

---

[1] Robert Thames and Douglas Webster, *Chasing Change: Building Organizational Capacity in a Turbulent Environment* (John Wiley & Sons, 2009), pp. 25–29.
[2] Ibid., pp. 29–33.

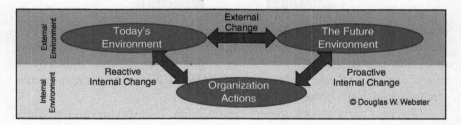

**FIGURE 3.1** Types of change. Source: © Douglas Webster. Used with permission.

may take training to prepare ourselves for future opportunities. We may also observe ongoing changes in society and consider how we can be better positioned to take advantage of those changes as they unfold.

Organizations similarly engage in reactive internal change to improve effectiveness and/or efficiency of their current operations. Improving internal controls on business processes is, for example, a reactive internal change intended to more consistently meet current business process requirements. Proactive internal change is also very important to organizations. A strategy is not static; it is dynamic. Proactive change is at the core of strategic planning and the setting of organizational goals and objectives intended to redirect existing and new resources to meet the needs of an evolving future environment and target new opportunities or manage potential problems and risks in that new environment.

Unfortunately, we too often focus our change efforts on reactive internal change to meet the needs of today while failing to position our organizations for success in a future environment. Consider the potential impact of such a limited point of view on change management, as depicted in Figure 3.2.

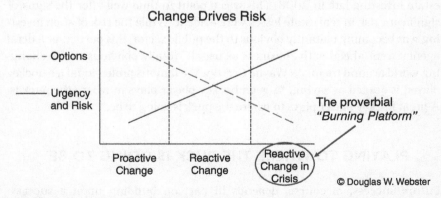

**FIGURE 3.2** Change drives value. Source: © Douglas Webster. Used with permission.

If we open our minds to considering what changes might best position our organizations for success in the future, we are likely to have more options available to us than if we are simply reacting to today's situation. We will also have more time to plan through our changes so that we are not constrained by an urgency to react. Of course, the worst situation is to have to implement reactive change when in the midst of a crisis.

History is rife with examples of organizations that reached an important level of success, yet failed to sustain that success by not responding to changes in the external environment. Names of American companies like Wang Labs, Circuit City, CompUSA, and Kodak immediately come to mind, and more recently Blockbuster and Toys R Us. Even the international financial crisis of 2008–2009 can be attributed to failing to respond to a changing external environment resulting from the US deregulation of financial institutions and bundling of risky subprime home mortgages as if they were safe investment instruments. While there are countless examples of private sector organizations failing to plan appropriately for the future, that challenge expands greatly in the public sector, including with government agencies.

Private sector organizations generally understand that they will cease to exist if they cannot effectively compete with competitors that better adapt to a changing environment. That dynamic is generally not present, however, in the public sector. Few public sector organizations "compete" for existence against other public sector organizations. While they may indeed compete for a limited overall budget, their very continuing existence is less likely at stake. As a result, a culture of considering only the "here and now" often permeates a public sector organization. As an example, one of this book's authors sat through a panel discussion sponsored by a US federal agency extolling the virtues of real estate investing late in 2008. This was a point in time well after the signs of significant risk in real estate losses were evident. While the risk of such investing was becoming blatantly obvious to the public sector, this particular federal agency went ahead with "business as usual," totally oblivious to the changing world around them. As Wayne Gretzky, the famous professional ice hockey player, is quoted as saying, "A good hockey player plays to where the puck is. A great hockey player plays to where the puck is going to be."

##  PLAYING TO WHERE THE PUCK IS GOING TO BE

Future success, of course, depends in part on building upon a successful present. If an organization cannot meet today's needs, it is particularly challenging to be successful in meeting tomorrow's needs. However, as has been stated, managing the present through reactive internal change is not sufficient to achieve such future success. We also need proactive internal change.

Because we are seeking to gain insights and make decisions regarding the future, we are operating in an environment of uncertainty. Managing the risk of that uncertainty in a meaningful manner is far too seldom considered a fundamental element of good management decision-making. Frequently, risk is considered only as a starting point for evaluating various options, or as an ending point to allow a decision that has already been tentatively made to proceed. In other cases, risk is treated as an afterthought once a decision has been made, or as a "check-the-box" exercise to meet some management or regulatory directive. Effective risk management requires much more. It requires an appreciation of how risk contributes to making an effective management decision aimed at generating increased, and ideally maximum, stakeholder value.

All organizations and their decision makers understand that organizational strategic objectives must be pursued, and hopefully achieved, while relying on limited resources. Cost-benefit analysis, whether conducted through a formal methodology or simply informal judgment, is always part of making management tradeoff decisions. However, except for certain business sectors, such as financial services and insurance companies, the explicit consideration of risk in arriving at a business decision has often been much less present. One of the challenges for the broader consideration of risk in decision-making has been the number of managers lacking exposure to more recent best practices in risk management. A strong case must be made to managers on the need for effective risk management as part of their day-to-day responsibilities for decision-making. Risk management must be understood to be a core management practice applicable to *every* decision maker, not simply a set of procedures conducted by a risk management department.

Making tradeoff decisions on the results delivered for products and services versus the costs of delivering those results are the typical cost-benefit considerations that every organization will exercise, even if informally. However, increasing stakeholder demands today in an environment that is more volatile and changing faster than ever (e.g., new and emerging technologies such as artificial intelligence) means that successful organizations will need more than cost-benefit analysis to sustain success. Instead they will need to understand the tradeoffs between results to be delivered through products or services, resources allocated to the delivery of those products and/or services, and the acceptable level of risk that supports delivering maximum value in the face of change.

**STRATEGIC PLANNING: AN ESSENTIAL ELEMENT OF NAVIGATING CHANGE**

In Chapter 2 we suggested that organizations are established to deliver value to their various stakeholders. However, that stakeholder delivery must be aligned with considerations of the organization's stated mission, and the products and services the organization produces, all while considering the effects of inevitable external second-order change.

The consideration of organizational mission and outputs (i.e., products and services) can often be modified or even radically changed in the private sector if doing so increases overall stakeholder value for the future. However, that is generally not true in government organizations, as missions and outputs are typically written into law or regulation, and significant changes need to come from stakeholders external to the organization.

Nevertheless, it must be recognized that there may be times in a national, state or provincial, or local government that the establishment of a new agency is under consideration. In these instances, the interactive balancing of unmet stakeholder needs, the definition of a proposed agency's mission, and the products or services the proposed agency would deliver are open to broad consideration and tradeoffs. In such a situation, it is likely that the discussion of stakeholder needs and the delivery of products and services to meet these needs would strongly affect the definition of the proposed organization's mission.

With this exception, however, the mission of any existing agency is generally well established and open to only relatively minor modification. Still, within the constraints of the existing mission, there may be opportunities to revise what are considered the primary products and services of the organization. There is certainly a need to understand stakeholder interests and needs as related to the purpose and outputs of the agency, which will in turn likely impact consideration of existing or proposed products and services and the means by which those products and services are delivered.

Regardless of the constraints placed on adjusting mission, outputs, and stakeholder interests, significant thought must be given to how these three factors interrelate, and changes to those relationships that could provide for greater value generation by the organization should be part of a strategic planning process. This is a core objective of the strategic planning process.

**LINKING STRATEGIC AND OPERATIONAL PLANNING**

The Balanced Scorecard Institute defines strategic planning as:

> an organizational management activity that is used to set priorities, focus energy and resources, strengthen operations, ensure that employees and other stakeholders are working toward common goals, establish agreement around intended outcomes/results, and assess and adjust the organization's direction in response to a changing environment. It is a disciplined effort that produces fundamental decisions and actions that shape and guide what an organization is, who it serves, what it does, and why it does it, with a focus on the future. Effective strategic planning articulates not only where an organization is going and the actions needed to make progress, but also how it will know if it is successful.

Particular attention should be paid to the idea that effective strategic planning is not only determining where an organization is going, but also to some extent "the actions needed to make progress." Too often organizations consider these steps as completely independent of one another by first setting direction, and only then giving any consideration to how to progress. For these organizations, "actions needed to make progress" are relegated to operational planning and the execution of a strategic plan already established. However, to develop an effective strategic plan, operational impacts and capabilities must be considered. The flaw in not considering operational impacts is that the development of operating plans is constrained by a strategic plan that did not consider operational capabilities. Establishment of any strategic goals must be set in the context of the abilities of the organization to deliver against those goals. This requires that strategic planning not be viewed solely as a boardroom or executive-level exercise that is not informed by lower levels of the organization, and as an exercise that is a top-down establishment of requirements without any bottom-up consideration of organizational capabilities, capacities, and need for change. To illustrate this two-way conversation that must take place in any large organization, let's reconsider Figure 2.5, repeated below as Figure 3.3.

The setting of top-level, long-term organizational objectives is certainly part of a strategic planning process. However, as potential strategic objectives are considered during the strategic planning process, consideration should also be

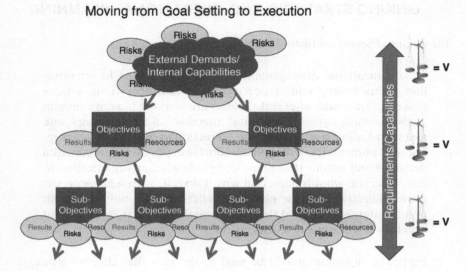

**FIGURE 3.3** Moving from goal setting to execution. Source: © Douglas Webster. Used with permission.

given to the subobjectives that must be achieved in order to successfully accomplish the highest-level objectives. As subobjectives are tentatively defined, those proposed subobjectives must be communicated to the next lower organizational level for review of feasibility of accomplishment with proposed resources and desired levels of risk. Pending preliminary agreement on subobjectives, those subobjectives should then be further decomposed and in turn discussed with the next lower organizational level to share expectations and agree on the proper balance of results sought, resources to be allocated, and risks deemed acceptable. As these top-level strategic objectives get decomposed and passed down to lower organizational levels for review and discussion, two important tasks are accomplished.

First, discussing objectives with those whose support is required to achieve the objective communicates the need for and rationale of the proposed change. This engagement helps ensure that lower-level actions on achieving objectives are informed by higher-level intents for those objectives. Second, these discussions may identify obstacles or challenges to accomplishing the objectives that were not identified and considered when originally proposed. Such a discussion by those who will be responsible for taking actions to achieve the objective may bring added insight into the challenges to achieving the proposed objectives.

By potentially increasing clarity on the level of results achievable, resources required, and risks to be faced, a more effective evaluation of the potential value to be delivered is likely. Moreover, such engagement between organizational levels can build support from those at lower levels from whom commitment will be required. Lower organizational levels typically want to know that their capabilities and concerns are understood by their next higher level of management, and that these capabilities and concerns are in turn taken into account in shaping higher-level objectives. This dialog thus becomes an important part of organization behavioral change to be addressed in more detail in Chapter 16.

It must also be noted that this passing of proposed requirements downward, and responding with capabilities and proposed adjustments to requirements upward, does not end at the top level of the organization. Conceptually, this movement could continue to the lowest levels of the organization. In large organizations, however, the number of conversations down through the organization and then back up to the executive level can take significant time, because these conversations must take place in series. The larger the number of organizational levels connected through these subsequent requirements/capabilities discussions, the more robust the final understanding and balancing of results, resources, and risks. However, this more robust understanding will require more time to achieve.

Careful consideration must be given to the time taken to plan for proactive change, as the external environment continues to shift in the meantime. In a rapidly changing environment, decisions made after passing discussions back and forth through many organizational levels may be out of date by the time those decisions are reached. Consideration must thus be given in balancing the improvements to understanding of the optimal balance of results, resources, and risks, and to the possibility that the optimized balance is applicable to when the strategic planning process started, but has since become inconsistent with a new external environment.

 ## THE QUEST TO OPTIMIZE STAKEHOLDER VALUE

While the determination of what constitutes value may be more challenging in the public sector than in the private sector, it is certainly no less important. Public sector organizations are generally faced with increasing demands for services in the face of ever-increasing budget challenges. While customers of private sector businesses can shift from one provider of products or services to a competitor when expectations are not met, that is generally not possible for citizens in the public sector. Expectations by customers of businesses can be high, and tolerance for failure low. Increasingly, citizens are having similar expectations as customers. There is an increasing impatience by taxpayers and governance boards with waste and inefficiency that is leading to demands for evidence of outputs, outcomes, transparency, and accountability. Terms like "more for less" are commonly heard.

It is thus essential that public sector managers understand the concept of stakeholder value and consistently seek to deliver that value. Simply spending the allocated budget – without concern for the outcome – is a certain road to failure. Accomplishing this objective requires considering that we are in a world of constant change, and future success will depend in part on successfully understanding future needs. A strategic planning process that vertically engages a sufficient part of the organization to ensure alignment between organizational objectives and capabilities will be required to successfully establish objectives delivering value in a world of constant change.

Chapter 4 describes in more detail one of the more popular strategy management methods that has the purpose of aligning the priorities and actions of managers and employees with senior leadership's strategy.

# CHAPTER FOUR

# The Strategy Map and Its Balanced Scorecard

THE BALANCED SCORECARD, THE methodology developed by Drs. Robert S. Kaplan and David Norton, recognizes the shortcoming of executive managements' excessive emphasis on after-the-fact, short-term financial results. It improves organizational performance by shifting attention from financial measures to managing nonfinancial operational measures related to customers, internal processes, and employee innovation, learning, and growth. These influencing measures are reported *during* the period when sooner reactions can occur. This in turn leads to better financial results.

The balanced scorecard is one potential approach to completing the linkage between the setting of strategic direction and the organization's ability to deliver on that direction, thereby supporting the full vision of VBM. Will the adoption rate of the balanced scorecard find the same difficulty crossing the chasms encountered by activity-based costing (ABC) systems in the 1990s? It took many failures in ABC system implementations before organizations learned what ABC is and how to shape, size, and level the detail of ABC systems before organizations began to get them ready and right for use. Are balanced scorecard implementations going to travel down the same bumpy road?

There is lack of consensus as to what a balanced scorecard is. To complicate matters, many organizations initially start with developing a balanced scorecard without first developing its companion and arguably more important strategy map from which the balanced scorecard's key performance indicators (KPIs) should be derived. Further complicating matters is that organizations confuse strategic KPIs that belong in a scorecard with operational performance indicators (PIs) that belong in a dashboard. The differences between KPIs and PIs are described later in this chapter.

##  LACK OF CONSENSUS

An early indication of trouble is the confusion about what a balanced scorecard is, and more confusion about what its purpose is. There is little consensus. If you ask executives whether they are using a balanced scorecard, many say they are. But if you next ask them to describe it, you'll get widely different descriptions. There is no standard – yet. Some executives say they have successfully transferred their old columnar management reports into visual dashboards with flashing red and green lights and directional arrows. Some realize a scorecard is more than that, and they have put their old measures on a diet, compressing them to a smaller, more manageable number of more relevant measures. Neither may be the correct method.

But how does anyone know if those measures – the so-called key performance indicators (KPIs) – support the strategic intent of the executive team? Are the selected measures the *right* measures? Or are they what you *can* measure rather than what you *should* measure? And is the purpose of the scorecard only to better *monitor* the dials rather than to facilitate the employee actions needed to *move* the dials?

Talk about balanced scorecards and dashboards seems to be appearing in business magazines, website discussion groups, and at conferences. Today's technology makes it relatively simple to convert reported data into a dashboard dial. But what are the consequences? What actions are suggested from just monitoring the dials?

In the VBM framework, results and outcome information should answer three questions: What? So what? And then what? Sadly, most scorecards and dashboards only answer the first question. Worse yet, answering the "what" may not even focus on a relevant "what." Organizations struggle with determining what to measure.

Organizations need to think deeper about what measures drive value and reflect achieving the direction-setting strategic objectives of their executive team. With the correct measures, organizations can then strive toward optimizing these measures, and ideally be continuously forecasting their expected results.

One of today's organizational problems is the disconnection and absence of alignment between *local* measurements of things a manager or employee can control or influence and the subsequent *organizational* results. Figure 4.1 reveals how dysfunctional measures create undesirable behavior and results. It illustrates the problem with a symbolic "wall of disconnects" that prevents the existing measures from aligning with the vision and strategy. The example used in the figure is a purchasing department. If you motivate the purchasing function to purchase the lowest-price supplies, equipment, and services, the purchasing function may look good, but other departments may end up having problems. You did not necessarily eliminate costs, but rather shifted costs elsewhere. Worse yet, you may have increased total costs. Strategy maps and a scorecard system remove this wall by selecting the few KPIs that point like vectors toward the organization's vision, mission, and strategy.

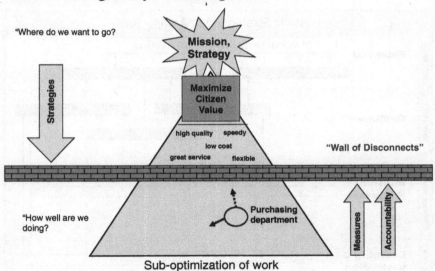

**FIGURE 4.1** Goal congruency and misalignment. Source: © 2019 www.garycokins.com. Used with permission.

**IMPLEMENTING TOO FAST AND SKIPPING KEY STEPS**

Why are so many people familiar with the term *balanced scorecard* but so few familiar with the term *strategy maps*? Strategy maps are orders of magnitude more important than the scorecard, which is merely a feedback mechanism. Why do executives want a balanced scorecard but without a strategy map? One possible explanation is the mistaken belief that those vital few KPI measures, rather than the trivial many, can be derived without first requiring employee teams and managers to understand the answer to a key question: "Where does the executive team want the organization to go?" This question is best answered by the executive team's vision and mission – and they must point to the direction they want the organization to follow them to. That is the executive team's primary job: setting direction. The strategy map and its companion scorecard are important, too, but their combination answers a different question: "How will we get there?"

Figure 4.2 illustrates a generic strategy map with its four stacked popular perspectives. Each rectangle represents a strategic objective and its associated projects or competencies to excel at plus their appropriate measures and targets.

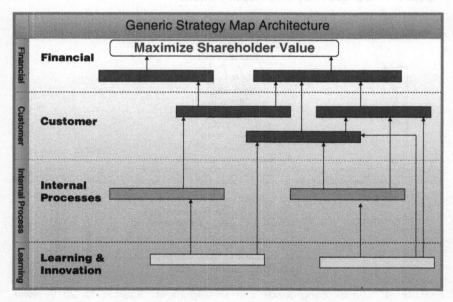

**FIGURE 4.2** Generic strategy map architecture. Source: © 2019 www.garycokins.com. Used with permission.

Note that there are dependency linkages in a strategy map with an upward direction of cumulating effects of contributions. The derived KPIs are not in isolation but rather have context to the mission and vision. To summarize a strategy map connects the linkages from the bottom perspective upward:

- Accomplishing the employee innovation, learning, and growth objectives contributes to the internal process improvement objectives.
- Accomplishing the internal process objectives contributes to the customer satisfaction objectives.
- Accomplishing the customer-related objectives results in achieving the financial objectives, typically a combination of revenue growth and cost management objectives.

The strategy map is like a force field in physics, as with magnetism, where the energy, priorities, and actions of people are mobilized, aligned, and focused. Its purpose is to fulfill the results for the VBM framework, leveraging cause-and-effect relationship linkages via feedback measurements to the organization.

The peril that threatens the success of this methodology is executive teams that are anxious to assign measures with targets to employees and hold them accountable. Executives typically skip three critical steps: (1) explaining their strategy to managers and employees so they understand it, (2) involving the managers and employees to gain their buy-in (and also commitment to the measures), and (3) the more critical prior step to identify the mission-essential projects and initiatives that will achieve the strategic objectives. The presence of enabling projects and initiatives goes to the heart of what distinguishes a strategic objective from just getting better at what you have already been doing. This linkage of using strategic goals to guide definition of supporting projects and actions is fully consistent with the decomposition of objectives discussed in Chapter 3 and shown in Figure 2.5.

An interesting question that is routinely asked is "Where is the organization's *strategy* defined and located on the strategy map?" The simple answer is that it does not appear. Why not? The reason is that the connected network of the strategic objectives is equivalent to the strategy! Strategic objectives suggest the actions that an organization must complete – or at least make much progress toward completing – or the core processes to excel at in order to achieve the organization's *strategy*, which in turn would realize its *vision*. The role of the strategy map is to communicate to employees and managers the direction the executives wish the organization to go. In short, the strategic objectives and supporting strategy map collectively are the strategy!

Figure 4.3 illustrates a modification of the strategy map for public sector organizations. "Maximize Community Value" replaces "Maximize Shareholder Value" for a private sector commercial company. Also, the financial perspective of the private sector strategy map is switched with a citizen/taxpayer/stakeholder perspective.

The list below displays the cause-and-effect flow of a strategy map's perspective from bottom to top.

■ A learning environment stimulates process excellence.
■ Process excellence leads to balancing of results achieved, resources/costs consumed, and risk accepted.
■ Balancing of results achieved, resources/costs consumed, and risk accepted creates value for citizens, taxpayers, and stakeholders.
■ The result is to maximize community value.

Figure 4.4 illustrates ideally who should be responsible for which one of five elements of each strategic objective: the executive team or the managers

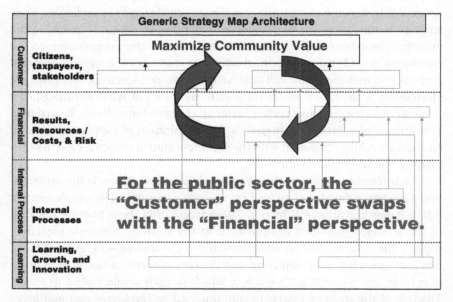

**FIGURE 4.3** Public sector strategy map. Source: © 2019 www.garycokins.com. Used with permission.

## Who Is Responsible for What?

| Measurement Period | 1st Quarter | | | | | |
|---|---|---|---|---|---|---|
| | Strategic Objective | Identify Projects, Initiatives, or Processes | KPI Measure | KPI Target | KPI Actual | Comments / explanation |
| Executive Team | X | ↑↓ | ↑↓ | X | | |
| Managers and Employees | | X | X | | *their score* | X |
| | | | | | <----- *period results* -----> | |

**A scorecard is more of a social tool than a technical tool.**

**FIGURE 4.4** Who is responsible for what? Source: © 2019 www.garycokins.com. Used with permission.

---

and employees. Sadly, many organizations neglect the first two elements identified in a strategy map. They begin with the third column to select KPIs without first constructing a strategy map. The performance management intelligence resides in the strategy map.

Strategy maps and their derived scorecard are navigational tools to guide the organization to *execute* the strategy, not necessarily to formulate the strategy. Executive teams are typically good at defining strategy, but a high involuntary turnover rate for chief executive officers (CEO) and the increasingly shorter tenure of CEOs are evidence of their failure to implement their strategy.

 **MEASUREMENTS ARE BOTH SOCIAL AND TECHNICAL**

Selecting and measuring KPIs are critical. You get what you measure, and strategy maps and scorecards serve a social purpose. Performance measures motivate people and focus them on what matters most.

Imagine if every day, every employee in an organization, from the cleaning person and janitor at the bottom of an organization to the CEO or managing director at the top, could answer this single question: "How am I doing on what is important?" The first half of the question can be easily displayed on a dial with a target; it is reported in a scorecard or dashboard. But it is the second half of the question that is the key – "on what is important" – and that is defined from the strategy map.

The risk and peril of the balanced scorecard involves the process of identifying and integrating appropriate cause-and-effect linkages of strategic objectives that are each supported by the vital few measures, and then subsequently cascading the KPIs down through the organization. KPIs ultimately extend into performance indicators (PIs) – operational performance indicators – that employees can relate to and directly affect.

The primary task of a strategy map and its companion balanced scorecard is to align people's work and priorities with multiple strategic objectives that, if accomplished, will achieve the strategy and consequently realize the endgame of maximizing shareholder wealth (or maximizing citizen value). The strategic objectives are located in the strategy map, not in the scorecard. The KPIs in the scorecard reflect the strategic objectives in the strategy map.

Debate will continue about how to arrive at the vital few KPIs for workgroups. Here are two approaches:

1. Newtonian-style managers, who believe the world is a big machine with dials, pulleys, and levers to push and pull, find appeal in looking at benchmark data to identify which relevant and unfavorably large performance gaps should therefore be areas for their focus. They want to know, "What must we get better at?" The KPIs are then derived. Strategies are then deduced from recognizing deficiencies.

2. In contrast, Darwinian-style managers, who believe the organization is a sense-and-respond organism, find appeal in having the executive team design the strategy map by applying a SWOT (strengths, weaknesses, opportunities, and threats) approach, which begins with the executive team freely brainstorming and recording an organization's SWOTs. They then cluster similar individual SWOTs into strategic objectives with causal linkages in the strategy map. Following this initial step, the middle managers and core process owners are then tasked with identifying the few manageable projects and core processes to improve that will attain the executive team's strategic objectives in the strategy map. After that step, those same middle managers can identify the KPIs that will indicate progress toward achieving the projects and improving critical core processes. This latter approach not only assures that mid-managers and employee teams will understand the executive's strategy, about which most mid-managers and employees are typically clueless, but it further generates their buy-in and ownership of the scorecard and KPIs since these have not been mandated to them from the executives. (Of course, the executive team can subsequently challenge and revise their lower

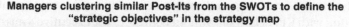

Managers clustering similar Post-Its from the SWOTs to define the "strategic objectives" in the strategy map

**FIGURE 4.5** Strategy map construction workshop. Source: © 2019 www. garycokins.com. Used with permission.

managers' selected projects and KPIs – debate is always healthy – but only after the buy-in and learning has occurred.) Figure 4.5 shows managers clustering their SWOTs into the strategic objectives with each perspective in the strategy map.

 ## SCORECARD OR REPORT CARD? THE IMPACT OF SENIOR MANAGEMENT'S ATTITUDE

Regardless of which technique or method is used to identify the KPIs, the KPIs ideally should reflect the executive team's strategic intent and not be reported in isolation disconnected, as typically the annual financial budget is disconnected from the strategy. This is the peril of the balanced scorecard. Its main purpose is to communicate the executive team's strategy to employees in a way they can understand it, and to report the impact of their contribution to attaining it. But starting with KPI definition without context to the executive's mission and vision denies this important step.

Research from Professor Raef Lawson when he was at the State University of New York, Albany, suggests that a major differentiator of success from failure in a balanced scorecard implementation is the senior management's attitude. Scorecard or report card? Will we use it for punishment or remedy? Do we work for bosses we must obey as if we were a dog ("roll over")? Or do we work for coaches, like on a sports team, and mentors who guide and counsel us?

As an example, is senior management anxiously awaiting those dashboards so they can follow the cascading score meters downward in order to micromanage the workers under their middle managers, acting like Darth Vader to see which of their minions may need to be cut off from their air supply? Or will the executives appropriately restrict their primary role and responsibility to define and continuously adjust strategy (which is dynamic, not static, always reacting to new insights) and then allow the empowerment of employee teams to select KPIs from which employees can actively determine the corrective interventions to align with the strategy?

The superior strategy map and scorecard systems embrace employee teams communicating among themselves to take actions rather than a supervisory command-and-control, in-your-face style from senior managers. An executive team micromanaging the KPI score performance of employees can be corrosive. If the strategy map and cascading KPI and PI selection exercise is done well and subsequently maintained, then higher-level managers need only view their own score performance, share their results with the employee teams below them, and coach the teams to improve their KPI and PI scores and/or reconsider adding or deleting KPIs or PIs.

 ## A DIFFERENCE BETWEEN VBM AND THE BALANCED SCORECARD

In Chapter 2 it was mentioned that the balanced scorecard is one of several methods used for strategy execution. Other examples are blue ocean strategy, "good to great," creating shared value, disruptive innovation, return-driven strategy, and reverse innovation. The authors chose to illustrate strategy execution using the balanced scorecard because it is a popular one.

VBM adds a variation to the balanced scorecard. Refer back to Figure 3.3, which is similar to how KPIs are cascaded downward to the managers and employee teams. These are also "subobjectives," which do not reside in a strategy map. The subobjectives are decomposed operational objectives that contribute to attaining the higher-level strategic objectives. Here is text from that chapter:

> This requires translating or decomposing strategic goals of value to stakeholders into operational objectives for the overall organization. These goals and objectives are in turn decomposed and cascaded downward to lower organizational levels that are focused on delivering more specific elements of the higher-level objectives.

Other than this variation the concepts remain similar.

 ## WHY NOT AN AUTOMOBILE GPS NAVIGATOR FOR AN ORGANIZATION?

Most new cars today have a global positioning system (GPS) route navigator. As with most new technologies, such as when handheld calculators replaced slide rules or laptop computers emerged, a GPS is another device that has evolved into a must-have for many of us. They get you to your destination without a hassle and offer a comforting voice to guide you along the way. Why can't an organization have a similar device? It can.

The refinement in usage of strategy maps and its companion balanced scorecard are becoming the GPS route navigator for organizations. For organizations the destination input into the GPS is the set of strategic goals. As earlier described, the executive team's primary job is to set strategic direction, and the "top" of their strategy map is their destination. However, unlike a GPS's knowledge of roads and algorithms to determine the best route, managers and employee teams must "map" which projects, initiatives, and business process improvements are best to get to the destination for achieving the strategic goals. In addition, when you are driving a car with a GPS instrument and you make a wrong turn, the GPS voice chimes in to tell you that you are off track – and it then provides you with a corrective action instruction. However, with most organizations' calendar-based and long cycle-time reporting, there is delayed reaction. The VBM includes a GPS.

Next, the organization as the automobile itself needs to be included. The motor and driveshaft are the employees with their various methodologies, such as customer value management and service delivery, that propel the organization toward its target. Collectively, the many methodologies, including lean management and activity-based costing, are two of the intermeshed gears of VBM.

But what important aspect of this automobile analogy is missing? Fuel efficiency. However, just like a poorly performing car with some broken gears, tires out of alignment, and gunky lubrication will yield poor gallons per mile (or liters per kilometer), the analogy is poorly integrated methodologies, impure raw data, and lack of digitization and analytics results in poor rate of shareholder financial wealth creation. The full vision of the VBM framework removes the friction and vibration plus weak torque, not only to optimize the consumption of the organization's resources – its employees and spending – but it also gets the organization to its strategy destination faster, cheaper, and smarter. The result? A higher shareholder wealth creation yield.

Finally, as mentioned earlier, a strategy is never static but is constantly adjusted. This means the destination input to the GPS navigator is constantly changing. This places an increasing importance on predictive analytics to determine where the best destination for stakeholders is located. How much longer do you want to drive your existing automobile when a VBM car with a GPS is now available to lift wealth creation efficiency and yield?

 ## FAILURES DUE TO ARROGANCE, IGNORANCE, OR INEXPERIENCE?

Some proposed management improvement methodologies, like the lights-out manufacturing factory touted in the 1980s, are fads that come and go. But the strategy map and its companion, the balanced scorecard for feedback, are most certain to be a *sustained* methodology in the long term. It only makes common sense that executive teams provide direction-setting and employee teams then take the actions to "get there." Are these early twenty-first-century missteps and misunderstandings in implementing the balanced scorecard due to arrogance, ignorance, or inexperience? This book proposes it is due to inexperience.

Conflict and tension are natural in all organizations. Therefore, it takes time among managers and employees to stabilize what ultimately is a behavioral measurement mechanism of cause-and-effect KPIs, to distinguish between KPIs and PIs; and to then get mastery with how to use both these types of measures to navigate, power, and steer as an integrated enterprise. As stated by the author Peter Senge, a thought leader in the field of organizational change management, the differentiator between successful and failing organizations will be the *rate*, and not just the amount, of organizational learning. Those intangible assets – employees as knowledge workers and the information provided to them – are what truly power the performance management framework.

 ## HOW ARE BALANCED SCORECARDS AND DASHBOARDS DIFFERENT?

There is confusion about what the difference is between a balanced scorecard and a dashboard. There is similar confusion differentiating key performance indicators (KPIs) from normal and routine measures that we can refer to as just performance indicators (PIs). The adjective "key" of a KPI is the operative term. An organization has only so much resources or energy to focus. To use a radio analogy, KPIs are what distinguish the signal from the noise – the measures of progress toward strategy execution. As a negative result of this confusion, organizations are including an excessive number of PIs in their scorecard system that should be restricted to KPIs.

A misconception about a balanced scorecard is that its primary purpose is to monitor results. That is secondary. Its primary purposes are to report the carefully selected measures that reflect the strategic intent of the executive team, and then enable ongoing understanding as to what should be done to align the organization's work and priorities to attain the executive team's strategic objectives. The strategic objectives should ideally be articulated in a strategy map, which serves as the visual vehicle from which to identify the projects and initiatives needed to accomplish each objective, or the specific core processes at which the organization needs to excel. After this step is completed, then KPIs are selected and their performance targets are set. With this understanding, it becomes apparent that the strategy map's companion scorecard, on its surface, serves more as a feedback mechanism to allow everyone in the organization, from frontline workers up to the executive team, to answer this question: "How are we doing on what is important?" More importantly, the scorecard should facilitate analysis to also know why. The idea is not to just *monitor* the dials but to *move* the dials.

## VITAL FEW VERSUS THE TRIVIAL MANY

Michael Hammer, the author who introduced the concept of business process reengineering, described the sad situation of measurement abuse in his book, *The Agenda: What Every Business Must Do to Dominate the Decade*:

> In the real world ... a company's measurement systems typically deliver a blizzard of nearly meaningless data that quantifies practically everything in sight, no matter how unimportant; that is devoid of any particular rhyme or reason; that is so voluminous as to be unusable; that is delivered so late as to be virtually useless; and that then languishes in printouts and briefing books without being put to any significant purpose. ... In short, measurement is a mess. ... We measure far too much and get far too little for what we measure because we never articulated what we need to get better at, and our measures aren't tied together to support higher-level decision making.[1]

Hammer is clearly not hiding his feelings. But has the cure been worse than the ailment? Simply reducing the number of measures can still result in an organization measuring what it *can* measure as opposed to what it *should* measure. But to determine what you *should* measure requires deeper understanding of the underlying purposes of a balanced scorecard relative to a dashboard.

## SCORECARDS AND DASHBOARDS SERVE DIFFERENT PURPOSES

The two terms – scorecards and dashboards – have a tendency to confuse, or rather get used interchangeably, when each brings a different set of capabilities. The sources of the confusion are:

- Both represent a way to track results.
- Both make use of traffic lights, dials, sliders, and other visual aids.
- Both can have targets, thresholds, and alert messages.
- Both can provide drill-down to other metrics and reports.

---

[1] Michael Hammer, *The Agenda: What Every Business Must Do to Dominate the Decade* (Crown Business, 2001), p. 101.

The difference comes from the context in how they are applied. To provide some history, as busy executives and managers have struggled to keep up with the amount of information being thrust at them, the concept of traffic lighting has been applied to virtually any and all types of reporting. As technology has improved, more bells and whistles have been added; an example is the ability to link to other reports and to drill down to finer levels of detail. The common denominator was the speed of being able to focus on something that required action or further investigation. The terminology evolved to reflect how technology vendors described what provided this capability. As a consequence, both dashboard and scorecard terms are being used interchangeably.

Figure 4.6 illustrates the difference between scorecards and dashboards using a taxonomy starting with all measurements in general. Scorecards and dashboards are not contradictory; they are used for different purposes.

At the top portion of the figure is the realm of scorecards. *Scorecards* are intended to be *strategic*. They align the behavior of employees and partners with the strategic objectives formulated by the executive team. In contrast, *dashboards*, at the bottom portion of the figure, are intended to be *operational*.

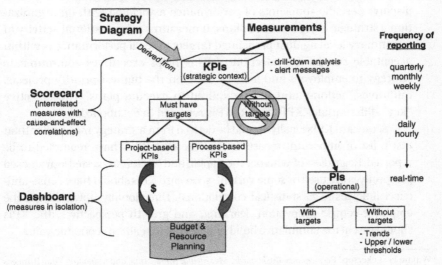

**FIGURE 4.6** Difference between KPIs and PIs: scorecard versus dashboard. Source: © 2019 www.garycokins.com. Used with permission.

Some refer to dashboards as "dumb" reporting and scorecards as "intelligent" reporting. The reason is dashboards are primarily for data visualization; they display what is happening during a time period. Most organizations begin with identifying what they are already measuring and construct a dashboard dial from there. However, dashboards do not communicate why something matters, why someone should care about the reported measure, or what the impact may be if an undesirable declining measure continues. In short, dashboards report what you *can* measure.

The selection and validation of the correct or best KPIs is a constant debate. Statistical correlation interaction analysis among KPIs can determine the degree of influence and "lift" that various cascaded KPIs have on the higher-level enterprise-wide KPIs; hence correlation analysis validates or improves the KPI selection. In addition, this type of analysis can automatically uncover previously unknown statistical relationships that may suggest cause-and-effect and can be used for predictive power. You want to make changes based on anticipated targets and constantly refocused outcomes so that employees can proactively make changes before unexpected events occur that would require a much more expensive reaction. In short, scorecards report what you *should* measure.

Here are some guidelines for understanding the differences:[2]

▪ **Scorecards chart progress toward strategic objectives.** A scorecard displays periodic snapshots of performance associated with an organization's strategic objectives and plans. It measures organizational activity at a summary level against predefined targets to see if performance is within acceptable ranges. Its selection of KPIs helps executives communicate strategy to employees and focuses users on the highest-priority projects, initiatives, actions, and tasks required to execute plans. The adjective "key" differentiates KPIs from the PIs reported in dashboards.

Scorecard KPIs ideally should be derived from a strategy map rather than just a list of important measures that the executives have requested to be reported. Regardless of whether the Kaplan and Norton suggested four stacked perspectives are used or some variant, scorecard KPIs should have cause-and-effect linkages (e.g., statistical correlations). Directionally upward from the employee-centric innovation, learning, and growth perspectives, the KPIs should reveal the cumulative build of potential to realized economic value.

There are two key distinctions of scorecards: (1) each KPI *must* require a predefined target measure; and (2) KPIs should comprise both project-based KPIs (e.g., milestones, progress percentage of completion, degree of planned versus accomplished outcome) and process-based KPIs (e.g., percent on-time delivery against customer promise dates). A scorecard comprised mainly or exclusively by process-based KPIs is not an efficient engine of change; it merely monitors whether progress from the traditional drivers of improvement, such as quality or cycle-time improvement, is occurring. Process improvement is important, but innovation and change are even more important.

■ **Dashboards monitor and measure processes.** A dashboard, however, is operational and reports information typically more frequently than scorecards and usually with measures. Each dashboard measure is reported with little regard to its relationship to other dashboard measures. Dashboard measures do not directly reflect the context of strategic objectives.

This information can be more real-time in nature, like an automobile dashboard that lets drivers check their current speed, fuel level, and engine temperature at a glance. It follows that a dashboard should ideally be linked directly to systems that capture events as they happen, and it should warn users through alerts or exception notifications when performance against any number of metrics deviates from the norm or what is expected.

The caution the authors have for organizations that are paying more attention to their performance measurements involves (1) the linkage of scorecard KPIs to the strategy diagram (often referred to as a strategy map) and also to the fiscal budget (as well as rolling financial forecasts); and (2) the linkage of dashboard PIs selected to influence behavior that will ultimately result in achieving or exceeding the KPI targets. Strategy diagrams and the budget are located in Figure 4.6 and are described below.

The authors observe a limitation of the balanced scorecard is that it does not include risk management and key risk indicators (KRIs). One can simply consider that if the KRIs are falling below their set targets, then there will be an adverse impact on KPIs. That is a simplistic view of the linkage of KRIs and KPIs where reporting of KRIs can be viewed as an early warning system that leads to impacts on KPIs.

## SCORECARDS LINK THE EXECUTIVES' STRATEGY TO OPERATIONS AND TO THE BUDGET

A strategy diagram is located in the upper left of Figure 4.6, which denotes that KPIs should be *derived from* the executives' strategic objectives and plans. If KPIs are selected independent of the strategy, then they will likely report only what *can* be measured as opposed to what *should* be measured. Failure to execute a strategy is one of a CEO's major concerns, and therefore KPIs should either reflect mission-critical projects and initiatives or core business processes that must be excelled at. (Hence there is the need for both project-based and process-based KPIs.)

The budget (and increasingly rolling financial forecasts) should be derived from the required funding of the projects (i.e., the nonrecurring strategy expenses and capital investments) and of the operational processes (i.e., the recurring operational capacity-related expenses that vary with driver volumes, such as workload demand from stakeholders, such as citizens).

Furthermore, the budget should also include spending derived from risk management. As was just mentioned, a limitation of the balanced scorecard is the absence of linkage to risk management. Chapter 6 in Part Four of this book is on risk management.

A strategy is dynamic, never static, as executives appropriately shift directions based on their new insights and observations. Reliably accurate forecasting is critical for both strategy formulation and future balancing of results, resources, and risks.

 ## DASHBOARDS MOVE THE SCORECARD'S DIALS

The organization's traction and torque are reflected in the dashboard's PI measures, the more frequently reported operational measures. Although some PIs may have predefined targets, PIs serve more to monitor trends across time or results against upper or lower threshold limits. As PIs are monitored and responded to, then the corrective actions will contribute to achieving the KPI target levels with actual results.

Cause-and-effect relationships between and among measures underlie the entire approach to integrating strategy diagrams (formulation), scorecards (appraisal), dashboards (execution), and fiscal budgets (the fuel).

## STRATEGY IS MORE THAN PERFORMING BETTER: IT INVOLVES DOING DIFFERENT THINGS

As mentioned earlier, strategy is dynamic, not static. The purpose of strategic objectives in a strategy map is to redirect the organization from the tyranny of maintaining the status quo. Strategy is about reacting to constant change. Strategic objectives are about the changes an organization should make to deliver maximum stakeholder value.

Dashboards and scorecards are not mutually exclusive. In fact, the best dashboards and scorecards merge elements from one another.

A simple rule is to use the term "dashboard" when you merely want to keep score, as in a sports event, and use the term "scorecard" when you want to understand the context of key scores in terms of how they influence achievement of strategic outcomes. A scorecard's measures will be fewer in number; they are strategic and carry more weight and influence. In contrast, the number of dashboard measures could number in the hundreds or thousands – you still need a way to focus on the unfavorable-to-target ones fast for tactical action. However, action with respect to a single metric in a dashboard is less likely to change strategic outcomes as dramatically compared to when reported in a scorecard.

 ## GETTING PAST THE SPEED BUMPS

The authors believe that the scorecard and dashboard components of commercial software should have predefined KPIs. However, for the integrated software component that reports measurements, the vendor's software should deliberately come with a limited rather than a comprehensive selection of KPIs that are commonly used by each type of industry. The purpose of providing standard KPIs should only be to accelerate the implementation of an organization's construction of their scorecard/dashboard system with a jumpstart.

The reason for *not* providing a comprehensive and exhaustive list of industry-specific measures is because caution is needed whenever an organization is identifying its measures. Measures drive employee behavior. Caution is needed for two major reasons:

1. Measures should be tailored to an organization's unique strategic goals.
2. Organizations should understand the basic concepts that differentiate scorecards from dashboards and KPIs from PIs.

Organizations should successfully implement and sustain an integrated strategic scorecard and operational dashboard system. Hence organizations should understand the distinctions described here. This is why the reader is cautioned against simply using an out-of-the-box list of various industries' common KPIs and PIs, regardless of their source.

As with any improvement methodology, experience through use refines the methodology's effectiveness and impact. The plan-do-check-act (PDCA) cycle is a great practice for learning organizations. With improvement methodologies, it's difficult to "get it perfectly right" the first time. There will always be a learning curve. Many organizations overplan and underexecute. With regard to KPI and PI selection, first learn the principles, and then apply them through selecting, monitoring, and refining the KPIs. Strategy maps and balanced scorecards are a craft, not a science.

# PART THREE

# Enterprise Performance Management

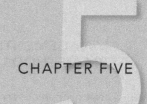

# CHAPTER FIVE

# Exceptional EPM Systems Are an Exception

TWO POPULAR TERMS FROM the last fifteen years are corporate performance management (CPM) and enterprise performance management (EPM). They are synonymous terms. The only difference is that the public government community prefers the latter because the former refers to "corporate," a word that can alienate government professionals because it appears to refer to commercial businesses. So, we will only use the term EPM.

In Figure 2.6, the enterprise performance management (EPM) methods were represented by an ellipse in "The Mechanism" floor of "The House of VBM." The depiction of EPM in this figure was intended to illustrate the role of EPM with the *balancing* of the three scales (results/resources/risks) required to maximize the delivery of stakeholder value. In this chapter we build upon that simple depiction to more completely describe the role EPM plays in ensuring this essential balancing of management considerations.

##  MANAGEMENTS' DELUSION THAT THEY HAVE EPM METHODS

Many organizations overrate the quality of their EPM methods and their IT systems, both in comprehensiveness and the degree of integration among the EPM methods. For example, when you ask executives how well they measure and report either costs or nonfinancial performance measures, most proudly boast that they are very good. This conflicts with surveys where anonymous replies from mid-level managers candidly score them as "needs much improvement." Every organization cannot be above average!

Let's not attempt to be a sociologist or psychologist and explain the incongruities between executives boasting superiority while anonymously answered surveys from their subordinate managers reveal inferiority. Rather, let's simply describe the *full vision* of an effective integration of EPM methods that organizations should aspire to possess.

First, we need to clarify some terminology and related confusion. EPM is not solely a process or a system. It is instead the *integration* of *multiple* managerial methods – methods that we earlier mentioned have mostly been around for decades, well before the term "performance management" was added to our business lexicon and arguably before there were even computer systems to support these methods. This is why we refer to EPM as being EPM methods. EPM is also not just a CFO initiative with a bunch of scorecard and dashboard dials. It is much broader. Its purpose is not about *monitoring* the dials of a balanced scorecard or dashboards but rather *moving* the dials.

Second, the authors of this book seek to share a broader vision for EPM – a vision that will more clearly add to generating stakeholder value across the entire organization. For those readers who have been previously introduced to the term Enterprise Performance Management, we ask you to put your current thoughts on hold for the time being and consider the following.

As we indicated in Chapter 2, the ultimate objective of any organization is the creation and delivery of maximum stakeholder value. As discussed in that chapter, this occurs when targets are set that will achieve that value. An organization then moves toward delivery of that future target value based upon wherever the organization is at a particular point of time. These are often referred to as the "As-Is" and "To-Be" states. The first step in this process can be represented as shown in Figure 5.1.

As seen in Figure 5.1, an organization needs to set a target for delivery of maximum value based on its proposed delivery of results, resources to be consumed, and risks to be accepted. This is reflected in the right side of the

## Improving Enterprise Value

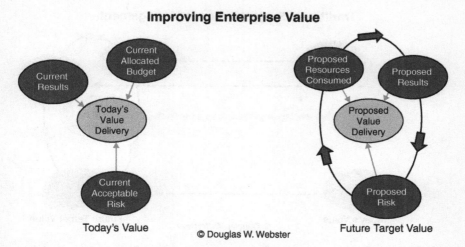

Today's Value · © Douglas W. Webster · Future Target Value

**FIGURE 5.1** Improving enterprise value. Source: Douglas Webster. Used with permission.

figure – the future target value. Setting these targets for results, resources, and risks needs to consider the multiple tradeoffs among these three considerations, as represented by the circles and arrows in the right side of the figure. Setting future targets also needs to consider the organization's current balance of results, resources, and risks, and determine a plan to get from the balance for "Today's Value" to that of the proposed "Future Target Value."

Moving from today's "As-Is" to the future "To-Be" may be a significant undertaking and require formal project management as the organization moves to revise processes and priorities in the delivery of results, allocation and consumption of resources, and the management of risks. This is reflected by the left-to-right horizontal arrows connecting the current and future states in Figure 5.2.

Finally, as we have noted previously, constant change is a fact of life. It is essential that as EPM seeks to move the organization from the "As-Is" state of "Today's Value" to the proposed "To-Be" state of the "Future Target Value," changes in the internal and external environments are evaluated and responded to in a timely fashion.

Progress in achieving results may be faster or slower, or more or less robust, than was originally planned. Similarly, the consumption of resources may differ from the original budget, and the assessment of risks may change over time. We thus need to monitor the progression of results, resources, and risks over time in

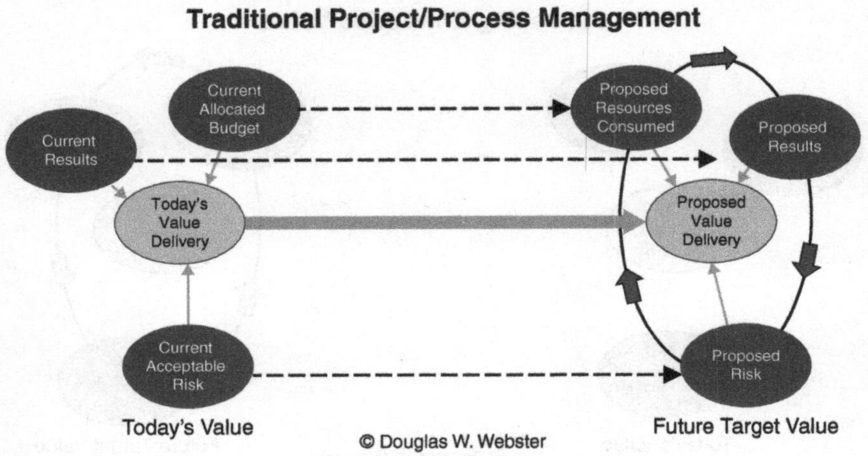

**Traditional Project/Process Management**

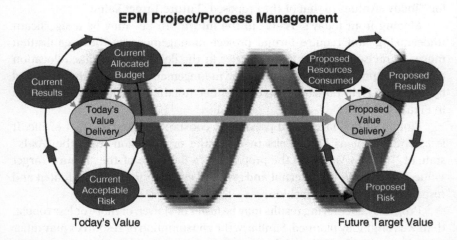

**FIGURE 5.2** Traditional project/process management. Source: Douglas Webster. Used with permission.

moving from the "As-Is" to the "To-Be," and make adjustments as necessary to maintain an optimal balance among our tradeoff considerations. This ongoing monitoring and adjustments (as appropriate) are reflected in Figure 5.3. As adjustments may become necessary in the journey toward value delivery, the projection of optimal results may need to be adjusted over time.

**EPM Project/Process Management**

**FIGURE 5.3** EPM project/process management. Source: Douglas Webster. Used with permission.

**EPM METHODS ARE LIKE MUSICAL INSTRUMENTS IN AN ORCHESTRA**

The authors like to think of the various EPM methods as analogous to musical instruments in an orchestra. An orchestra's conductor does not raise the baton to the string, woodwinds, percussion, and brass instruments and say, "Now everyone play loud." They seek balance and guide the symphony composer's fluctuations in harmony, rhythm, and tone.

Here are five primary components of the EPM methods as they apply to government. They are the musical instrument sections:

1. **Strategy execution.** This component was described in Chapters 3 and 4. It is where a strategy map and its associated balanced scorecard with key performance indicators (KPIs) fits in. The authors recognize that there are several strategy management methods, but since the strategy map and its balanced scorecard are a prominent one, we selected it to describe. (It was discussed in detail in Chapter 4.) Together a strategy map and its balanced scorecard serve to translate the executive team's strategy into navigation aids necessary for the organization to fulfill its vision and mission. The executive's role is to set the strategic direction to answer the question "Where do we want to go?" Through use of correctly defined KPIs with targets, the priorities, actions, projects, and processes of managers and employee teams become aligned with the executives' *formulated* strategy to *execute* their strategy.

2. **Cost visibility and driver behavior.** This component will be discussed in detail in Chapter 8, "Resource and Cost Management." For commercial companies, this is where profitability analysis fits in for products, standard service-lines, channels, and customers. For public sector government organizations, this is where understanding is necessary that processes consume resource expenses in the delivery of services and report the output costs, including the per unit cost, of their services. Activity-based costing (ABC) principles model cause-and-effect relationships based on cost drivers. This involves progressive, not traditional, managerial accounting such as ABC rather than calculating costs with broadly averaged cost factors without causal relationships. Cost visibility does not end with calculating only the costs of services. It includes "full costing" to detect different types of citizens or stakeholders who disproportionately consume an agency's expenses across a spectrum of being difficult (i.e., high demanding) or easy (i.e., low demanding) at the end extremes.

3. **Risk management.** This component will be discussed in greater detail in Part Four. Risk management serves as a brake to the potentially unbridled gas pedal that EPM methods are designed to step hard on. For commercial businesses, risk mitigation projects and insurance require spending, which reduces profits, which in turn adversely impacts compensation incentive bonuses for executives. For public sector organizations, risk management is one of the three balancing scales. It takes discipline to ensure adequate attention is placed on appropriate risk management practices.

4. **Forecasting, budgeting, and predictive analytics.** This component will also be discussed in detail in Chapter 13. Data mining typically examines historical data "through the rear-view mirror." This EPM component directs attention forward to look at the road "through the windshield." The benefit of more accurate forecasts is reduced uncertainty, which is an aspect of risk management. This contributes to the balancing of the three scales – results, resources, and risks. Forecasts for the future volume and mix quantities of services for citizens and other stakeholders are core *independent variables*. The costs are the *dependent variables*. In complex environments forecasting may rely on predictive analytics (e.g., regression analysis). Based on those forecasts with which so many dependent variables have relationships, process-related costs derived from the resource expenses can be calculated and managed. Examples of dependent variables are the future headcount workforce and spending levels with suppliers and contractors. CFOs increasingly look to capacity-sensitive driver-based budgeting and rolling financial forecasts grounded in ABC principles using this component.

5. **Process improvement.** This component will be discussed in Chapters 7 and 12. This is where business process reengineering (BPR), lean management, and quality management (e.g., Six Sigma) initiatives fit in. Their purpose is to remove waste and streamline processes to accelerate and reduce cycle times. They create productivity and efficiency improvements.

What makes for exceptionally good EPM is that its multiple managerial methods are not only individually effective, but they are also seamlessly integrated and imbedded with analytics of all flavors.

Examples of analytics are segmentation, clustering, regression, and correlation analysis.

## ENTERPRISE PERFORMANCE MANAGEMENT (EPM) METHODS IN GOVERNMENT

Enterprise performance management (EPM) methods serve as enablers for VBM. Their primary focus is on two of the three "scales" in Figure 2.1 (i.e., costs). The EPM methods assist an organization to align its resources and their associated costs to achieve policy and strategic objectives, measure results against targets, and identify the best opportunities for improvement. However, organizations that have been implementing improvement methods in isolation of one another miss the increased value from the synergy of seamlessly integrating the EPM methods with IT technologies to facilitate achieving *the full vision* of the VBM framework.

The good news is that EPM methods are not *new* methods that everyone now has to learn, but rather they are the assemblage and integration of *existing* methods with which most managers are already familiar. They may not have yet implemented some (or any) of the EPM methods in their agency, but they may likely be aware of other agencies who have implemented such management approaches.

With EPM methods, organizations can proactively manage their risks, costs, processes, and programs by monitoring performance and exploring problems or issues that are obstacles to achieving the "Results" scale in Figure 2.1. All of this information can be used in turn to develop and justify budgets, which involves the "Resources" scale in Figure 2.1.

Government agencies can expect to improve their processes and achieve service-level expectations and overall program success by focusing on the following: communication of results, performance optimization, insight into prioritization and resource allocation, cost reduction through cost analysis and cost management, and collaboration among managers and employee teams to collectively improve performance.

The authors were tempted to call this book *Enterprise Performance Management in Government*. But that title does not provide a sufficient and complete description. What is needed is to place an emphasis on value: creating value for all stakeholders. Hence, "Value" is in the book's title.

Using the two terms – VBM and EPM – introduces a problem of nomenclature and semantics. The analogy of an automobile provides a way to grasp the terms. The EPM methods are like a car's engine, chassis, and tires. They are needed for motion. VBM is like the fuel, global positioning system (GPS), and the driver. The fuel represents the capacity of resources (e.g., expenses such as salaries and supplies). The GPS represents navigating the direction the government agency is headed to achieve its objectives. The driver is needed to manage, including reacting to unplanned events. The EPM method involving costs is not fuel itself. Costing and budgeting methods determine the type and quantity of the fuel needed for VBM.

Traction, direction, control, and speed: the EPM methods provide the traction and speed; VBM provides for the direction and control. As described in Chapter 2, VBM is about balancing performance (for stakeholders), costs (resources expenses consumption), and risk.

One can think of the EPM methods as a closed-loop integrated framework that spans the complete management planning and control cycle, including the processes, metrics, methods, systems, and software tools that collectively manage implementing an organization's strategy and its policies. Also, EPM methods have existed in organizations for decades, well before the term "performance management" was added to our business lexicon and arguably before there were even computer systems to support these methods. What is different in the twenty-first century is that information technologies can electronically link EPM methods into an integrated technology platform. This topic will be described in Chapter 15.

 ## SEAMLESS INTEGRATION OF EPM METHODS AND IT SYSTEMS AS AN ASPIRATION

CFOs often view financial planning and analysis (FP&A) as synonymous with EPM. It is more appropriate to view FP&A as a subset of the EPM methods. And although better cost management and process improvements are noble goals, an organization cannot reduce its costs forever to achieve long-term prosperity.

The important message here is that EPM methods are not just about the CFO's organization. The message is that what is needed is the seamless integration of all the often siloed and self-serving functions and departments of the organization chart. Silo behavior is typical in any organization.

Look again at the five EPM components described above. Imagine if the information produced and analyzed in each of them were to be seamlessly integrated. Imagine if they were each embedded with analytics, especially predictive analytics. Then powerful decision support is provided for insight, foresight, and actions. That is the *full vision* of how VBM can be supported by the EPM methods to which government agencies should aspire in order to achieve the best possible performance.

Today, outstanding EPM systems are an exception despite what many executives proclaim. If organizations have effective and sound leadership and their management teams all work hard and smart enough, then in the future EPM methods as a seamlessly integrated system will be common and standard to support VBM.

 ## THE THREE Rs OF VBM

EPM can generate significantly greater value when it serves in a role to integrate considerations of results to be achieved, resources to be allocated, and risks to be accepted, all in the pursuit of delivering the greatest possible stakeholder value. The next three chapters of this book will take the reader through a description of the balancing and integration of these components of stakeholder value. The three components that are the 3 Rs of VBM are risk, results, and resources.

# The Three Rs: Risk, Results, and Resources

# 6

# Risk Management

F OR MANY, TODAY'S PUBLIC sector management challenge is greater than at any time in our lives. That is certainly true in the United States, but is also true for much of the developed and developing world. Decades of deficit spending resting on the belief (or at least the hope) that "investments" would result in increased productivity generating revenues greater than costs have failed to come true. National governments have awoken, even if slowly, to the recognition that nations, just like individuals, cannot spend indefinitely at a rate higher than incoming revenues. While local governments may not be able to engage in deficit spending, they are nevertheless impacted by national governments that do so.

We have long heard the calls from leaders and consultants to "do more with less." Yet such a goal requires productivity to increase faster than the rate of reduction in budgets. For most of our lifetimes that was feasible. Increasingly, however, it appears that budget challenges are making such a goal no longer credible. Given our introduction of the concept of value-based management, this battle cry should change to "do more of value with fewer resources." While perhaps not as memorable, this phrase is much more meaningful in terms of solutions to the challenges that lie ahead.

Leaders must be driven not by a focus on spending less or doing more, but rather on creating increased stakeholder value through the balancing of results sought, resources available, and risks accepted.

Risk management, as indicated in the discussion of the value-based management framework in Part One, is an inherently critical element of any decision-making process that seeks to maximize stakeholder value. While balancing desired results and available resources/budget will always be part of the decision process, too often risk is left out of serious consideration. It is important to understand the challenges to meaningfully incorporate risk considerations in business decisions. However, before beginning that discussion, it is vitally important to define exactly what we mean by "risk."

*Risk* is a very commonly used term, but a term that can mean considerably different things once one gets into the details of its definition. For the purposes of this book, we choose to use the word "risk" as defined in the international risk management standard ISO 31000: "the effect of uncertainty on objectives." Defining a word such as "risk" in advance of a discussion using that term is important because many organizations and individuals have defined that term in different and inconsistent ways. The average person might think of a risk as a threat to safety or achieving an objective, in contrast to a possible opportunity or benefit. However, in defining risk as uncertainty, we are including both the downside (i.e., threat) and the upside (i.e., opportunity) associated with such uncertainty. Given that some degree of uncertainty is involved in almost every business decision, why does it not always naturally occur as part of the decision-making process?

There are many reasons for the traditionally diminished role of risk management in management decision-making. Thinking seriously about risk is not something that many decision makers have learned as a practice. They (1) simply ignore risk either because of a lack of awareness or concern of the uncertainty in achieving a desired objective, or (2) they briefly consider risks and assume them to be negligible and unworthy of serious consideration. Some decision makers may recognize that risks exist, but simply bypass proactively addressing risks and instead take a reactive approach that deals with risks only after they transition into adverse events (if a threat). Such decision makers also do not integrate an uncertain upside to risk (opportunity) as part of their decision-making process.

Additionally, many organizations – particularly those in government – desire not to acknowledge the existence of risk in delivering services to and on behalf of their various stakeholders. This unwillingness to address risks to the public thus transfers over into an unwillingness to manage those risks as part of planning and operations. This narrow-sighted approach to risk management in the public sector must cease if government leaders are to maximize the value delivered in exchange for limited resources. Pretending to their constituency that we live in a riskless world will come back to haunt many government leaders if risks are not consciously and proactively managed.

## THE EVOLUTION OF RISK MANAGEMENT

Whether primitive humans were managing the risk of attack by adversaries or wild animals, the concept of risk – and the effort to manage that risk – is as old as humankind. Early examples of a more formal approach to risk management can be seen in the Code of Hammurabi (circa 1755 BCE), which provided the underpinnings of maritime insurance contracts. The concept of risk and considering how to manage that risk further developed over the centuries. Marine insurance appeared in Italian port cities as early as the twelfth century, and an organization in Belgium in 1310 was the first in that country to offer marine insurance for their merchants. The establishment of the Fire Office in London, possibly the first company offering fire insurance, was a likely response to the Great Fire of London in 1666. The development of probability theory in the seventeenth and eighteenth centuries allowed for the calculation of quantifiable risks, which did much to formalize the practice of risk management and open it to a much larger area of application.

Despite an ability to trace the concern over risk in a very broad sense dating back several millennia, the focus until the mid-twentieth century was generally on insurance-related risk – those risks that could be insured by transferring to another party. The development of modern risk management focused on organizational functions beyond insurance has been a much more recent occurrence.

The trail to financial risk management was blazed by the actuarial profession beginning in the mid-nineteenth century. However, risk in the eyes of the actuarial and accounting professions maintained a relatively narrow and limited focus. In the 1950s there were no textbooks on the broader topic of risk management, and no university courses offered on the subject. The first book published on what we think of as risk management nowadays in the broader business context was *Risk Management in the Business Enterprise*, written by Robert I. Mehr and Robert A. Hedges in 1963. This book appears to have been the first formal use of the term "risk management." Moreover, the book was the first to propose steps to the risk management process that can be seen reflected in the various risk management standards of today. These proposed steps were:

1. Identifying loss exposures
2. Measuring loss exposures
3. Evaluating the different methods for handling risk:
   ■ Risk assumption
   ■ Risk transfer
   ■ Risk reduction

4. Selecting a method
5. Monitoring results

Financial risk management developed rapidly beginning in the 1970s with the use of derivatives to manage insurable and uninsurable risks, and many additional practices developed in the remaining years of the twentieth century. While much of the development of risk management in this period took place in the arena of finance and insurance, other areas developed strong risk management practices and procedures as well, such as engineering.

In 1995, Australia and New Zealand jointly published the world's first formal risk management standard, AS/NZS 4360. This standard considered risk as applicable to all endeavors, not only finance and insurance. Members of the committee that developed AS/NZS 4360 included communities of interest as diverse as the Australian Computer Society, Australian Customs Service, the Australian Department of Defense, Australian and New Zealand engineering associations, universities, and others. In short, this initiative included a broad cross-section of society that had a strong interest in and need for effective risk management. In 2004, the United Kingdom's HM Treasury published "The Orange Book: Management of Risk – Principles and Concepts." Both AS/NZS 4360 and the HM Treasury Orange Book highly influenced the creation in 2009 of the International Organization for Standardization's risk management standard, ISO 31000. This standard was subsequently updated in 2017.

As risk management has matured over the past half-century, so, too, has the general concept of "risk" grown. As noted, early risk management was focused on insurable risk – that risk that could be transferred to another party in exchange for a risk premium. In more recent years, however, the concept of risk has increasingly focused on the idea of uncertainly, rather than simply potential loss. This important distinction recognizes that we may often knowingly and willingly take on the acceptance of loss in order to have the opportunity for gain.

No race car driver can take on the possibility of a win without considering the possibility of car damage or even bodily harm. How much risk such a driver undertakes depends in part on how much risk he or she is willing to take. A lower degree of risk would yield a lower chance of bodily harm, but also a lower likelihood of winning. We all typically face decisions on a daily basis of balancing the upsides and downsides of uncertainty (even if without such impactful consequences), but we recognize this should always be an upside benefit to taking on a potential for downside consequences. This broader definition of risk as uncertainty, rather than threat or loss, ensures that this balancing act is part of the decision-making process.

## TRADITIONAL RISK MANAGEMENT

The management of risk in various functional areas has become increasingly sophisticated over the years. Whether concerned about fraud, financial reporting misstatements, expected return on investments, inability to accomplish program requirements, adequately managing cyber-security, or countless other needs, the necessity to manage risks to achieving specific objectives has become broadly recognized. Not until the 1990s, however, did risk management begin to be considered broadly across the organization and not limited to specific functional or programmatic areas of concern. Australia and New Zealand jointly developed and published the first risk management standard, AUS/NZS 4360, in 1995. This standard in turn directly led to the international risk management standard ISO 31000 published in 2009. In the meantime, COSO developed and published the COSO ERM-Integrated Framework in September 2004, and the United Kingdom published the Treasury Orange Book in October 2004.

## THE RISK MANAGEMENT PROCESS

While these various risk management standards are all unique and have slightly different approaches and terminology for elements of the risk management process, their description of the risk management process can generally be portrayed as illustrated in Figure 6.1. This figure was developed by the US's White House Office of Management and Budget and is influenced by both the United Kingdom Treasury Orange Book and ISO 31000. The two outside rings are typical for a federal agency, but should be adapted for a state or local government organization. While this diagram is not intended to be prescriptive, it does illustrate the steps that are typically included in the risk management process:

1. *Establish the Context.* Consideration must be given to the internal and external environments relative to the organization in which risks are to be managed. Depending on the objectives and associated risks to be considered, the subject organization could be a large agency, a division or other organizational element of the agency, or even a smaller subcomponent of an agency for narrowly focused objectives and associated risks.

   Examining an organization's external context (i.e., outside the boundaries of the specific organization in question) may include factors such as an understanding of the influence of the social, cultural, political,

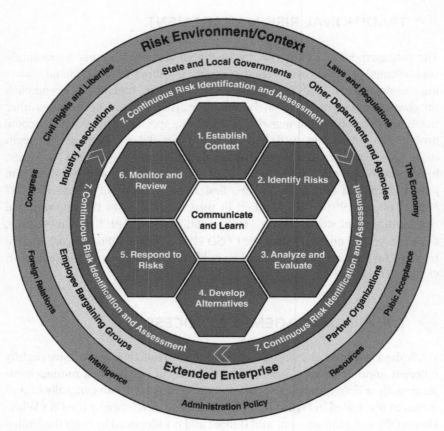

**FIGURE 6.1** Example risk management process. Source: Office of Management and Budget Circular A-123, White House (US federal government).

legal, regulatory, financial, technological, economic, and competitive environments. It will also include an understanding of the key drivers and trends affecting the objectives of the organization: the relationships, perceptions, values, and expectations of external stakeholders; and contractual relationships and commitments.

The organization's internal context may include but not be limited to vision, mission and values, governance processes, organizational structure, strategies and policies, capabilities (such as budget allocation, time, people, processes, and technologies), relationships with internal stakeholders, organizational culture, and contractual relationships and commitments. The context also includes consideration of the organization's risk appetite, which forms the basis for evaluating acceptability of risks to the organization's objectives.

Defining the organization's objectives and the overall risk appetite for achieving various objectives is an important part of the context. Clearly defining objectives is a critical element of establishing the context, because the identification of risks to achieving objectives – the purpose of the following step in the risk management process – cannot be achieved until the organization first establishes what those objectives are intended to be.

Also, along with understanding what objectives the organization seeks to accomplish, an understanding of the level of risk the organization finds appropriate in seeking to accomplish those objectives is essential. This appropriate level of risk to be accepted by an organization, which is known as "risk appetite" and was mentioned above, can be defined as the amount and type of risk that an organization is prepared to pursue, retain, or take. A risk appetite statement is a higher-level statement that broadly considers the levels of risk that management deems appropriate.

Establishing and communicating an organizational risk appetite is a critical and often missed step in the risk management process. A risk appetite is the basis for judging whether or not an existing risk is at an acceptable level, and whether or not further risk treatments are appropriate. If that risk appetite is not clearly defined and used to guide decisions across the organization, different managers will make risk treatment decisions in different and inconsistent ways. The level of risk an organization is willing to take in pursuit of objectives is not a trivial matter and should not be an ad hoc process exercised by individuals inconsistently across the organization.

The "appropriate" level of risk should be determined after considering tradeoffs between the upside potential for new opportunities versus the downside potential for adverse impacts. This is not a "one-size-fits-all" proposition. For example, the United States knew full well in the 1960s that seeking to land a man on the moon was fraught with great risk. However, the upside opportunity for new knowledge was deemed greater than the downside possibility of loss, including the loss of human life. It would be inappropriate to take such risks for most other ventures. An individual starting up a small business typically wants reasonable assurance that they will profit from their venture. Lacking such expectation, such individuals might be more inclined to work as an employee for another company that has decided to take such business risks.

While the overall risk an organization finds appropriate to accept in pursuit of objectives should be considered and communicated across the organization, this level of risk may appropriately vary from one part of the organization to another. For example, an organization may be compelled to knowingly accept large uncertainty in pursuit of certain program objectives, as the upside potential is much greater than the downside. Scientific research and exploration is an area of human endeavor that easily falls into this general category. At the same time, the organization may have a far lower risk appetite for cyber-security or the loss of personally identifiable information (PII). It is thus appropriate – and often critical – to tailor an overall enterprise risk appetite statement to various functional or programmatic areas of the enterprise. This tailoring, however, should be a coordinated process that incorporates enterprise stakeholder interests, and is not done on an isolated basis by individual functional or program managers having no awareness of or commitment to the overall enterprise risk appetite.

A related consideration for the context step is risk tolerance. Risk tolerances set the acceptable level of variation around specific objectives. Risk tolerance is thus focused on specific objectives and is typically quantifiable in setting measurable boundaries for acceptable variation in those objectives.

2. *Initial Risk Identification.* Using a structured and systematic approach to recognizing where the potential for undesired outcomes or opportunities can arise relative to organizational objectives.

Once the context has been established, elements at all levels of the organization should identify risks to achieving objectives set for their particular part of the organization. There are numerous risk identification techniques, such as:

- Brainstorming
- Interviews
- Checklists
- Structured "What-if" Technique (SWIFT)
- Scenario Analysis
- Fault Tree Analysis (FTA)
- Bow Tie Analysis
- Direct Observations
- Incident Analysis
- Surveys

3. *Analyze and Evaluate Risks.* Considering the causes, sources, probability of the risk occurring, the potential positive or negative outcomes, and then prioritizing the results of the analysis.

   Once risks are identified, they must be analyzed in terms of their likelihood of occurrence and the impact if those risks do transition into actual events. In practice, the risk identification and risk analysis steps frequently overlap, as the techniques for identifying risks often yield insight into the likelihood and impact of the risk. In addition to the techniques identified under *Initial Risk Identification*, various specialized techniques relevant to particular types of risks (e.g., credit, information technology, engineering, project management and others) may be used, often enabling more quantifiable analyses.

   After risks are analyzed for likelihood and impact, they must be evaluated by comparing the identified risks to the established risk appetite, and prioritizing those identified and analyzed risks in terms of potential treatment. This prioritization takes into account the level of risk compared to the risk appetite.

4. *Develop Alternatives.* Systematically identifying and assessing a range of risk response options guided by risk appetite.

   Based upon the risk analysis and evaluation, various options are considered for treating any particular risk. Options for treating risks can be categorized into one of four categories:

   A. Avoid. An entity can choose to avoid the activities that create the risk. For example, accepting cash payments for goods or services has inherent risk. Some people are willing to lie, cheat, and steal to take cash. One way to address that risk is to stop accepting cash payments. In recent years, the airlines have virtually all decided to avoid the risk of cash payments for various items on planes, in part to reduce the administrative cost of handling cash. If you want to purchase a meal or an alcoholic beverage on a plane, you must pay for it with a credit or debit card.

   B. Mitigate. An entity can elect to implement procedures to reduce the risk. For example, if you gamble at a casino and give the dealer a 100-dollar bill, it will almost certainly be immediately deposited in a lockbox under the table, and the dealer will alert someone that a bill is being deposited. Cash moving about is still a risk, of course, but that risk is reduced by getting higher-value bills off the tables quickly. Also, in a casino, all activity is closely monitored through a video system, whereby everything is watched and recorded in real time. Risk mitigation can focus on reducing the likelihood of an event occurring, the impact of the event if it does occur, or both.

C. Share or transfer. A homeowner will be required by a mortgage company to insure his home against fire. This action shares the risk of a home fire with the insurance company, who will bear the risk of repairing fire damage in exchange for an insurance premium. Sharing risk often is beneficial when the likelihood of an adverse event is small, but the potential impact is unbearable without significant damage to the organization.

D. Accept. There will be frequent occasions when reducing the risk not only reduces the threat of an adverse action, but simultaneously reduces the opportunity to achieve beneficial results. Anyone interested in playing a competitive game, for example, may mitigate the risk of a loss through training and experience. However, they ultimately must accept a level of risk of a loss if they are to enjoy the thrill of the competition.

5. *Respond to Risks.* Making decisions about the best option(s) among a number of alternatives, and then preparing and executing the selected response strategy.

There may be a number of options developed in the prior step to potentially address any particular risk. In responding to a risk, choices are made by the organization as to how to treat a particular risk. Key considerations in determining the selected treatment include both (1) whether or not the risk treatment will reduce the treated risk to within the organization's risk appetite, and (2) the return on investment when considering the level of risk reduction versus the cost of achieving that reduction. Generally, risk treatments are selected that ensure risks stay within the risk appetite, and that maximize the return on investment in treating the risk. Treatments should never cost the organization more to implement than the increased value offered by reducing risk.

It must be noted that even when risks are within the risk appetite of the organization, there may be times when further treatment of the risk will generate a positive return on investment (ROI). This occurs when further treatment of a risk yields benefits in excess of the costs of additional treatment.

6. *Monitor and Review.* Evaluating and monitoring performance to determine whether the implemented risk management options achieved the desired level of remaining risk.

Starting down the road to implementing a risk treatment by applying the preceding risk management steps is essential. However, it is then required that risk treatment plans are monitored on a timely basis to ensure schedules for treating risks are met, and that the proposed risk treatment is actually implemented and achieves the intended result. This requires periodic monitoring of risk treatment plans to ensure plans are progressing on schedule to meet desired deadlines, or changes are made as needed to achieve intended results.

A final and critical element of managing risk is a consistently used approach to documenting risks and risk treatments. For this purpose, organizations typically use what may be referred to as a risk register or risk profile. Too many organizations, however, fall into the trap of simply listing risks. Identifying a risk is but a small part of the risk management process. Meaningful risk management requires all of the following:

1. The specific objective that is at risk
2. The specific risk to achieving the objective without treatment (i.e., current state)
3. The likelihood of the risk occurring in its current state
4. The impact of the risk, should the risk in its current state transition into an actual event
5. The current relative rating of the risk, considering the combined effects of likelihood and impact
6. The proposed risk treatment if the current level of risk is not considered acceptable
7. The proposed risk likelihood after completion of the risk treatment
8. The proposed risk impact after completion of the risk treatment
9. The proposed risk rating after completion of the risk treatment
10. Responsible party for taking action on risk treatments
11. Target date for completion of the risk treatment

Typically, a register will list risk vertically as rows in the register, while the above elements of the register serve as columns.

The risk register/profile plays a critical role in risk management by allowing management to see all key risks at once to:

1. Understand the current overall level of risk to the organization's objectives
2. Compare risks to the organization's risk appetite
3. Prioritize risks for potential treatment
4. Document (at a summary level) risk treatments for specific risks
5. Set targeted risk remaining after treatment

6. Establish accountability for risk treatment (by individual or organizational element)
7. Establish targeted date of completion for proposed risk treatment
   Moreover, having all key risks documented in a consistent manner using the above elements will enable risk managers across the organization to consider risk treatment in a consistently documented manner. This will become critical if the organization choses to implement enterprise risk management, as discussed below.
7. *Continuous Risk Identification.* Must be an iterative process, occurring throughout the year to include surveillance of leading indicators of future risk from internal and external environments. This includes evaluation of prior risk responses to ensure they were successful in meeting the targeted level of risk. If not, the risk management process would be repeated for these risks and risk responses.

Finally, risk management is not a one-time activity. New risks constantly arise that may not have been evident or even present when organizational risks were previously reviewed. Because the environment within which every organization operates is constantly changing, new risks are constantly arising. It is thus essential for organizations to understand that risks must be identified and managed on an ongoing basis.

How frequently risks to objectives should be reviewed, as well as how frequently existing risk treatment plans are reviewed, is dependent on the nature of the organization and the environment within which it operates. Rapidly changing environments – whether that change is a result of political environment, advancing technology, changing financial conditions, or other considerations – means the organization's risks should be reviewed more frequently. Typical public sector organizations review organization-wide risks on a quarterly or semiannual basis. Organizations operating in a rapidly changing environment, or where risks must otherwise be tightly controlled, will want to monitor organization-wide risks on a more frequent basis.

Just as risks change over time, so do organizational risk appetites. Whether due to a change in the external environment within which an organization operates, a new strategy for achieving results, or simply a difference in leadership, the organization's stated risk appetite should occasionally be reviewed. While there is no prescriptive timeline for such a review, and the "ideal" frequency of review is certainly related to the rate of change in the organization's environment, it is suggested that the risk appetite statement initially be reviewed on an annual basis, with that frequency being revised as deemed appropriate.

## THE ROLE OF INTERNAL CONTROLS

Certainly, no discussion of risk management would be complete without including the role of internal control. However, the relationship between internal control and the broader topic of risk management is frequently misunderstood.

Just as with risk management, the concept of internal control can be traced back many centuries to ancient Egypt and Babylonia. Written records were kept, and an elaborate system of internal controls required that the records of one official agreed with those of another. Accounts were audited by officials, and gross irregularities were severely punished, even by death. Over the years, internal controls have been an important element of ensuring the accuracy of record keeping. Stated in terms of risk management, internal controls have helped limit the risk of incorrect or inaccurate records. For this reason, internal controls have become an important element of the accounting and audit profession.

The American Institute of Accountants (AIA, now the AICPA) was the first to offer a definition of internal control in 1936: "Those measures and methods adopted within the organization itself to safeguard the cash and other assets of the company as well as to check the clerical aspects of the book-keeping." This definition was broadened and made more binding on the accounting and audit profession in a number of revisions in subsequent years.

In 1992, the Committee of Sponsoring Organizations of the Treadway Commission (COSO) published the "Internal Control – Integrated Framework." The document defined internal control as:

> a process, effected by an entity's Board of Directors, management, and other personnel, designed to provide reasonable assurance regarding the achievement of objectives in the following categories:
>
> 1. Effectiveness and efficiency of operations
> 2. Reliability of financial reporting
> 3. Compliance with applicable laws and regulations

The 1992 COSO document was a major step forward in formalizing the concept of internal control as having much broader applicability to risk management than accounting and auditing. Moreover, the COSO framework contained the following five control components:

1. Control environment
2. Risk assessment

3. Control activities
4. Information and communication
5. Monitoring

These elements of internal control clearly influenced formalization of the broader elements of general risk management reflected in AS/NZS 4360, the UK HM Treasury Orange Book, and ISO 31000.

It is important to recognize, however, that the context of internal control in which these control components are set is narrower than that intended in the referenced risk management standards. At their core, internal controls are focused on controlling risks internal to the organization or created within or by the organization. Any major new initiative, especially those calling for innovation and addressing new challenges, will face significant risks. As noted in Figure 3.2, we must always consider both reactive change and proactive change. Internal controls typically have a major role in managing reactive change, because we are generally seeking to manage or improve how we do business in today's environment. Improving the processes we have in place to meet today's needs is a key element of reactive change, and an area in which internal control is critical.

However, most organizations face many risks far beyond the boundaries of their current operations and processes. Strategic decisions such as which line of business an organization should pursue, how well customers will accept new product or service offerings, what impacts possible future regulatory changes will have on a business or government organization, and even the likelihood of a future economic recession are all potential risks, but not ones for which controls can be established. In short, control of such risks is often not within the ability of the organization to manage. At best, one can only hope to influence in some manner such external risks. Even if controls cannot be set in place for such risks, however, it is essential that these risks be considered in the decision-making process and decisions and actions adjusted accordingly.

 ## THE EVOLUTION OF ENTERPRISE RISK MANAGEMENT

If the above description of the risk management process is pertinent to the good practice of risk management in general, what then does the concept of enterprise risk management (ERM) add to the discussion? More specifically, what is the difference between traditional risk management and ERM? To answer this question, we can begin with a short history of what prior generations felt might be missing from traditional risk management. Perhaps the first visualization of the concept of ERM was from Gustav Hamilton, the risk manager for Sweden's State Company Limited. In 1974 he created a "risk management circle" in which he sought to graphically describe all elements of the risk management process (see Figure 6.2). This is the earliest known effort to show the interconnectedness of various categories of risk across the organization.

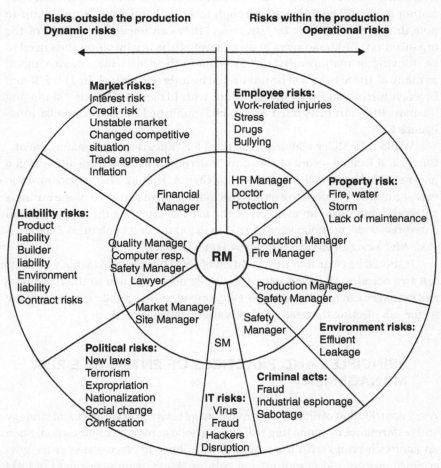

**FIGURE 6.2** Gustav Hamilton's "Circle of Risk."

It would be almost two decades later, however, before the idea of an integrated approach to the management of risk, including strategic risks, was formally addressed. This occurred in 1992 in a journal article titled "A Framework for Integrated Risk Management in International Business" by K.D. Miller. This paper clearly laid out the much broader landscape of risk in general beyond that of internal control. General environmental uncertainties such as political instability, government policy instability, social uncertainties, and natural uncertainties were included. So, too, were various industry uncertainties, such as market uncertainties. While such risks cannot generally be managed through internal controls, it is important to note that while they may be "strategic," they can impact every level of the organization. Risk managers at every level of the organization thus need to be thinking of management risk external to their immediate environment, as many of those risks will be unaffected by internal control. In 1995, James Deloach further added to the literature with his journal article "Managing Business Risk: An Integrated Approach," published by the Economist Intelligence Unit.

While K.D. Miller addressed the need for "integrated risk management," the earliest located record of the term "enterprise risk management" was in a paper so titled and published in 1996 by Glyn A. Holton. That paper, however, was arguing for the need to exercise risk management across all of the business enterprise, but made no mention of the need to integrate these risks into an enterprise-wide, portfolio view of risk. In 2000 the first book titled *Enterprise-Wide Risk Management* was written by James Deloach.

It should be clear that the evolution of ERM has occurred largely over the last two decades. However, what specifically does ERM add to the traditional risk management process to support any organization – public sector or private sector – in meeting the needs of their various stakeholders?

 ## PRINCIPLES AND PRACTICES OF ENTERPRISE RISK MANAGEMENT

A key contribution of ERM is improved linkage between organizational strategy and performance by managing risk as a portfolio across the organization. Such an approach brings with it a requirement to have in place a supportive governance process and organizational culture. A recurring assessment of ERM practices will aid the organization on opportunities to further improve and benefit from the potential advantages of ERM over traditional risk management practices. Following are some key elements necessary for meaningful implementation of ERM.

▪ **Strategy and Performance.** The key distinction between traditional risk management and ERM is that the latter seeks to manage risk in a holistic, collaborative fashion across the entire organization. This more collaborative approach is intended to optimize the ability of the overall organization to deliver maximum stakeholder value by ensuring organizational strategy is directly linked to and informed by the tradeoffs of results sought, resources allocated, and risks accepted across the enterprise. In contrast, traditional risk management is often focused on meeting lower-level organizational, functional, or programmatic needs without consideration of how to balance those needs with resource availability and risk appetite across the overall organization. This more integrated approach to considering risk facilitates the use of consistent best practices across the organization. Perhaps more importantly, however, ERM facilitates a discussion horizontally across all elements of the organization to ensure that decisions on managing risks are aligned with top organizational strategy and stakeholder value.

▪ **The portfolio management of risk.** Linking risks across the organization in a manner that maximizes value aligned with strategic priorities requires a portfolio management approach to risk. Most individuals who invest in retirement plans are already engaged in portfolio management, whether they realize it or not. The typical investment will seek to balance risk and reward by diversifying their investments across a number of individual investments. The ultimate goal is not to maximize the return on any single investment, but for the portfolio of investments overall. To accomplish this, an individual may invest some of their retirement funds in stocks, other funds in bonds, and yet other funds in other opportunities, all in an effort to balance risks with overall rate of return. So, too, should organizations seek to maximize their overall return on investment by balancing delivery of products or services, available resources, and acceptable risks. This portfolio view of overall organizational risk is central to the concept of ERM.

▪ **Governance.** ERM requires communication across organizational, functional, and programmatic boundaries. This in turn requires an ongoing collaboration across those boundaries to prioritize risks and associated risk treatments in a manner that maximizes benefits for the overall enterprise. Such an integrated approach to management of risk across the enterprise requires a governance structure that enables such a cross-organizational communication and prioritization of risk management consistent with organizational strategic goals and objectives. An effective governance structure for ERM will support the integration of internal controls with broader risk management concerns horizontally across the enterprise, and vertically from the lowest levels of the organization (where many risks originate) up to the top of the organization (that must ultimately ensure management of the most critical risks).

■ **Culture and Organizational Change Management.** Perhaps the largest challenge to overcome in the effective implementation of ERM is not the development of policies, training, implementation of risk management processes, or governance. Such tasks are relatively straightforward and achievable for most organizations. Experience has instead shown that the largest challenge to implementation is typically changing behaviors of individuals that impede effective ERM implementation. ERM requires transparency across the organization in sharing with others the risks that each portion of the organization faces. Without such transparency, judgments made on prioritizing risks and risk treatments in a portfolio approach across the organization is not feasible. Ensuring the necessary organizational culture to apply and benefit from ERM will often require an awareness-building program across the organization on the need for effective risk management, the value of a strategically aligned portfolio approach to risk management enabled by ERM, the establishment of appropriate governance processes, and the modification of individual performance incentives (where appropriate) to motivate a willingness to identify, share, and manage risks for the benefit of the overall organization.

■ **Monitoring Progress.** Full implementation of ERM can be a long-term journey, particularly because of the organizational behavioral change management challenges that must be overcome in many cases. It can thus be useful to assess the level of maturity of an organization's ERM program at any point in time, and then to monitor progress over time in the adoption of ERM good practices. Some organizations use a simple four- or five-point scale, beginning with only ad hoc actions on managing risks, up to an integrated ERM program closely linked to strategic planning, budget allocation, performance measurement, and so on. However, it is quite likely that one of the elements of a successful ERM program may be more relatively mature than other portions. For example, policies for ERM could be relatively mature, organizational elements have a strong awareness of risk and need to manage that risk, yet detailed procedures are lacking or the organization culture seeks to contain the management of risk in close organizational silos. Regardless of how sophisticated an ERM maturity model may be, it is important that organizations self-assess to understand how far down the road to ERM they have traveled, and which next steps should take priority.

 **RISK AND MORE**

As we have stated, organizations need to maximize stakeholder value, and doing so requires a careful balancing of the risks accepted, results sought, and resources allocated for any particular objective. We began our more in-depth discussion of these three considerations with this chapter's focus on risk. The choice to discuss risk first was not that it was more important than the other two; all three considerations are equally important. If we are to generalize among these three balancing factors, perhaps the easiest differentiator is that risk is the least understood of the three and the most frequently ignored in decision-making. It is thus appropriate that we began with risk. However, there are of course results (performance) and resources (cost) to consider. Chapter 7 will discuss the results management element of the three Rs: the management of activities within the end-to-end business processes designed to set and achieve a particular result

7

# Results Management

O NE OF THE THREE Rs scales to be balanced in seeking to maximize organizational stakeholder value under VBM is what the authors have termed "results management." While this may be a new term to the reader, it will surely not be a new concept. Just as risk management is the management of risk, and resource and cost management are the management of resource usage and their costs, so, too, is results management the management of activities within the end-to-end business processes designed to set and achieve a particular result for stakeholders.

To be clear about the context of the word "results" in this chapter, we remind the reader that we are referring to a "result" as what an organization aspires to achieve through a particular decision and associated actions, and not the cost or risk of successfully achieving that result. In short, it is the "return" element of a risk-adjusted return on investment analysis as originally shown in Figure 2.3 and repeated here as Figure 7.1.

While the need to manage toward the delivery of desired results will surely be recognized, the authors present a new concept for how those results need to be achieved as part of a larger set of considerations. This larger set of considerations was discussed as part of enterprise performance management (EPM) in Chapter 5 and graphically presented in Figure 5.3. That figure is repeated as Figure 7.2. In this chapter we focus more specifically on one element of that EPM

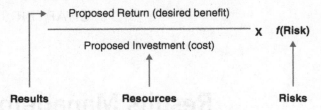

Value = Risk-Adjusted Return on Investment =

$$\frac{\text{Proposed Return (desired benefit)}}{\text{Proposed Investment (cost)}} \times f(\text{Risk})$$

**Results**          **Resources**          **Risks**

**FIGURE 7.1**   Risk-adjusted ROI.

## EPM Project/Process Management

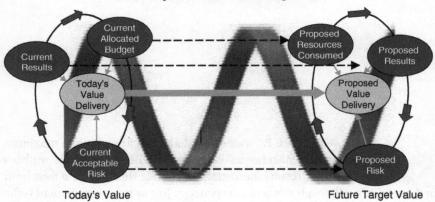

**FIGURE 7.2**   EPM project/process management.

effort: results management. To describe in further detail what we mean in our use of the term "results management," let us further elaborate on Figure 7.2.

As introduced in Chapter 5, "current results" are those results currently being delivered. In many cases, evaluation of these current results raises questions on whether the balance among results, resources, and risks is ideal for the delivery of maximum stakeholder value. In such cases, organizations typically engage in considerations to adjust results, resources, or risks as a means of improving overall stakeholder value. Such discussion frequently leads to establishing targets (e.g., KPIs) for a proposed new balance of results, resources, and risks to improve stakeholder value. This is of course normal for any organization and represents the very source of organizational progress. In an organization employing VBM, specific proposed targets will be set for proposed results, proposed resources consumed, and proposed risks accepted, as discussed in Chapter 5 on EPM.

**MANAGING RESULTS WITHIN EPM**

Managing results is simply one of the three elements of EPM. It is important to recognize that a "proposed result" is what we intend to accomplish for one or more stakeholders. It is the setting of targets and the intended consequence of actions yet to be taken, not the final consequence of those actions. In other words, it is what we intend to deliver at a future point in time as a result of our efforts, not what we will have actually delivered after completion of those actions. Once we have delivered a set of results, we refer to those as "results accomplished." Keep in mind that the "proposed results" of which we are speaking could be a new or improved product or service going to an external stakeholder outside of the overall organization; a product or service to an internal stakeholder that is being delivered from one part of the organization to another part of the organization (e.g., recruiting services offered by the human resources department to other portions of the organization); or even a revised process that results in the same end product or service but is delivered more cost effectively or with lower risk.

Ideally, results sought and results accomplished are identical. However, any manager typically faces unexpected challenges that may cause results accomplished to differ from results sought as initially envisioned. The results achieved may be better or worse in terms of contributing to stakeholder value than when originally set in the balancing with resources allocated and risks accepted. This change in results accomplished versus results planned and predicted may necessitate consideration of changing resources allocated or risks accepted if maximum potential stakeholder value is to be maintained. Results management is thus simply managing the activities to deliver a set of results in response to those originally sought, as illustrated in Figure 7.3, as well as the reengagement with resources management and risk management through EPM activities as changes over time may require.

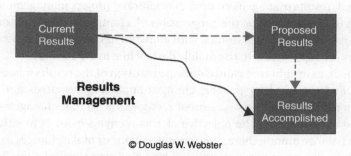

© Douglas W. Webster

**FIGURE 7.3** Results management.

**FROM PROPOSED RESULTS TO RESULTS ACCOMPLISHED**

If results management thus provides an ongoing reassessment of what "mid-course corrections" may be needed to ultimately deliver maximum potential stakeholder value, how are these adjustments accomplished? First, results management is actively engaged with risk and resource management in the ongoing reevaluation of the current level of results expected to be delivered. This enables consideration of tradeoffs given the current level of resources allocated to achieve those results and the risks currently being accepted. In order to have such an engagement, however, the results management process must understand the current capability of the organization in delivering results that contribute to stakeholder value. This engagement is represented on the left side of Figure 7.2 as "Today's Value."

Second, results management considers how stakeholder value could be increased by changing the currently delivered value of products, services, or processes. To accomplish this, results management engages with resource management and risk management activities to consider options for changing and rebalancing results, resources, and risks in a manner that would improve overall stakeholder value. For example, might a new product or service be offered that creates new value for stakeholders? Might an existing product or service be modified in such a manner that a reduced consumption of resources or decreased risk to delivery of the product or service increase value to stakeholders? Could the processes used to deliver a particular product or service result in lower production cost or higher quality? Setting the targets for proposed value thus requires active engagement from a results management perspective, as well as resource management and risk management. This discussion and projection of a proposed rebalancing is represented on the right side of Figure 7.2 as "Proposed Value."

Third, results management applies traditional project management activities to guide and monitor the progression of changes needed to move from current results to proposed results, with adjustments made as necessary. These activities are represented in the middle dashed line in Figure 7.2.

Fourth, as insights are gained during execution of the results management process and the need for possible changes impacting resources and/or risk becomes evident, results management reengages with risk management and resource management. The objective of this reengagement is to either confirm the balance among these three considerations or make changes as needed in order to deliver maximum stakeholder value upon completion. This last activity, represented by the red helix in Figure 7.2, results in the integrated EPM process, reflected by the green arrow in the figure.

Moving from "current results" to "results accomplished" thus reflects in part traditional project management activities. However, in an organization applying value-based management, project management additionally incorporates the rebalancing of resources, results, and risks on an ongoing basis as the insight into these three elements evolves and adjusts over time. The goal, of course, is to deliver maximum stakeholder value at the point of delivery and not be constrained by assessments of proposed results, resources, and risks that may have become inaccurate over time. The need for this ongoing reengagement among results sought, resources allocated, and risks accepted should not be new to any experienced project manager. VBM simply makes this balancing act explicit, and ties the need for such a three-way balance to strategy not just within a specific project, but vertically across all levels of the organization and horizontally across all functional and programmatic areas of the organization.

It should be noted that the changes reflected in the solid line of Figure 7.3 do not necessarily reflect a reduction in results or value over time, but simply a change. As project management occurs to change current results to proposed results, new opportunities or insights may arise that were not available or envisioned when the proposed results were first established. The solid line in Figure 7.2 is thus simply a recognition that effective results management requires ongoing adjustments to evolving challenges and opportunities.

 ## OPTIMIZING RESULTS IN VALUE-BASED MANAGEMENT

As was discussed in Chapter 2, optimizing value across the overall organization requires a portfolio view of how value is created and delivered on behalf of the organization's stakeholders. This requires an integrated view of the balance of results sought, resources allocated, and risks accepted across the organization, both horizontally across all functional and programmatic areas of the organization, as well as vertically from the top of the organization to the bottom. Accomplishing this integrated view begins with an understanding of what constitutes stakeholder value at the highest levels of the organization, and then cascading those value-based strategic goals and objectives downward through the organization in terms of supporting elements results, resources, and risk.

Relative to the management of results, this requires determination of what proposed results are for the highest levels of the organization, and

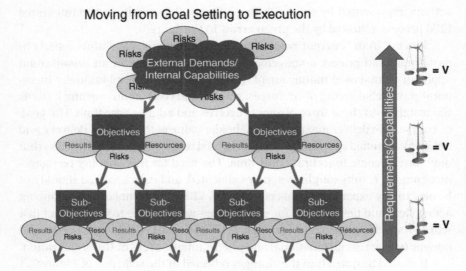

**FIGURE 7.4** Moving from goal setting to execution.

then decomposing these desired results into subordinate results that must be achieved in order to accomplish the higher-level results. This decomposition of results, which at every level of decomposition must be balanced with risks and resources, was illustrated in Figure 2.5 and is repeated here as Figure 7.4.

##  PROCESS IMPROVEMENT: A RESULT SOUGHT OR PART OF RESULTS MANAGEMENT?

The authors have referred above to the management of actions to achieve proposed results as "project management." This is because project management can be thought of as management of a process or set of processes designed to accomplish a particular output. In this case, project management is a set of coordinated, time-constrained actions required to achieve the delivery of "proposed results." Considering how to run a project designed to deliver a proposed result effectively and efficiently is thus a process and a candidate for formal process design and control.

However, it is important to recognize that process control and improvement could also be a desired result. For example, an organization may decide that a significant strategic goal could be to improve effectiveness and efficiency of existing processes. A desired result thus need not be limited to a new product or service. Simply delivering an existing product or service more effectively or efficiently through improved process control and redesign can be a justifiable result sought.

##  LEAN, QUALITY, AND BUSINESS PROCESS MANAGEMENT

As noted, process improvement can be an end-objective, and consideration of results desired, resources allocated, and risks accepted can inform the implementation of such a goal. However, during the reengagements to pursue the proposed results, the existing end-to-end processes are frequently involved. This includes productivity *improvement* typically from cycle time reduction and quality improvement. This involves programs referred to as lean management, quality management, often using Six Sigma techniques, and business process management (BPM). To clarify the last one – BPM – it is not another synonym with EPM. EPM is associated with being strategic and is holistically enterprise-wide. In contrast, BPM is associated with being operational and tactical, focusing on various end-to-end processes to remove waste and increase effectiveness and efficiency.

Much has already been written about these, so they will not be described in any depth in this book. They are simply referenced here so that they are not completely omitted, because they do serve a role in balancing the three Rs and maximizing stakeholder value – the end game of VBM.

Resource management (including cost management) will next be addressed in Chapter 8, which examines the aspects of capacity management and the language of money – financial information.

CHAPTER EIGHT

# Resource and Cost Management

T HIS CHAPTER CONCLUDES THE description of VBM's three Rs of risk, results, and resources in Part Four. It is an introductory chapter to cost management. It describes the utility and benefits from cost management in government using progressive management accounting practices and methods to manage costs.

The preface mentioned that VBM's three Rs are balanced. Part Five, Chapters 9 to 14, involving cost management, will give an impression they are imbalanced. This is because author Gary Cokins has substantial experience with management accounting methods and practices, including writing several books and many articles on this subject.

The extensive length of Part Five is a deep dive into management accounting in government. It is intended to educate practitioners (including consultants) with the "how," not just the "why," to design and implement progressive management accounting in organizations. If you are not directly involved with the CFO's department, then the authors suggest that perhaps you read only this Chapter 8 and share the entire Part Five (Chapters 9 to 14) with accountants whom you care to influence to implement what is written in this chapter.

Most organizations – particularly in government agencies – need better resource and cost information to take advantage of the VBM framework.

## COMPLIANCE WITH COSTING'S "CAUSALITY PRINCIPLE"

One way to derive a solid understanding of resource spending expenses is through appropriate cost assignment methods such as project/program accounting and activity-based cost management (ABC/M), and subsequently applying analytics on them to generate insights and make judgments. For costing environments that involve nonrecurring projects/programs, "make-to-order" manufacturing of one-of-a-kind products (e.g., a space satellite), or with projects/programs (e.g., a government project, house construction, law and consulting firms), then project accounting applies as a high form of direct costing. (However, ABC/M can be included with project accounting to trace indirect expenses based on causal relationships for full costing of the projects.) ABC/M applies to organizations that have repetitive processes and typically addresses the indirect expenses, although ABC/M can also be applied for direct expenses.

Figure 8.1 illustrates some alternative ways in which costs can reflect the diversity, variation, and differences of the cost objects (e.g., products,

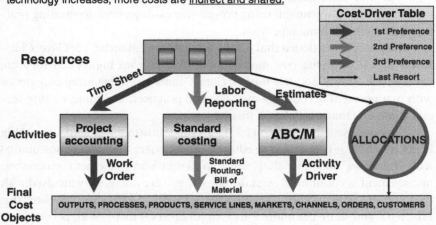

**FIGURE 8.1** Improved accuracy via greater direct costing. Source: Copyright 2019 www.garycokins.com.

services, outputs, projects, programs, work orders, service recipients, citizens, or customers) that consume expenses. Any cost distribution or reassignment, popularly called a *cost allocation*, will always involve three elements: the origin, the transfer mechanism, and the destination (i.e., cost objects). In costing lingo, the resources "supply" capacity as expenses to work activities as calculated costs, whereas the products, services, projects, or citizens/customers/beneficiaries "consume" the capacity as work activity costs. It is a demand and supply relationship, where there may be some excess or unused supply capacity (e.g., buffer capacity for spikes in demand).

Resource expenses can be thought of as payroll, employee benefits, materials, operating supplies, or energy utilities; these represent the available capacities and capabilities that are supplied to the work activities that produce outputs. Resource expenses are initially captured in a general ledger accounting or fund accounting system, a method of accumulating transactions into the ledger's expense account balances.

Figure 8.1 shows the continuum of differences among cost assignment approaches. These include the two popular direct costing methods, project/program (job order or work order) accounting and standard costing, followed by the ABC/M assignment method based on causality.

The applicability of the direct costing method ranks, left to right in the figure, from the most preferred to least preferred method. Note that *cost allocations* located at the far right are discouraged. There is no great mystery here. If the work activity was not consumed by or has no valid consuming relationship with a cost destination, then no meaningful assignment can exist. There is no cause-and-effect relationship. This is referred to as costing's *causality principle*. In practice, the basis or factors for many cost allocations are often at best directional (e.g., allocated by number of output units produced or delivered, employees, or square feet) and at worst arbitrary possessing no correlation – no causality. That is why *cost allocations* in Figure 8.1 are termed in the cost driver table as a "last resort."

 ## PROJECT ACCOUNTING AND WORK ORDERS

Public sector organizations have for years been using project accounting and work order management accounting systems. Direct costing of highly direct labor and material costs is not a foreign concept to them. But what has been surprising is the increasing shift and magnitude from direct into indirect costs. Indirect and support overhead expenses are trickier to trace and assign than direct costs.

Project accounting or its equivalent twin, job order costing, is the highest form of direct costing with regard to accuracy of costs. This assignment method simultaneously captures the *intersection* of the resource's time-usage duration with the project plan's work step or with its recipient, such as a job/service work order, product, or service. That is, both the work activity *and* its recipient are coupled at the cost intersection. This form of costing is more applicable in law, consulting, or auditing firms as well as in contractor environments. In manufacturing, work order costing is popular in job shops where, at the extreme, the organization is building a one-of-a-kind. Project accounting is also prevalent and often regulated in compliance with laws stipulated by government agencies such as the Department of Defense or the Department of Energy.

With this form of direct costing, the time length of life of the cost object (e.g., a project or program) has a beginning and an end: a complete life cycle unto itself. Expenses are continuously charged while the work is in progress, and costing concludes by "closing out" when the project, program, or job is complete.

ABC/M and project accounting can be combined and blended. All of these cost assignment methods involve a form of direct costing that apply calculated costs from expenditures into outputs.

 ## ACTIVITY-BASED COST MANAGEMENT (ABC/M)

Activity-based cost management (ABC/M) is a management accounting method of using reasonably accurate and reliable cost information and combining it with other sources of VBM data to gain insights and influence decision making. Cost management should be performed in the context of VBM. It is one of the three scales in Figure 2.1.

Reporting an agency's cost center expense spending against its budget from its fund accounting system (which is the equivalent of a commercial company's general ledger accounting system) is now recognized as using structurally deficient information. It reports *expenses*. It does not report the calculated *costs* of the business processes (or of the work activity costs that belong to them) or of the costs of their outputs and outcomes. It does report budget spending variances, but this fact does not make managers any smarter about how to influence or control the costs. If they are using ABC/M information, which computes the costs of processes, outputs, and outcomes, then they have insight into (1) the cost drivers that cause expenses to be consumed, and into (2) the per-unit costs of the outputs, which are valuable for benchmarking and tracking cost trends across time.

Some government accountants may claim they already calculate output costs, but these costs are usually distorted and flawed by using broadly averaged cost allocation factors like the number of service units delivered, square feet, or the number of employees. ABC/M's math resolves these error-causing cross-subsidies by tracing the activity costs within each process to the outputs using cause-and-effect activity cost drivers. Complying with costing's *causality principle* is fundamental for valid management accounting.

ABC/M provides an approach for organizations that enables them to recognize the work activities performed – by their employees, contractors, and equipment – and see what resources (such as time, budget dollars, salary, or materials) are consumed in conjunction with the activity. Further, ABC/M reveals who or what is driving costs.

It is important to note that ABC/M is often used at both the program and organizational levels to help organizations minimize costs. ABC/M information complements balanced scorecard and the VBM framework by linking costs of activities and operations to strategy. For example, some KPIs in the balanced scorecard can come from ABC/M.

 ## THE UTILITY AND BENEFITS FROM ABC/M IN GOVERNMENT

In recent years government organizations have begun to look to private industry for ideas on how to improve their business practices and their efficiency in resource use. ABC/M is an important component of VBM being introduced in the effort to achieve these ends. ABC/M provides fact-based information.

Many senior managers have gotten used to making decisions without good information, so they think they do not need better cost information. But the pressure to make better decisions and use resources more intelligently has increased. ABC/M provides valuable information that can be used to make a broad range of decisions, spanning from outsourcing decisions to operational planning and budgeting.

ABC/M has often met with a mixed response in its initial stages, despite widespread discontent with traditional management accounting methods and despite its proven track record elsewhere. Part Five of this book explains what ABC/M is intended to do – and what it is not – in the hope that such enlightenment will help in applying a powerful costing method to the critical problems now facing much of the public sector.

Activity-based concepts were introduced nearly two decades ago, but their development was sidetracked by the headlong gold rush of consulting and software firms clambering to sell services and products that were based on immature and incomplete ideas. The results were high-cost, limited-value solutions whose success fell far short of expectations.

Activity-based concepts and principles provide a powerful tool for creating valid economic cost models of organizations. By using the "lens of ABC/M," organizations of all sizes and types can develop the valid economic models required for their executives and managers to make value-creating decisions and take actions to improve their productivity and resource usage – and ultimately to better serve their stakeholders and constituencies.

In this chapter, we touch lightly upon the pressures for improved cost accounting in government, misapprehensions, and other sources of resistance against ABC/M. Many of the subjects introduced will be examined more closely in the chapters in Part Five, most particularly those dealing with the mechanics of designing an ABC/M system. In the end, the authors hope to have convinced the reader that ABC/M in government is an idea whose time has come to be adopted.

 **POLITICAL PRESSURES TO HOLD DOWN COSTS**

Public sector organizations at all levels and of all types are facing intense pressure to do more with less. Federal, national, state, county, municipal, and local governments in almost all the countries in the world are feeling some sort of fiscal squeeze. This includes departments, administrations, legislative bodies, branches, foundations, and agencies.

The pressure on spending has many sources. It can come from politicians aiming to win taxpayers' approval or directly from taxpayer special-interest groups. For example, there is pressure from the competition with other cities to attract homebuyers or with other counties, states, or nations to attract businesses. In the United States, the cities don't just compete against other cities – each city competes against its own suburbs. And the suburbs often have an advantage in attracting residents and businesses. The suburbs may offer lower taxes, better schools, and less crime. As residents and businesses relocate, the cities and towns they departed from lose a little more of their tax base. Less spending is available unless tax rates are raised.

Additional pressure may come from declining demand, regardless of the reasons. An example is rural road maintenance. In these cases, economies of scale are less easily achieved.

In the United States, the federal government is shifting some responsibilities to state and local governments but providing only limited funding to fulfill those obligations. Regardless of where the pressure is coming from, the message is: better, faster, cheaper – hold the line on raising taxes, but don't let service slip.

Meeting this daunting challenge often requires:

- Determining the true and actual costs of services
- Implementing process improvements
- Evaluating outsourcing or privatization options (i.e., is it better to deliver internally or purchase outside?)
- Aligning manager and employee activities to the organization's mission and its strategic plan

The solution for governments under pressure cannot be to simply uncover new sources of revenue or to continuously raise tax rates. Some governments have succumbed to these quick fixes, only to meet with a downward spiral as more businesses and families move to more economically attractive locations. Governments must get a handle on their problems. Holding the line on raising taxes will need to be more than a hollow campaign slogan; it may become an absolute requirement to retain the tax base. This restriction will create more reasons to understand costs. Efficiency and performance, once reserved for the private sector, will increasingly be part of the language of the public sector.

ABC/M offers potential solutions to the problem. Providing meaningful, fact-based management accounting information to government officials, managers, and employee teams can be an effective means of bringing about beneficial change and improved performance in government and not-for-profit environments. Intuition and political persuasion are becoming less effective as means for decision-making.

The pressure on the public sector is undeniable. People want government to work better and cost less. To do so, public sector managers will have to change their way of thinking about the true costs – and value – of the services they provide.

 ## AN EXCESSIVE FOCUS ON FUNCTIONS

When a new mayor takes office in a city, he or she may be told by the city managers that the finances are reasonably healthy. Expenditures and resources are in balance; there is no fiscal deficit. But can those same managers tell the new mayor how much it costs to fill a pothole, to process a construction permit, or to plow a highway mile or kilometer of snow?

The reference to the cost of outputs will repeatedly resonate throughout the chapters in Part Five. It is inescapable. The need to consider outputs, not simply the level of manpower, equipment, and supplies, is what is forcing the awareness and acceptance of ABC/M. At a very basic level, ABC/M is simply a converter and translator of expenditures as inputs restated as outputs.

ABC/M answers fundamental questions such as "what do things cost?" and "why?" It further answers "who receives them?" and "how much costs did they each receive?" Examples of output costs are the unit cost per each type of processed tax statement or the unit cost per each type of rubbish disposal pickup. ABC/M serves as a calculation engine that converts the expenses of employee salaries, contractor fees, and supplies into the costs of outputs. The work activities are simply the mechanism that produces and delivers the outputs. The work of people and equipment is foundational. All organizations do work or purchase it. All work has outputs. This topic of outputs will be constantly revisited. It is a critical aspect of ABC/M.

The dilemma for many not-for-profit and government agencies, branches, administrations, and departments is their fixation with determining budget levels for spending without sufficient facts to base them on. From the budget requestor's perspective, an annual budget negotiation is usually an argument to retain or increase the level of resources relative to the recent past's existing level. Regardless if this behavior is due to an ego display by ambitious or fearful managers or a lack of any better means to determine resource requirements, it is the rare manager who accepts a reduction in anything – except maybe a reduction in headaches caused by his daily problems. Defending one's budget was not the way it worked in the beginning. Let's now revisit the past and understand some history about budgets.

##  THE EVOLUTION OF ANNUAL BUDGETS

Organizations seem to go through an irreversible life cycle that leads them toward specialization and eventually to turf protection. When organizations initially begin, things are fairly straightforward. With the passing of time, the number and variety of their services change as well as the needs of their customers and service recipients (e.g., citizens and taxpayers). This introduces complexity and results in more indirect expenses to manage the complexity.

Following an organization's initial creation, all the workers are reasonably focused on fulfilling the needs of whatever created the organization in the first place. Despite early attempts to maintain flexibility, organizations slowly evolve into functions (e.g., departments). As the functions create their own identities and staff, they seem to become fortresses. In many of them, the work becomes the jealously guarded property of the occupants. Inside each fortress, allegiances grow and people speak their own language – an effective way to spot intruders and confuse communications.

With the passing of more time, organizations then become internally hierarchical. This structure exists even though the transactions and workflows that provide value and service to the end recipients pass across internal and artificial organizational boundaries. These now-accepted management hierarchies are often referred to, within the organization itself as well as in management literature, as "silos," "stovepipes," or "smokestacks." The structure causes managers to act in a self-serving way, placing their functional needs above those of the cross-functional end-to-end processes to which each function contributes work. In effect, the managers place their personal needs above the needs of their service recipients.

At this stage in the organization's life, there is less sensitivity to the sources of demand placed on the organization from the outside and to changes in citizen or customer needs. In other words, the organization is in danger of losing sight of its raison d'être. The functional silos compete for resources and blame one another for any of the organization's inexplicable and continuing failures to meet the needs of their customers or service recipients. Their arguments about the source of inefficiencies are little enlightened by the conflicting priorities involved.

By this evolution point, there is poor end-to-end visibility regarding what-drives-what inside the organization. Some of these organizations evolve into intransigent bureaucracies. Some functions become so embedded inside the broader organization that their work level is insensitive to changes in the number and types of external requests that were the origin of why their organization was originally created. They are somewhat insulated from the outside world.

As will be described throughout Part Five, the actual or planned spending levels reported by the general ledger or fund balance accounting system eventually emerge as the primary financial view for each of the functional managers. This has become the only way that functional managers can think about what level of spending can satisfy the needs of citizens or stakeholders relying on them for good service. Most managers are reasonably confident in the reported numbers underlying this view. They roughly know their employee salaries and benefits, have authorized most of the purchasing requests, and understand (but may despise) the allocation for support overhead expenses that they are charged with. That is, the managers understand the bookkeeping system, including its archaic cost-chargeback schemes. Figure 8.2 illustrates the limited view that many managers have of their fiscal condition.

The traditional accounting structure mirrors the hierarchical organizational structure. Each function is a cost center of sorts, and the accountants consolidate the functional department expenses into totals with elegant roll-up procedures. But is managing a cost structure all about focusing on the supply-side of resource expenses, which is basically the organization's capacity to serve? Or should the focus begin with reacting to the demands for work placed on the organization from citizens and service recipients? ABC/M brings visibility and understanding to the latter – fulfilling the needs of the citizens and service recipients who consume the organization's outputs.

The ABC/M view is a radical departure from the norm for governments and defense organizations. Consider how politicians campaign for votes. They

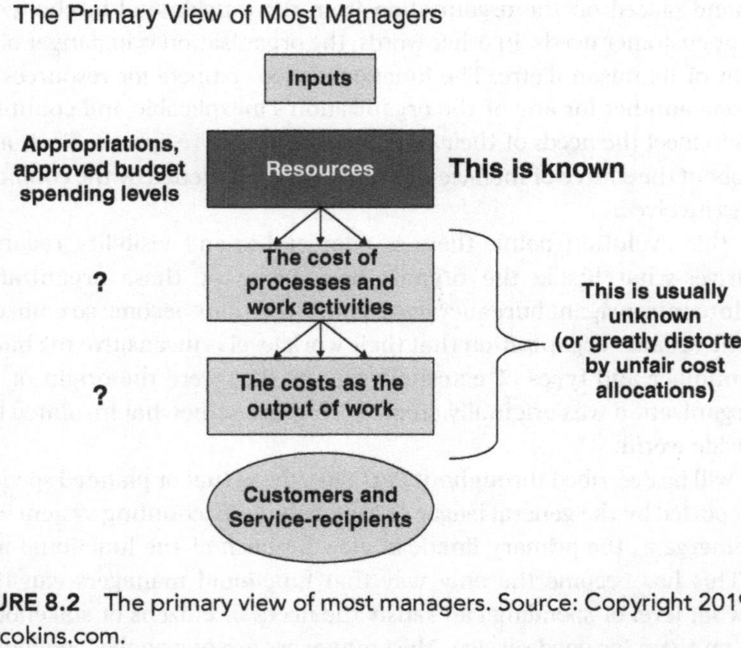

**The Primary View of Most Managers**

FIGURE 8.2 The primary view of most managers. Source: Copyright 2019 www.garycokins.com.

communicate in terms of inputs. Politicians who want to be viewed as tough on crime will propose spending more money on police forces and prisons. Those who want to be perceived as kind and generous will offer more money for social programs. This fixation with inputs does not conclude with the election. Following an elected politician's campaign rhetoric, press releases applaud the funding of programs as if the money going in automatically ensures that desired results will come out the other side.

In the military services, newly assigned field commanders regularly arrive at their military bases sharing a single interest: they lobby for a bigger budget. They may be granted the money. But holding them accountable for the results or how efficiently they use the government's money is a separate matter.

Government employees and managers often view the annual fiscal budgeting process with cynicism. ABC/M practitioners have learned that it is better if buyers and consumers, including government buyers and procurement agents, purchase outputs instead of the inputs. Fortunately, the focus within the public sector has begun to shift from budget management to performance-based results measurement. Chapter 13 will discuss traditional budgeting and describe how capacity-sensitive driver-based budgeting can leverage an ABC/M system and produce more credible and valid budget planning of resource needs and utilization.

## REMOVING THE BLINDFOLD: OUTPUTS, NOT JUST RESOURCE EXPENSES

The traditional financial accounting system has evolved in such a way that all public sector managers reasonably know what expenditures they have spent in past time periods. But none of them know what the costs were either in the aggregate or for the individual outputs. So, what are the costs of outputs? What is the cost of each output on a per-unit basis? How does one accurately calculate these costs?

To simplify semantics, resources are capacity that is consumed, and expenses or expenditures are incurred when money is exchanged with third-party suppliers and with employees for the resources. Costs are always "calculated." Costs restate the expenses as work activities and ultimately as outputs. Expenses and costs must equate in total, but they are not the same things.

Figure 8.3 illustrates how management's limited view can be extended beyond the resources' expenditure amounts. Traditional financial management systems focus on the expenses of labor, supplies, and so on, rather than on

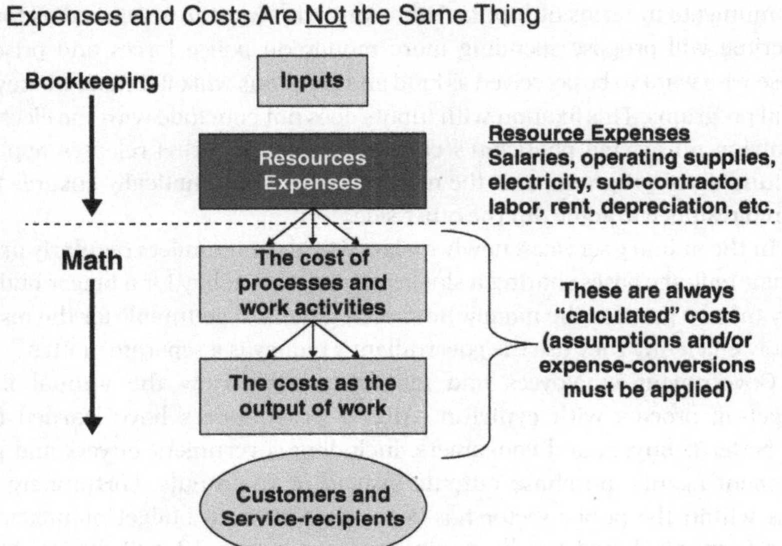

Expenses and Costs Are <u>Not</u> the Same Thing

FIGURE 8.3 Expenses and costs are not the same thing. Source: Copyright 2019 www.garycokins.com.

what work is performed and the outputs resulting from using these resources. ABC/M makes visible what has been missing in financial reporting by using management accounting

Governments adhere to and comply with standard government accounting principles similar to statutory and regulatory compliance accounting. For example, fund accounting is similar to the general ledger bookkeeping that commercial businesses use, except that fund accounting adds an extra step. In most simple terms, fund accounting first establishes a planned or budgeted spending ceiling for various funds and their accounts. (Funds are comparable to responsibility cost centers in general ledger accounting.) Approved spending often comes in the form of appropriations.

The extra step involves requisitions. Managers basically use requisitions for spending; if the spending ceiling has been reached, or if the requisition fails other tests, then the purchase is prohibited. In effect, government and not-for-profit accounting adds an extra level of spending control. However, although these extra controls deter government managers from committing fraud or stealing money, they do little to stop them from wasting it.

The accounting system reports overhead and support costs and allocates them to the final outputs of the organization. The basis for how the cost allocation is distributed is usually convenient for the accountants but does not reflect the unique and relative relationship between resource expense consumption and the final output costs, much less the work processes involved. This violates costing's causality principle.

In the end, many managers dismiss the calculated cost from their accounting system as mistruth. It may accurately reconcile in total for the organization, but not in the pieces. Unfortunately, these same managers have little choice but to go along with these flawed and misleading costs. They have little influence or control over their accountants. The accountants count the beans, but they are not tasked to grow the beans.

When managers and employee teams do not reliably know what the costs are for their current outputs, including per-unit of output costs, they have a difficult time knowing what the future costs may be for future levels of demand or for changes in requests for their outputs. This is discussed in Chapter 13. Most managers consciously or subconsciously stick with the primary view of the costs they are familiar with – their spending. And the accounting system, structured to report spending this way, reinforces this view. As mentioned, no managers willingly volunteer to continue into a future year with fewer resources, so they fight for the same or (usually) more resources at the annual budget planning time.

When managers receive their monthly responsibility center report calculating the favorable or unfavorable expense variance between their actual spending and their budget, what does that information really tell them? When they look at their variances, they are either happy or sad, but they are rarely any smarter! ABC/M extends the minimal information in the departmental spending reports to make managers and employee teams more informed and smarter. This extended information is then used for gaining insights and making decisions – better decisions than are made without the ABC/M information.

Decisions always affect the future. The past has already happened. ABC/M's strength is giving insights based on understanding past costs, not just spending, and then applying the same information to make better decisions.

Let's add some more realities to this description of government and defense organizations as service providers. Let's now include the key players – public sector workers, taxpayers, citizens, and users of the government services:

- The civil service worker or military member might simply prefer the status quo or whatever may be a little bit better for him or her.
- The taxpayer prefers to be taxed less.
- The user of government services desires more and higher-quality service.
- The functional manager is defending the existing level of his resources and fiscal budget.

It is a no-win situation. Something has to give. The combination of these disparate interests creates tension and conflict. How does one untangle the knots? Untangling is difficult when the primary financial view that is used by management only shows spending for resource expenses. There must also be an *equivalent* financial view of the outputs and their costs. Questions and discovery begin when the costs of outputs can be made visible and compared with other output costs including from other departments or agencies. A more reasonable discussion about spending levels occurs when you can *equate* the spending and what the citizens and service recipients get for the spending.

And even if two outputs, such as the per-unit cost for rubbish disposal for two neighboring houses per month, appear to be the same amount, each house may have consumed a different workload. One may have had fewer containers but with cumbersome items, like wood blocks and metal rods, for the material handlers to deal with. The other may simply have more containers, but with standard contents. Alternatively, compare two municipal rubbish disposal services with the identical number of residential stops and identical work crew staff at similar weekly wages. All things being equal, if one crew averages six hours per day while the other averages eight hours, the cost per house disposal is equal for each municipality, but the work material handling content is not. The former crew has more unused capacity than the latter crew. The former has a lower disposal cost per residential home for the productive work excluding the two hours of unused capacity.

By adding the management accounting view of the outputs to the financial view of the resource expenses, managers and employee teams can much better understand the behavior of their cost structure – what causes and drives the costs. The visibility that comes from knowing the costs of outputs becomes the stimulant for understanding the cost structure and economics. Outputs are the linkage to the external service recipients as well as to the internal work activities. The distribution of workload adapts to changes in demand levels for outputs. Output costing can also benefit the cross-functional processes. An ABC/M information system gives visibility to all of these relationships (and even more with the additional capability to score or tag costs with ABC/M's attributes discussed in Chapter 12).

##  BUT OUR DEPARTMENT DOES NOT HAVE OUTPUTS

It is a bogus statement by some departments that, presumably due to the nature of their work, they have no outputs. There is no dichotomy between workers who think and plan and workers who deliver services and tangible products. Managers and workers who think, plan, and give directions conclude that since their work deals with intangibles, not things, then there is no definable output from their work. But outputs can be intangible. Many are. What is the output of a university education? Is it the diploma? Is it each professor's course? Is it the learning by each student? These may all appear to be intangible. But the financial cost for each one is measurable.

Employment by government is not an entitlement program for its workers. The value of the contribution of work must be understood and compared among alternatives.

The purpose here is not to get emotional or political or to tug on heartstrings. ABC/M does not take sides. It just reports the facts. People can then debate their own positions about what is the value of it all. But ABC/M does provide the basis for determining cost/benefit tradeoffs and thus allows comparison with other services competing for tax budget money. This type of dialogue and discussion cannot easily occur when funding is simply stated in the form of salaries, supporting expense, and supplies. Dialogue is better stimulated when costs are stated in other terms, such as the per-unit costs for each output, permitting comparisons to be made.

A recognized need to shift emphasis from inputs to outputs is leading some civilian and defense organizations to adopt financial funding relationships based on pay for performance – rather than simply disbursing cash to service providers as if they were entitled to it. As an example, one city government had historically funded one of its social service agencies based essentially on inputs. The mission of this particular social service organization was to prepare and place unemployed people into jobs as workers. Historically the agency billed the city's central funding authority based on the number of unemployed candidates interviewed and the number of hours of job training provided. Whether any of these candidates actually got a job was irrelevant to the agency getting paid. The basis for payment to the agency was the events involved in the process, rather than the relevant results – successful hirings – that the city had hired the agency to produce.

The city government altered the payment arrangement to one based on the number of job hirings lasting for at least six months that were secured

## A Case Study About Defining Outputs

Several years ago at one of the US government laboratories where high-paid physicists wrestle with theory and scientific advances in their field, a business-process effectiveness study was conducted. There was debate about how to map inputs, processes, and outputs. Some of the physicists believed their work was unmappable. The physicists argued that one could not rigorously define the brain's thinking process when it comes to innovation. That is not the point with ABC/M.

All work has outputs. For example, when one of this same government laboratory's experiments is conducted, there is a "completed" experiment. When a research paper is written and submitted by a physicist, there is a "completed research paper." There may have been lots of thinking, preparation, typing and copying support, and so on to "finish" the research paper, but these costs can be appropriately traced and assigned to a type of output. When the report is done, the aggregate output can be described as a "completed research paper."

Moreover, all completed research papers are not equal in the time, effort, and support needed and used. There can be great diversity and variation. ABC/M measures that variation and links the costs back to what the organization spent in paying for salaries and supplies. The focus is not on who funded that spending, although there is a clear audit trail back to the source. ABC/M cares that spending did occur and went somewhere and into something for somebody.

Seeing the true cost of outputs can produce some organizational shock. To exaggerate, if a "completed report" at this government laboratory, after all the time and support is traced into it, costs let's say $325,000, that may be a surprise. If it is read by only three young advisors to a US senator, and they brief the senator in a quick hallway conversation without any more use of that report, it makes you wonder whether the report was worth it. You cannot be sure, but at least you have a significant piece of information that you did not have before – the true cost to produce that particular report. The $325,000 price tag would clearly make some other government service provider – let's say one that may be very strapped on budget and whose mission is feeding and caring for children in need – really think about whether appropriations are fairly distributed.

for these former welfare recipients. This output-based solution worked. The agency recognized that it needed to customize its training according to individual needs and shortcomings. In the end, the agency benefited as well with increased revenues.

## ABC/M USES (AND SOME PITFALLS)

A significant lesson learned from previous implementations of ABC/M is the importance of working backward with the end in mind. That is, it is to management's benefit to know in advance what its organization might do with the ABC/M information before the calculation effort is launched. The end determines the level of effort required to collect, validate, calculate, and report the information.

Although ABC/M is basically just information, one of its ironic shortcomings is the wide variety of ways the information can be used. Different uses require more or less detail or accuracy. Accordingly, the system should be built with a clear idea of the types of decisions, insights, or assessments that the ABC/M information will be used for to support. Some ABC/M implementations may miss the mark by being initially designed as either overly detailed or not detailed enough.

Eventually, as the ABC/M information is applied as an enabler for multiple uses, the size of the system and level of effort to maintain it stabilizes at an appropriate level. Through using the information, the ABC/M system gets right-sized and self-balances the tradeoff between the level of administrative effort to collect, validate, calculate, and report the information and the benefits as it meets various users' needs. Designing and implementing a "right-sized" ABC/M system is discussed in Chapter 14. The technique involves rapid prototyping an initial ABC/M model, followed by iterative remodeling, to arrive at a repeatable and reliable ABC/M system in weeks, not in months.

Here are examples of the more popular uses of ABC/M by governments and defense organizations:

- **Fees for service/cost-to-serve** to calculate costs of specific outputs as a means of pricing services provided to customers and other functions/ agencies. This applies to agencies tasked with full cost recovery of their expenses via prices charged.
- **Outsourcing/privatization studies** to determine which specific costs will actually remain or go away if a third party were to replace an existing part or all of an organization. Increasingly, commercial companies are positioning themselves to perform services once viewed exclusively as a public-sector domain. Some government agencies are learning that it is better to proactively measure their costs to prevent the possibility of a poor

decision by an evaluation team. For example, the team may mistakenly conclude that outsourcing makes the most sense and discover after the fact that more accurate information would have reversed that decision. ABC/M can also help a government organization bring its costs in line with those of a commercial provider; its governing authority may allow a grace period for doing so.

- **Competitive bidding:** Increasingly, commercial companies are positioning themselves to perform services, such as operating prisons, that were once exclusively the domain of the public sector. But the reverse is possible, too. Some government departments, such as those performing road maintenance or tree trimming, may excel and compete with commercial companies.
- **Merging/diverging agencies or functions** to identify administrative services that could be shared or combined among multiple agencies or functions.
- **Performance measurement** to provide some of the inputs of KPIs to balanced scorecards designed to improve performance and accountability to taxpayers.
- **Process improvement/operational efficiency** to optimize resource use and, at times, to serve as a key to an agency's survival. Some agencies are facing budget cuts (or taking on additional activities due to consolidation) and are unclear about the costs of their internal outputs. What does it cost to process a new registrant versus a renewal? Why might these two costs be so different? Do both costs per each event seem too high?
- **Budgeting** to routinely plan for future spending not based on the current rate of spending but, more logically, on the demand volume and mix of services anticipated.
- **Aligning activities to the strategic plan** to correct for substantial disconnects between the work and service levels that an organization is supplying and the activities required to meet the leadership's strategic goals. It can be shocking for organizations to discover to what extent they are very, very good at things they do that are deemed very, very unimportant to the strategic plan.

There are many uses for management accounting. The idea here is not to start an ABC/M implementation process just because it seems to feel right or because an authority commands or dictates it. Know in advance what problems the better cost information will be solving.

## COST INFORMATION IS EMPOWERING

When senior leadership, managers, and employee teams are provided with reliable views of not only their resource expenses spending but also the costs of work activities, costs of processes involved in these activities, and the total and per-unit costs of the outputs deriving from the activities, they have so much more basis for making decisions. Compare all of those sources of cost information to what they have now. Today they only have the expense spending view, but no insight as to how much of that spending is or was really needed or why. Managers need to know the causal relationships – the drivers of costs. And when employees have reliable and relevant information, managers can manage less and lead more.

An ABC/M system provides a good starting point for any nonprofit or government organization to model its cost behavior. ABC/M can be thought of as a solution looking for problems, and all organizations have problems. ABC/M provides a top-down look at how an organization's resources get used – and why, and by whom, and how much. This is so logical and fundamental.

In your mind, divide resource spending into two categories: resources used and resources unused (i.e., idle capacity). For the first category, resources used, a cost can only be incurred if some person or piece of equipment does something. In other words, if you want to understand your cost behavior, you must understand which activities your organization performs, which other work activities or services these activities support, what outputs derive from these activities, and the characteristics of who is requesting and using these outputs. There are linkages. An ABC/M system models these linkages and reports the results as calculated costs. One gains multiple views of the costs, plus an understanding of the relationships.

Today, this type of management information can be provided with commercially available software products that link to existing fund accounting, cost, and metric systems. And ABC/M software can flexibly deliver meaningful reports to an individual's workstation – whether through integrated systems or web delivery. This is a cost-effective way of achieving performance improvement.

## DEALING WITH THE DARK SIDE: DOWNSIZING PUBLIC SECTOR EMPLOYEES

Many organizations experience an illusion that if they introduce productivity improvements and streamlining actions, they will automatically save costs. But being more efficient does not equate to realized savings in expenses – as opposed to costs – unless resources are removed (or when volume increases, extra resources do not have to be acquired).

Where do cost savings come from? All things being equal, and if there are no significant changes in revenues or funding following a change in services, then the only positive impact on cash flow must come from reduced variable costs. If purchased materials and supplies are reduced a certain percentage, those costs are totally variable and consumed as needed. The financial savings are real. That is, the cost savings are truly realized as cash outlay expense savings.

But when an organization works more efficiently and manpower staffing remains at a constant number, then basically there is a freeing up of unused capacity in the workers. These workers are more available to do other things. But as long as they continue to get paid their salary and wages, the organization realizes zero expense savings. Unlike the totally variable "as-needed" purchased materials, workers are "just-in-case" fixed costs where their full capacity is in effect contracted in advance of the demand for their services. If they are not totally needed all the time, the government pays for their idle capacity time as well.

As efficiencies are realized, manpower cost savings or future cost avoidance can only be realized by management in two ways:

- It can fill the freed-up worker's time with meaningful work, ideally addressing new volume of demand.
- It can remove the capacity. That means remove the workers (i.e., terminate them) to realize the savings in expense.

The issue here is that of transferring employees, demoting them, or removing them. One of the most difficult political issues stemming from privatization and outsourcing is the loss of public-employee jobs. This problem can be mitigated, however, if government and its private-sector partners work together to ensure the least pain and most gain for the individuals displaced.

The loss of jobs should be dealt with openly, compassionately, and comprehensively. There are several ways to accomplish this. Ideally, in an outsourcing situation, the private-sector company can rehire a portion of the existing government employees who are, after all, already experienced in the outsourced activities. The problem of inefficiency and lack of innovation is often not caused by worker incompetence but by weak processes or a heritage of poor managerial styles. Much of that changes when a new group of managers takes over.

Additional ways to address the loss of jobs is through transfer and attrition. Some employees can be placed in growth areas of the organization or elsewhere in the government as opportunities arise. In the interim, some organizations will set up a temporary "job bank" that uses the displaced workers in a meaningful way until attrition or new needs create job openings. Some employees are not totally wed to their employer, and the thought of quitting to do something else may be appealing to them. A financial incentive to quit can be just the stimulant to help them make that decision for themselves.

Ultimately, there may be no alternative but to terminate some employees. Grievances and threats of lawsuits may result, but an organization should never fear these if not guilty. Finally, remember that there are outplacement services with job training, paid for and cost-justified as part of the transition, that employees needing extra help in job relocation can use.

Not every transition to privatization goes smoothly. But people's lives are involved here and must be considered, too. Good approaches to addressing the loss of jobs are opportunities to soften the impact of entering into a partnership with the public sector. Compassion exhibited here may reduce the pace of realizing cost savings, but minimizing the short-term trauma of job displacement can bring longer-term benefits.

Finally, if an organization is downsizing, do not neglect the employees who remain to operate the organization. There is an old message that these people have heard: "The good news is you are the survivors. The bad news is you are the survivors." Sometimes management removes the bodies but not the work caused by external drivers. And the old methods and old systems often remain in place. Management may have met some short-term objectives, but they need the remaining workforce to operate with the long term in mind. Try to understand the processes, workload, and capacity before making radical changes.

 ## WHY CHANGE NOW

It may sound glib to say that change is the only constant, but it is so often true. The question for the public sector is whether it will drive change or be driven by it. In the United States, large federal budget deficits and new regulations, such as the Government Performance and Results Act (GPRA), have acted as catalysts for change in the way that government agencies perform their functions. Competition from the private sector will place additional pressures on governments, agencies, and the military to provide good service economically.

Without visible, relevant, and valid information, it is difficult for organizations to stimulate ideas and evaluate what options are available – and their financial impact. ABC/M provides fundamental information that is part of the solution. Applying ABC/M may well be critical to an organization's survival.

The authors believe that government is moving past the initial stage of rethinking what government does and how it does it. Restrictive funding pressures have already jump-started that. Government agencies are adopting a greater performance orientation and are replacing a detailed micromanagement style with a more practical approach where the costs are justified by the benefits. ABC/M is now and will continue to play an important role in helping government to manage its affairs.

The authors hope that this chapter and those in Part Five provide additional thought on how ABC/M systems can contribute to serving the public sector as a whole. Part Five will describe changes in the economics of an organization that has created the need for progressive management accounting methods and practices, including activity-based cost management (ABC/M).

# Management Accounting in Government

# CHAPTER NINE

# Understanding ABC/M: A Few Basic Truths

I N PART FIVE, BEGINNING with this chapter, the full spectrum of management accounting will be discussed not only for measuring past period costs but also the forward-looking future view of budgeting and "what-if" tradeoff analysis. Chapter 14 will describe a practical approach to implement a progressive, repeatable, and reliable production management accounting system in a few weeks, not months. This is intended to dispel the notion that the extra benefits from the extra effort to implement a progressive management accounting system is not cost-justified. But by reducing the effort relative to the benefits, it can make sense to proceed.

## THE NEED FOR MORE QUANTITATIVE AND FACT-BASED FINANCIAL INFORMATION

At the federal level in the United States, the President's Management Agenda, Office of Management and Budget (OMB), the Government Accountability Office (GAO), and Congress are demanding transparency and accountability of effectiveness of government programs. Federal agencies are required to assess and determine performance. And funding will increasingly be determined according to demonstrated results.

The purpose is to improve performance and program management by creating a focus on results. Ineffective programs are being reformed or constrained, or are facing closure. Programs deemed ineffective or with questionable results are losing budget funding and face poor publicity. Agencies find themselves defending program missions and their budgets to the US Congress.

Agencies at the state and local level in the US face similar pressures. In many states, the governor, state legislature, and the public are impatient and demanding accountability and transparency of government effectiveness, as well as improved efficiency.

All government agencies globally are faced with the daunting challenge of determining and proving program effectiveness. In addition, they are asked to assess costs, justify budget requests with performance information, and communicate expected and tangible results. They are being held accountable for every taxpayer dollar going toward their services and programs. The need for more quantitative and fact-based financial information, a strength of ABC/M, is undeniable.

Government organizations are intrigued – or perhaps feeling threatened – by the prospect of adopting a new, better management accounting method such as ABC/M. Experience has shown that eliminating some common misconceptions about ABC/M substantially eases the path to its acceptance and use. This chapter describes some simple truths about the purpose of ABC/M, its scope, and its applicability to public sector enterprises as well as to private industry.

Remember that rules are many and principles are few. ABC/M is a management accounting method based on the costing's causality principle of cause-and-effect relationships, similar to the law of physics that states every action involves an equal and opposite reaction.

##  WHAT IS ABC/M?

First, let us look at some of the concrete benefits that accrue to an organization when it adopts ABC/M. The system serves a variety of purposes. After reading Chapter 8, some benefits should be obvious, but others may be less clear.

ABC/M is an alternative to the tyranny of traditional cost allocations. Imagine that you go to a restaurant with three friends. You order a little salad and they each order a great big and expensive prime rib steak or lobster. When the waiter or waitress brings the bill, they all say, "Let's split the check evenly." How do you feel? Not fair to you. Not equitable.

Well, that is how many product and service lines also feel in a traditional cost accounting system when the accountants and comptrollers group allocate the typically large indirect support and overhead expenses as costs using broad averages without much (or any) logic. They spread those indirect expenses like butter across bread. There is minimal or no linkage between the true proportional consumption of the expenses and their allocation to the individual products, service lines, or end users. This is unfair. It is unfair in what is being costed, and it is unfair to people who use this information for insights and to make decisions.

ABC/M is a method that gets it right. In our restaurant example, ABC/M divides the check more fairly. It creates four individual checks – you pay for only what you consume. You don't subsidize the others or receive a generous gift from the others. To many ABC/M practitioners, the word *allocation* is one they wish had never existed. It implies inequity to so many people because of past abuses in their organization's accounting practices. The word *allocation* practically means misallocation, since that is usually the result. ABC/M practitioners often say that they do not allocate expenses; instead they *trace* and *assign* expenses into costs based on cause-and-effect relationships – costing's *causality* principle.

Many operations people cynically believe that accountants count what is easily counted – but not what counts. Outdated, traditional cost accounting obstructs managers and employees from seeing much of the relevant costs that are accurately attributable to their outputs. This problem has become increasingly significant as indirect expenses have ballooned relative to direct expenses.

Figure 9.1 reveals that, over the last few decades, indirect and overhead expenses have been displacing direct, recurring expenses as the major share of total expenses as organizations mature. Under the traditional cost accounting system, the organization has a reasonably clear view of direct expenditures for front-line labor and for material purchases. It has little insight, however, into the causes of its support and overhead spending.

For example, a banking institution is experienced at monitoring the work of its tellers and other employees who perform recurring work that is closest to the products and services benefiting its customers. It uses cost rates and performance-related factors, such as labor variance reporting, to calculate standard costs that are output-related. Many banks consequently know their standard cost per each deposit, per each wire transfer, and so on. They do not, however, have comparable financial information for the many vice presidents working on the second floor to the top of their building! The only financial

## The Need for ABC

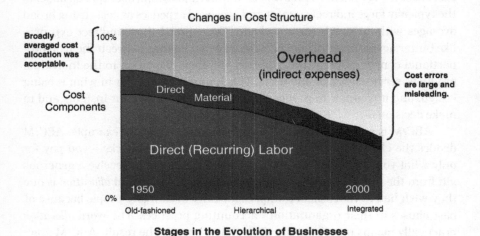

**FIGURE 9.1** The need for ABC. Source: Copyright 2019 www.garycokins.com.

information applied for those expenses is the annual budget plan, under which spending is monitored for each department or function only to see if the spending is under or over the budget.

When you ask people why, in their view, indirect and overhead expenses are displacing direct expenses, they almost invariably say that it is due to technology, equipment, automation, or computers. In other words, organizations are automating what were previously manual jobs. This cause is only a secondary factor. The primary cause for this displacement shift reflects the gradual proliferation in the diversity and variation of products and service lines that have occurred over the last few decades. Organizations now offer a greater variety in products and services and use more and different types of distribution channels to serve a wider variety of end users and service recipients. For example, manufacturers offer products with more colors and sizes. As another example, 20 years ago most entry-level soldiers in the US military were considered similar. But today, not only are extra expenses associated with the corps' composition (e.g., the influx of women), but there are many more different functions for which entry-level soldiers must be trained.

Greater variation and diversity (i.e., heterogeneity) creates complexity and in turn requires more indirect and overhead expenses to manage the complexity. Thus, a larger overhead component of expense does not automatically mean that an organization is becoming inefficient or bureaucratic. It may simply mean that it is offering more variety of products and services to a broader and more diverse array of recipients: citizens and stakeholders.

If you're not convinced by this explanation, the authors ask you to interview a long-time employee who is soon to retire. Ask someone in a manufacturing company, "How thick was your company's product catalog when you joined the organization, and how thick is it now?" For government employees, ask what types of citizens or government agencies the organization served at its creation, and how many more types it serves now. Their answers will reveal that the real reason for increasing overhead becomes evident. It is a result of increasing complexity needing to be managed.

Whatever the derivation of indirect support and overhead expenses, it is clear that traditional cost accounting methods have failed to meet the challenge. What ABC/M does is extend the visibility now pertaining to direct spending to illuminate what has for many organizations become the lion's share of spending – the indirect expenses. ABC/M then becomes an organization-wide method for understanding true work-activity costs and thus provides a reliable basis for predicting the outcome of decisions affecting the future.

ABC/M can also be used for calculating the output costs from direct expenses when the organization is not applying cost accounting.

ABC/M is a better gauge than benchmarking with blinders. Some governments and government organizations fool themselves into thinking that they are efficient when they benchmark their activities against similar activities performed by other governments or organizations. Their consulting firms sometimes even maintain benchmarking databases that are restricted to government agencies. The cost rates may be unfavorable relative to private sector companies, but without such comparisons, government agencies relying on benchmarked data may unknowingly continue to believe there is little room for improvement.

ABC/M can be used effectively either as an alternative to benchmarking or as a means of improving benchmarking as an informative tool. Alone, it gives management a true picture of cost/benefit relationships and thus a firm basis for effecting beneficial change. It can also serve as an essential adjunct to accurate and useful benchmarking. ABC/M requires standard activity and output "dictionaries." These standard definitions enable apple-to-apples comparisons, rather than apples-to-oranges.

Acquiring accurate information about costs is one of the biggest hurdles for public officials trying to save money and improve services, particularly for newly elected or appointed officials. Reasonably accurate information about costs is a key to making almost every other change initiative possible. ABC/M information is an effective enabler. Yet most governments and government organizations simply do not have sufficiently good information about their costs – perhaps about their expenses, but not their costs.

 ## WHAT ABC/M IS NOT

It is a mistake for ABC/M project teams to refer to ABC/M as an improvement program or a new change initiative. When that occurs, managers and employees often label the new project as a fad, fashion, or "flavor of the month." ABC/M information is simply used as a means to ends. It makes visible the economics of the organization and the consumption of resource expenses by its work activities and the outputs that consume them. Money is continuously being spent on organizational resources whether ABC/M measuring is present or not.

ABC/M is analogous to a physician's stethoscope that allows listening to one's lungs and heartbeat. Your heart is beating and you are breathing regardless of the presence of the stethoscope. In a similar way, an organization is continuously burning up its resource expenses through its processes and the work activities that belong to them, and it then traces the activity costs to who or what is consuming the resources. This is occurring whether ABC/M is monitoring these events or not.

The authors are deliberately dumbing down and understating ABC/M for an important reason. In the early 1990s, when ABC/M was beginning to get serious attention, the management consulting community began selling the system as consulting services. Unfortunately, in those days the consultants hyped and oversold ABC/M as a magic pill that could possibly solve all of an organization's problems. This raised management's expectations too high. If the consultants did not solve the problems that their client thought it had engaged them for in the first place, the blame fell on ABC/M for not working. But ABC/M worked just fine. It is simply full absorption costing, but done correctly – complying with costing's causality principle. It was just that some of the consultants did not accurately sell the system to their client – nor at times adequately understand how to interpret and use the ABC/M information. But that has changed now. The consultants have realized that their value-add is to help their clients solve their problems, and the ABC/M information is an important enabler to the solutions to those problems.

In many cases, organizations oversized the initial ABC/M system (e.g., with 1,000+ activities) well beyond the size needed to see results and get quick hits. It is important that an organization realize early on that ABC/M provides fundamentally good information to be used for understanding, discovery, and decision-making. Then ABC/M is better positioned for longer-term and wider acceptance. Chapter 14 describes the rapid prototyping with an iterative remodeling implementation approach that prevents oversizing ABC/M with a "right-sized" costing system that is good enough for better decision-making.

So, the authors are deliberately managing expectations about ABC/M by reducing one's perceptions that it provides all the answers. ABC/M restacks the costs but does not root them out. ABC/M's information can be a great enabler for providing answers; the key phrase is that it is an enabler.

There are many acronyms related to organizational improvement, TQM for total quality management and BPR for business process reengineering, to name a couple. They all focus on continuing improvement of work and the pursuit of excellence in daily operations. Many of these programs emphasize the following:

■ Management of processes rather than resources
■ Elimination of waste

One common thread runs through all of these improvement techniques: a focus on work activities and their relationship to services or products provided to customers or citizens. ABC/M information can turbocharge all of these performance improvement programs. When ABC/M is combined with operational information, such as performance measures (e.g., the balanced scorecard's KPIs), it becomes an even more powerful tool in making sensible and substantial changes.

In the authors' opinion, it is inevitable that all organizations will eventually rely on some form of an ABC/M information system to assist in effectively managing their affairs. So there is no reason to hype or overstate the power of ABC/M. It will continue to claim widespread global acceptance simply based on its merits and based on the utility and benefits that the ABC/M information provides.

 ## LET THE "HOW" AND "WHY" DRIVE THE EFFORT

In the end, 90 percent of ABC/M is organizational change management and behavior modification, and 10 percent of it is the math. This will be further discussed in Part Seven. Unfortunately, most organizations initially get those two functions reversed. They spend way too much time defining and constructing their ABC/M information system and very little time thinking about what their organization will do once they have the new ABC/M information. This presents a problem.

Poor implementation has adversely affected the rate of adoption of ABC/M. When ABC/M systems fall short of manager and employee teams' expectations, it is usually because the initial ABC/M system design was, as mentioned, substantially overengineered in size. The typical initial ABC/M system is usually excessively detailed and is well past diminishing returns on extra accuracy for each additional incremental effort of extra work to construct the ABC/M system. One manager reacted to seeing his first ABC/M report by saying, "I feel like a dog watching television. I don't know what I'm looking at!" With a fraction of the effort and in a much shorter timeframe, the implementation team could have started to produce reasonable and comprehensible results.

It is important to start getting results from ABC/M quickly because of the potential organizational shock that managers and employees may experience when they receive and view the new ABC/M information. That is, it is important to start realizing what kind of new (and possibly disturbing) information might come from ABC/M.

When people see the ABC/M information for the first time, they will see things they have never seen before – even though some of it will not be pretty. For example, there may be a manager who for years believed that his or her services were very efficient relative to those of other departments, functions, or agencies. But when ABC/M finishes more properly tracing the true consumption of expenses, the result may be an unpleasant surprise. The total costs of that manager's department services, as well as the calculated per unit costs per each output of service, may be well above comparable benchmarked costs of similar services elsewhere! That manager will not be happy to see this information, nor happy with whomever reported that information. Do not underestimate the level of resistance that can come from exposing managers and employees to the ABC/M information. You are dealing with human nature.

There is an important lesson here. Treat the ABC/M information responsibly. ABC/M is not an accounting police tool or a shame-and-blame tool, but rather an organization-wide managerial information system to be used for self-improvement. Its information is not intended to embarrass anyone and should not be used to punish anyone. In many cases no one really knew what the true costs were. Many suspected that the existing expense and cost allocations were wrong, but they did not know what the correct calculations would reveal. ABC/M finally gives managers and employee teams the hope that they can see the truth and reality. But seeing the information and using the information are not the same thing. There is much more thinking required when it comes to using the ABC/M information for managing and decision-making.

There is an old fable that says that all truth passes through three phases:

1. First, it is ridiculed.
2. Next, it is violently opposed.
3. Finally, it is accepted as being patently obvious.

Whether the perceived villain is the ABC/M method, or the costs of output information computed by the ABC/M system, keep this in mind. There will be resistance to ABC/M. And the resistance is not so much due to people being afraid of change – although that is a factor – but that they are afraid of uncertainty. The irony is that ABC/M information provides truth and reality, but until the ABC/M information is revealed, people are not sure what will be shown or how it might be used.

In short, even if an ABC/M system is in place, do not expect changes to automatically follow. Using the information is the hurdle.

##  COMMERCIAL BUSINESSES VERSUS GOVERNMENT ENTITIES

ABC/M advocates generally find the doubting Thomas syndrome more prevalent in the public sector than in the business world. In making their argument against the applicability of ABC/M to their work activities, government employees often cite two facts: (1) government does not operate with a profit motive in mind, and (2) government is normally a supplier of services rather than products. Both are true. In this part, we will look at these and other differences among ABC/M users as well as the growing similarities.

ABC/M has a different flavor when applied to not-for-profit organizations and governments rather than to commercial businesses. The general concepts of ABC/M remain foundational. But there are some different purposes and conditions that alter the focus and even the design of ABC/M for government organizations.

A significant difference in contrast to commercial businesses is a government agency's absence of a profit- and wealth-maximization motive. The system of reporting layers of profit contribution margins used by commercial organizations to focus on opportunities is meaningless. Some quasi-private public sector organizations, such as a military base commissary, pursue full cost recovery through pricing and fees, and do not have to maximize profit to enhance the owner's or investor's wealth. Just breaking even with the sales revenues recovering the total costs may be the goal.

Many other public sector organizations have no fee or price structure and no revenues from buyers or consumers. The organization is funded with a spending budget issued by an authorized body, such as a municipal board of directors or the US Congress, and it delivers services to other agencies or citizens without any exchange of payments. A local police or fire department and a national aviation agency are examples. Citizens are not expected to purchase their safety in pieces or on an as-needed basis; it is an expected service.

Another difference between the private and public sectors involves the targeting of specific markets and customers. Not-for-profit and government organizations usually do not have the luxury of determining whom they wish to serve. Tax authorities deal with all taxpayers, and their work is defined by law. Public hospitals are required to attend to all patients, water municipalities cannot easily withhold their product from different groups in society, and so forth. Not-for-profits cannot simply abandon or ignore certain types of recipients of their products or services, even those making relatively high demands. Hence, they cannot easily adjust their cost structure by simply targeting certain groups to serve or to avoid in the way that commercial businesses can.

Despite these differences, the similarities between commercial and not-for-profit organizations are substantial and growing with time. There is a convergence with their uses of modern managerial improvement methods. Some public sector agencies are managed indistinguishably from for-profit businesses. They are increasingly adopting private sector business practices, and in some cases are competing with commercial businesses. They can and do benefit from the same management tools and techniques used by the private sector. For example, when a government agency introduces a previously nonexistent surcharge or converts to a fee-for-service arrangement, isn't this comparable to a commercial business charging higher prices to those willing to pay more in exchange?

 ## SERVICE-BASED VERSUS PRODUCT-BASED ORGANIZATIONS

In an earlier reference to outputs such as "finished reports" that may be intangible but can still be defined, we were distinguishing between cost structures of product makers and of service providers. As pointed out, ABC/M and its costing principles are applicable to either case. This is because ABC/M is concentrating on how any output is consuming the work activities, including whatever expenses support those work activities.

However, a few differences between a service provider and a product maker/distributor with a high reliance on equipment are important:

▪ In service organizations, the resources generally are more flexible and interchangeable than in capital-intensive organizations where equipment may be dedicated to making only certain products or only doing certain things. In service organizations, some people can multitask or move among different tasks. In contrast, in capital-intensive companies that make and distribute products, the moment that their equipment is purchased, they have committed themselves to a certain level of available capacity (and cash outlay expenses) regardless of the level of subsequent use of that equipment. Service companies effectively have the luxury of "postponing" the addition of resources – mainly workers – until they are needed. In short, service companies can more quickly adjust the level of their capacity. With people as their most flexible resource, it is also the capabilities, not just the capacity, of their workers that allow more variety of outputs to be delivered. The more capabilities, the more flexibility. That is one reason that organizations are increasingly investing in training and education of their workforce, and even their suppliers' and contractors' workforces.

▪ When an organization is operating at near full capacity and needs to significantly alter its own cost structure, service organizations have an advantage over a hard goods provider. Presuming that the service organization in this case is truly as lean and agile as it can be, it can still alter its own cost structure by influencing the "future demand workload" side of the supply-and-demand equation. It may be able to offer a greater number of service level options (with varying prices or promotional features) to induce customer behavior more in harmony with its cost structure. Providing service-level options would be similar on a personal basis to choosing to ship a package with overnight delivery or with two-day, three-day, or other rates. By inducing the customer or service recipient to make the appropriate choices, an organization can shift the demand workload away from workers operating at full capacity and toward workers with some idle and unused capacity.

In the end, if one steps back and views service sectors versus product making sectors, the two forms appear to converge. There are more similarities than dissimilarities. ABC/M can be easily modeled for both forms using common ABC/M principles. If anything, service organizations arguably have some advantages in adapting to the guidance provided by use of an ABC/M model. Chapter 10 will expand on applications of ABC/M.

# CHAPTER TEN

# If ABC/M Is the Answer, What Is the Question?

O NE CAN ONLY REFER to "ABC/M" for so long before needing to visualize it and understand it as a cost-flow mechanism. Chapter 9 described what an ABC/M system looks like and how it calculates costs. In this chapter we address some of the questions that invariably loom large in the minds of organizational planners contemplating ABC/M application to their problem-solving. The chapter introduces some of the concepts and terms that are basic to understanding ABC/M as an accounting tool and, more importantly, as a management tool for encouraging behavioral change.

##  SO, WHAT IS THE BIG PROBLEM?

Why do some public sector managers shake their heads in disbelief when they think about their organization's cost accounting system? The authors once heard a public official complain, "You know what we think of our cost accounting system? It is a bunch of fictitious lies – but we all agree to them." Of course, he was referring to the misallocated costs based on those broad averages violating costing's causality principle that result in flawed and misleading information. What a sad state it is when the users of the accounting data simply resign themselves to a lack of hope. And unfortunately, many of the accountants are comfortable if the numbers all foot-and-tie in total; they care less if the parts making up the total are correct. The total is all that matters to them, and any arbitrary cost allocation can tie out to the total expenses.

Imagine if you were a roving reporter and asked managers and employee teams throughout your organization, "How happy are you with the financial and accounting data that now support policy decisions aimed at improving effectiveness, efficiency, and performance?" Thumbs up or down? Many would give it thumbs down. When you have the *wrong* information coupled with the *wrong* measurements, it is not difficult to make *wrong* decisions.

How can traditional accounting that has been around for so many years all of a sudden be considered so bad? The answer is that the cost information is not necessarily bad so much as somewhat distorted, woefully incomplete, and partly unprocessed. Figure 10.1 provides the first hint of a problem. The left side shows the classic monthly responsibility cost center report that managers receive under the general ledger system. Note that the example used is a back-office department of a license bureau, such as for driver or hunting

## The General Ledger View:
### *It Is Structurally Deficient for Decision Analysis.*

| Chart-of-Accounts View | | |
|---|---|---|
| **Insurance Claims Processing Department** | | |
| | **Actual** | **Plan** | **Favorable/ (unfavorable)** |
| Salaries | $621,400 | $600,000 | $(21,400) |
| Equipment | 161,200 | 150,000 | (11,200) |
| Travel expense | 58,000 | 60,000 | 2,000 |
| Supplies | 43,900 | 40,000 | (3,900) |
| Use and occupancy | 30,000 | 30,000 | — |
| Total | $914,500 | $880,000 | $(34,500) |

**When managers get this kind of report, they are either happy or sad, but they are rarely any smarter!**

**FIGURE 10.1**  The general ledger view. Source: Copyright 2019 www.gary cokins.com.

licenses. It is a factory, too, only its outputs are not tangible products but documents. This is to demonstrate that, despite misconceptions, indirect white-collar workers produce outputs the same as factory workers do. You can substitute any department, government or commercial, for the license bureau department in the example and the lessons will hold.

If you question managers who routinely receive this report, "How much of these expenses can you control or influence? How much insight do you get from this report into the content of your employees' work?" they will likely answer both questions with a "Not much!" This is because salaries and fringe benefits usually make up the most sizable portion of controllable costs, and all that the manager sees are those expenses reported as lump-sum amounts.

When you translate those "chart-of-account" expenses shown under the general ledger or fund accounting system into the actual work activities that consume these expenses, a manager's insights begin to increase. The right side of Figure 10.2 is the ABC/M view that is used for analysis and as the starting point for calculating the costs both for processes and for diverse outputs. In effect, the right-side ABC/M view begins to resolve the deficiencies of traditional financial accounting by focusing on work activities. ABC/M is very work-centric, whereas general ledger and fund accounting systems are expenses transaction-centric.

## Each Activity Has Its Own Cost Driver

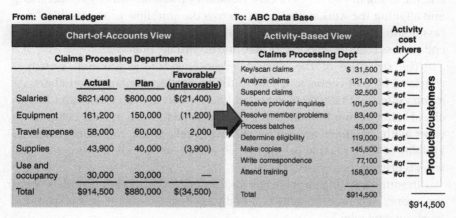

**FIGURE 10.2** Each activity has its own cost driver. Source: Copyright 2019 www.garycokins.com.

Another key difference lies in the language used to depict cost allocations (i.e., absorption costing). ABC/M describes activities using an "action verb-adjective-noun" grammar convention, such as "process building permit" or "open new taxpayer accounts." This gives ABC/M its flexibility. Such wording is powerful because managers and employee teams can better relate to these phrases, and the wording implies that the work activities can be favorably affected through change, improvement, or elimination. General ledger and fund accounting systems use a chart-of-accounts, whereas ABC/M uses a chart-of-activities as its language. In translating the data from a general ledger or fund accounting system into the information of activities and processes, ABC/M preserves the total reported budget funding and costs but allows the individual elements to be viewed differently.

To be further critical of the left side chart-of-accounts view, notice how inadequate those data are in reporting the costs of processes that run cross-functionally and penetrate through the vertical boundaries of a government agency's organization chart. The general ledger and the fund accounting system are organized around separate departments or cost centers. This presents a reporting problem. For example, with a city's department of public works, what is the true total cost for processing equipment repair requisitions that travel through so many hands? For a service organization, what is the true cost of opening a new account for a citizen or service recipient?

Many organizations have flattened and de-layered such that employees from different departments or cost centers frequently perform similar activities and multitask in two or more core workflow processes. Only by reassembling and aligning the work-activity costs across the workflow processes, like "process home buyer permits" or "open new taxpayer accounts," can the end-to-end process costs be seen, measured, and eventually managed.

The structure of the general ledger and fund accounting system is restricted by cost-center mapping to the hierarchical organization chart. As a consequence, this type of reported information drives vertical and hierarchical behavior, not the much more desirable end-to-end process behavior. In effect, with traditional accounting systems, public sector managers are denied visibility of the costs that belong to their end-to-end workflow processes – and what is driving those costs.

In summary, the general-ledger and fund-accounting view describes "what was spent," whereas the activity-based view describes "what it was spent for, to whom, and why."

##   HOW DO COST DRIVERS WORK?

Much additional information can be gleaned from the right-side view of Figure 10.2. Look at the second activity, "analyze licenses," at a total cost of $121,000 and ask yourself what would make that cost significantly increase or decrease. The overall answer is the number of licenses analyzed. That is that work's activity driver. Figure 10.2 illustrates that each activity on a stand-alone basis has its own activity driver. At this stage, the costing is no longer recognizing the organization chart and its artificial boundaries. All the employees' costs have been combined into the work performed. The focus is now on the cost of that work and on what influences and affects the level of that workload.

There is yet more that can be gained from this view. Let's assume that 1,000 licenses were analyzed during that period for the department shown. Then the unit cost per each analyzed license is $121 per license. If one specific group – senior citizens over the age of 60, for example – was responsible for half those claims, then we would know more about the sources of demand (i.e., workload). The senior citizens would have caused $60,500 of that work (500 claims multiplied by $121 per claim). If married couples with small children required another fraction, married couples with grown children a different fraction, and so on, then ABC/M will have traced all of the $121,000. If each of the other work activities were similarly traced, using the unique activity driver for each activity, ABC/M will have piled up the entire $914,500 into each group of beneficiaries. This reassignment of the resource expenses will be much more accurate than any broad-brush "butter spreading" cost allocation applied with traditional accounting systems that use broad averages.

This cost assignment network is one of the major reasons that ABC/M calculates costs of outputs more accurately. The assignment of the resource expenses also demonstrates that all costs actually originate with the ultimate end user, service recipient, or beneficiary of the work. That location and origin of costs could be a citizen, welfare recipient, new home buyer seeking permits, or another government agency relying on those services. This is at the opposite end from where people who perform "cost allocations" think about costs. They think it begins with the expenses.

Traditional cost allocations are structured as a one-source-to-many-destinations redistribution of costs. They ignore that the destinations are actually the origin for the costs. The destinations, usually outputs or people, place demands on work, and the work draws on the resource capacity (i.e., the spending); hence the costs measure the effect by reflecting backward through the ABC/M cost assignment network. In sum, accountants have historically allocated "what we spend" from the general ledger, whereas ABC/M assigns "what it costs."

 ## WHAT ARE COSTS?

Although the two cost views – the cost assignment and the process view – seem logical, people who design or use ABC/M systems often have difficulties deploying the power of these two views. In practice, they often confuse the two.

Part of the problem in defining and designing costing systems involves understanding just what exactly costs are. What are costs, anyway? Costs themselves are abstract and intangible. We cannot see costs or hold a couple of them in our hands. Yet we all know they are there. Like an echo, we know they exist whether we measure them or not.

We know that costs increase or decrease as changes in the workload affect the activity costs via changes in the quantity or frequency of their cost drivers. Work activities are triggered by events, and the costs react as the effect. In one sense, since costs are not tangible, ABC/M operates as "an imaging system" similar to radar, sonar, or an electrocardiogram. Like a digital camera, ABC/M records the image.

As just stated, costs measure effects. And costs measure effects more than they illuminate root causes. However, ABC/M systems can provide an enterprise-wide image of all the collective effects plus the causal relationships that result in an organization's costs. So, costs give insights to root causes, but mainly through their inferences. This may sound ironic, but "cost management" can be considered an oxymoron (such as "jumbo shrimp" and "hospital food") – a contradictory phrase. You do not really manage costs; you understand the causes (and drivers) of costs. Then you manage the causes.

So, in effect, an organization does not manage its costs; it manages: (1) what causes those costs to occur (i.e., its cost drivers), and (2) the effectiveness and efficiency of the organization's people and equipment in responding to those causal triggers.

It is sort of amazing that, when one designs a cost measurement system, the resulting information is actually measuring something intangible and invisible! But in its own way, ABC/M makes tangible the data to represent things that most people believe are intangible.

To sum up, in one sense, the report on the left side of Figure 10.2 represents more of an "accounting police" or "budget police" command-and-control tool. This is the most primitive form of control. Have you overspent your budgeted target? If you have, who says that budgeted target amount was fair when it was initially imposed? As previously mentioned, when managers receive the left-side cost center report, they are either happy or sad but rarely any smarter. That is unacceptable in today's world, which expects much more out of organizations than in the past. We will all witness the emergence of the "learning organizations," not ones that are straightjacketed with spending restrictions. The right side of our graphics in the Figure 10.2 restates the same expenses as on the left side, but the costs are reported in a much more useful format and structure for decision support.

When expenses are expressed as activity costs, they are in a format to be traced into outputs. Expenses are transformed into calculated costs. As a result, employees can never say, "We couldn't care less about what anything costs." People care more when they know what things cost and believe in the accuracy of those costs. Cost accounting is outside their comfort zones. ABC/M makes "cost" understandable and logical.

##  HOW DOES ABC/M INTERSECT WITH TRADITIONAL COST ACCOUNTING?

Figure 10.3 uses the analogy of an optical lens to show how ABC/M serves as a translator of general ledger and fund accounting system data to provide more focused information for improved decision support. The lens not only translates the ledger expenses into a more useful and flexible format but provides more sensory information. The information from the ABC/M lens can serve as an early warning detector that some resource level of spending may be out of alignment, perhaps with the goal or strategy of the organization or with the needs of its customers. For quality managers, ABC/M makes visible all the work related to the cost of quality (COQ) – for example, where quality-related costs are located and which outputs and products the COQ costs have gone into.

As shown in Figure 10.3, ABC/M is not a replacement for the traditional general ledger and fund accounting system. Rather, it is a translator or overlay that lies between the traditional expense account accumulators and the end users. Examples of end users include the government agency's own managers and employee teams who apply cost information in decision making, as well as governing authorities or oversight committees who may evaluate how to better redeploy spending budgets.

## ABC/M Doesn't Replace the Accounting System

**An ABC/M system does not replace the accounting system.
It restates the same data and adds operating relationships to
more effectively support decision making.**

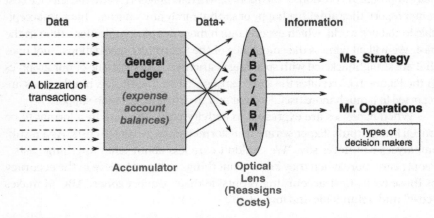

**FIGURE 10.3** ABC/M doesn't replace the accounting system. Source: Copyright 2019 www.garycokins.com.

ABC/M translates expenses into a language that people can understand: into elements of costs, namely the work activities, which can be more flexibly linked or assigned to processes or cost objects based on demand-driven consumption patterns. It is not a simplistic and arbitrary system of broad average cost allocations.

The reason ABC/M is becoming popular in government and public sector organizations is that general ledger and fund accounting systems are now recognized as being structurally deficient. The data from those systems are not in a format that will provide good managerial information for decision support. Traditional accounting is a sound mechanism for collecting and accumulating transaction-intensive expenses, but not for converting those into costs for useful decision-making support.

In the simplest terms, the general ledger or fund accounting system acts like a checkbook. One can read the amount of money spent but not really know the what-for's and why's of any individual "check." And, unfortunately, the spending ledger's largest "check" amounts are employee payroll-related, which gives managers virtually no visibility into the content of the employee work activities being performed. Further, the payroll-related costs do not reveal the interrelationships of that work with other work or with products and service lines for service recipients or beneficiaries. Moreover, there are no insights into what events cause or drive variations in work activity costs. Since an organization's work activities probably represent the costs most subject to management control, it is critical to know and to understand them.

An ABC/M system does not replace the accounting system. It restates the same data and adds operating relationships to support decision-making more effectively. In contrast to traditional accounting, ABC/M focuses on the work activities associated with operating and managing any institution, including those in the not-for-profit or government sector. As noted, ABC/M is work-centric, whereas the general ledger or fund accounting system is expenses transaction-centric. Both have their place and purpose, but the data provided by traditional accounting are too raw to be considered business intelligence for decision support. ABC/M solves that problem and does much more. Just translating the ledger account expenses into their work activities is an incomplete view of ABC/M. The total picture includes ABC/M's linkage of these activities into networks to calculate the cost of outputs useful for performing analysis, for determining tradeoffs, and for making decisions.

The modern movement toward "managing with a process view" has created a growing need for better managerial and costing information. Managing processes and managing activities (i.e., costs) go together. By current definition, a workflow process comprises two or more logically related work activities intended to serve end-receivers and beneficiaries; thus, a means of integrating processes, outputs, and measured costs has become an even more important requirement for managers and employee teams. ABC/M information provides a logical way to visualize and report on these linkages.

In sum, ABC/M resolves the structural problem of data inherent in the general ledger and the fund accounting system by first converting account balances into activity costs. ABC/M then assigns the activity costs to cost objects or reassembles the activity costs across processes. These new and transformed cost data can be used to identify operating relationships that are key to making good decisions affecting products, service lines, and customers.

##  WHY THE INCREASED INTEREST IN ABC/M?

In the early 1980s, many organizations began to realize that their traditional accounting systems were generating inaccurate or incomplete costing information. The typical organization's cost structure had been changing substantially as overhead and indirect costs increased and displaced direct labor and material costs. As alluded to earlier, the three primary causes for this shift were: (1) increasing organizational complexity resulting from proliferation in the variety of product and service-line offerings, (2) a more diverse group of delivery channels and service recipients, and (3) increased automation, new technologies, and new methodologies.

In the past, the system of calculating costs by using simplistic volume-based cost allocations may have been acceptable and may not have introduced excessive error. The rapid rise in indirect and overhead expenses changed all that. The traditional costing method became increasingly invalid because of its failure to tie actual consumption costs to the broadening array of products and standard service lines. The unfavorable impact of these costing distortions was becoming much more intense than in the past.

Some managers understood intuitively that their outdated accounting system was distorting product and service line costs, so they sometimes made informal adjustments to compensate. Some created their own "shadow" cost reporting separate from the accounting department's reports. However, with so much complexity and diversity, it was nearly impossible for managers to predict the magnitude of adjustments needed to achieve reasonable accuracy. ABC/M was seen as the way to resolve the problem of poor indirect and overhead cost allocations and to provide additional information that would serve as a basis for positive actions, both strategic and operational.

The rise in ABC/M is also the result of external factors. The level of performance and service that is expected of most organizations has increased dramatically. In the past, many organizations were reasonably comfortable with making mistakes. There was adequate time or resources to mask the impact of any wrong or poor decisions. In many cases, there simply was no accountability with consequences. Errors and poor service were more easily tolerated.

Today the pressure has intensified, and the margin for error is slimmer. Governments and not-for-profit organizations cannot make as many mistakes or use excess capacity and expect that they will not be noticed. Cost estimates for new projects, capital investment decisions, technology choices, outsourcing, and make-versus-buy decisions today all require a sharper pencil. More private sector organizations are behaving like predatory competitors. These companies are becoming strong rivals to government institutions by better understanding the cause-and-effect connections that drive costs and by fine-tuning their processes and competitive bid prices accordingly.

The resulting squeeze from the existence of more and possibly better options for service recipients is making life for some government organizations much more difficult than in the past. Budget tightening has worsened the problem. Knowing what products, service lines, and service recipients truly cost is becoming key to survival. With ABC/M visibility, organizations can understand what drives their costs and identify where to remove waste, low-value-adding costs, and unused capacity. These topics will be discussed in Chapter 12.

Today an organization's road is no longer long and straight; it is winding, with bends and hills that do not give much visibility or certainty to plan for the future. Organizations need to be agile and continuously transform their cost structure and work activities. This is difficult to do if they do not understand their own cost structure and economics.

 ## HOW DOES ABC/M YIELD MORE ACCURACY?

As previously described, ABC/M was developed as a practical solution for problems associated with traditional cost management systems. In traditional cost accounting, the indirect expenses are usually too aggregated to serve any purpose, thus ruining any likelihood of an accurate calculation of cost by type of output.

Moreover, these overhead cost allocations are generally determined by applying broad-brush average cost rates to a volume-based factor, such as the number of employee labor hours or department expenses. Overall, this system may reflect inputs used or outputs produced but will not accurately measure the segments. This flawed basis for allocating costs rarely reflects the specific cause-and-effect relationship between the indirect overhead expense and the product, service line, channel, or service recipient (i.e., the cost object) that is actually consuming the cost. Many managers are tired of the "allocation food fights."

Because allocating is a zero-sum error game, the result of inaccurate cost allocations is that some cost objects get overcosted while the remainder must be undercosted. In practice, the undercosting of some cost objects can be substantial. That is because these service lines, service recipients, or perhaps even other government agencies require far more technical attention or consume more employee time than the broad-brush averages applied. Some people refer to traditional cost allocations as spreaders. In effect, we have allowed the accounting profession to construct a costing scheme that distorts reality and violates costing's causality principle as a manager understands it.

ABC/M corrects for these flaws by identifying the work activities that are responsible for costs. It builds a cost-flow assignment network, which allows the work activity costs to be continuously reassigned or passed on only if the

products, service lines, or service recipients, or in some cases other work activities, actually use and consume the activity. Remember the restaurant example?
Figure 10.4 shows a diagram popularly called the ABC/M cross, which is critical to understanding this concept.

Costs represent the belief system of the organization. Many employees
accept the reported costs as true strictly because the accountants report them.
Other employees are suspicious. An allocation-free cost system is like a smoke-
free environment: no pollution. In short, don't allocate – prorate. ABC/M
brings in the "myth grenades" that blow up the old flawed beliefs and replace
them with real facts.

The ABC/M cross reveals that work activities, which are located in the
center intersection of the cross, are integral to calculating and reporting both
the costs of workflow processes and the costs of cost objects. Cost objects are the
persons or things that benefit from incurring activity costs; examples are products, service lines, internal or external recipients (e.g., citizens and customers),
stakeholders, and outputs of internal processes. Cost objects can be thought of
as for what and for whom work is done.

Figure 10.4 lists the questions that the vertical cost-assignment view answers.
The vertical cost-assignment view explains what specific things cost, whereas the
horizontal process view explains what causes costs to exist and to fluctuate.

### The Activity-Based Cost Management Framework

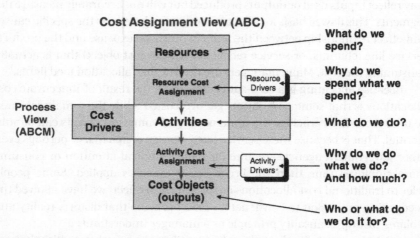

**FIGURE 10.4**   The activity-based cost management framework. Source: © 2019
The Consortium of Advanced Manufacturing International (CAM-I). All Rights
Reserved; used with permission.

The vertical axis reflects costs and their sensitivity to demands from all forms of product and service-recipient diversity. The work activities consume the resources, and the products and services for the end users, citizens, and beneficiaries consume the work activities. The vertical ABC/M cost-assignment view is a cost-consumption chain. After each cost is traced based on its unique quantity or proportion of its driver, then all of the costs are eventually reaggregated into the final cost objects.

The horizontal view of the ABC/M cross is the workflow-process view. A workflow process is defined as two or more activities or a network of activities with a common purpose. Activity costs belong to the workflow processes. Across each process, the activity costs are sequential and cumulatively additive. In this orientation, activity costs satisfy the requirements for popular flowcharting and process-modeling techniques and software. Process-based thinking, tipping the organization chart 90 degrees and flowing across the organizational chart "boxes," now dominates managerial thinking. ABC/M provides the cost elements for process costing that are not available from the general ledger and the fund accounting system.

Figure 10.5 illustrates the mechanism of the vertical axis of the ABC/M cross. It reveals that an activity cost has an output cost rate that is synonymous with the activity driver rate.

## Activity Drivers

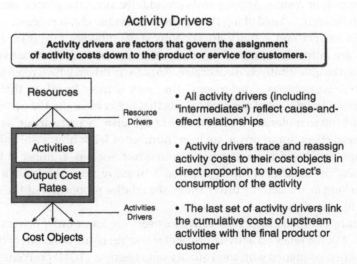

Activity drivers are factors that govern the assignment of activity costs down to the product or service for customers.

Resources

Resource Drivers

Activities

Output Cost Rates

Activities Drivers

Cost Objects

- All activity drivers (including "intermediates") reflect cause-and-effect relationships

- Activity drivers trace and reassign activity costs to their cost objects in direct proportion to the object's consumption of the activity

- The last set of activity drivers link the cumulative costs of upstream activities with the final product or customer

**FIGURE 10.5**   Activity drivers. Source: Copyright 2019 www.garycokins.com.

##  WHAT ARE DRIVERS?

Other than "activity," there probably is no term that has become more identified with activity-based cost management than the term "driver" and its several variations. The problem is that it has been applied in several ways with varying meanings. To be very clear, a cost driver is something that can be described in words but not necessarily in numbers. For example, a storm would be a cost driver that results in much cleanup work, which in turn has related costs. In contrast, the activity drivers in ABC/M's cost assignments must be quantitative, using measures that apportion expenses into costs. In the ABC/M vertical cost-assignment view, there are three types of drivers, and all are required to be quantitative:

- **Resource drivers** trace expenditures (cash or fund outlays) to work activities
- **Activity drivers** trace activity costs to cost objects
- **Cost object drivers** trace final cost object costs into other final cost objects.

In the ABC/M cross's vertical cost-assignment view, activity drivers will have their own higher-order cost drivers. Events or other influences, which are formally called cost drivers, cause work activities. Think of a cost driver as a work order that triggers the work activity, which in turn uses resources to produce outputs or results. Activity costs are additive along the process and therefore can be accumulated along the business and value chain process.

Cost drivers and activity drivers thus serve different purposes. Activity drivers are output measures that reflect the usage of each work activity, and they must be quantitatively measurable. An activity driver, which relates a work activity to cost objects, "meters-out" the work activity based on the unique diversity and variation of the cost objects that are consuming the activity. It is often difficult to understand whether use of the term "activity driver" is related to a causal effect (input driver, such as "number of labor hours worked") or to the output produced by an activity (output driver, such as "number of licenses processed" or "number of meals prepared"). In many cases, this is not a critical issue so long as the activity driver traces the relative proportion of the activity cost to its cost objects.

Figure 10.6 illustrates how activity drivers are lower-order drivers of cost drivers. ABC/M relies on activity drivers for tracing costs. Collectively they are useful when combined with total quality management (TQM) problem-solving tools for identifying root causes.

## Activity Drivers Have Cost Drivers

**Activity drivers have their own cost drivers. It is best to use "symptomatic" and physical output drivers in the ABC model to measure unit driver rates and segment the diversity of the cost objects...**

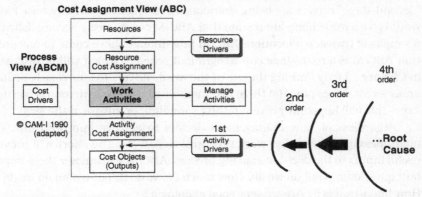

**...and rely on employees to determine the "nth order" drivers using TQM problem solving techniques outside of ABC's cost flowing.**

FIGURE 10.6  Activity drivers have cost drivers. Source: Copyright 2019 www.garycokins.com.

Driver data, whether it is cost-driver or activity-driver information, sparks root cause analysis. Generally, the activity drivers used for ABC/M costing are output-based. Therefore, as the quantitative measures of the drivers rise or fall over time, ABC/M can report the historical trend in terms of per-unit cost of work rates for the activity outputs and ultimately for the products as a whole. Alternatively, it can also provide the per-unit cost of each output rates for use in predictive planning and what-if scenarios, which are popular uses of the ABC/M information.

Cost estimating with ABC/M is very natural because the activity costs react and behave linearly with changes in their activity drivers. Too often with traditional costing, the cost rates do not directly vary with changes in volume; this fault then results in misestimates and ultimately in errors resulting in poor decisions.

As mentioned, in the vertical cost-assignment view, the term "driver" is prefix-appended in three areas. The first – called a resource driver – deals with the method of assigning resource costs to activities. The second – an activity driver – deals with the method of assigning activity costs to cost objects. The third – a cost object driver – applies to final cost objects after all activity costs have already been logically assigned. Note that cost objects can be consumed or used by other cost objects.

In this context, references to old 1990s language of "first-stage" and "second-stage" drivers are being abandoned as being obsolete. Their use today would give a misleading impression that ABC/M can be easily accomplished as a simplistic two-step allocation. ABC/M practitioners have come to recognize that ABC/M is a multistage cost assignment scheme (which will be discussed in Chapter 11). By limiting the use of the word "driver" to four clearly defined areas – cost driver plus the three just mentioned as appearing on the vertical axis – this will hopefully prevent misinterpretation or misuse of the term.

Regardless of how management decides to achieve improvements, the main message here is that work is central to ABC/M. The effort will provide useful inputs to the decision-making process. ABC/M will answer these important questions: What do we do? How much do we do it? For whom do we do it? How important is it? Are we very good at doing it?

## WHY IS MINIMIZING THE SIZE OF THE ABC/M SYSTEM IMPORTANT?

In practice, ABC/M systems will sometimes trace work activity costs to two or more other intermediate work activities that consume the work upstream from the ultimate products and services that initially trigger the demands on work. The reassignment network of cost-segmented consumption is key to ABC/M's superior costing accuracy. ABC/M can tolerate reasonable cost-driver estimates as proxies for actual-transaction detail drivers because the error does not compound – it dampens out on its way to the final cost objects. Although counterintuitive, with ABC/M, precision inputs are not synonymous with accurate outputs. This property significantly lightens the workload for data collection. And this is why the mantra of ABC/M is: "It is better to be approximately correct than precisely inaccurate!"

Figure 10.7 illustrates the impact of the error-dampening property. The figure shows several asymptotic curves that all have the same destination: 100 percent perfectly accurate cost results. The vertical axis represents the accuracy level while the horizontal axis represents the "level of effort." For each incremental level of administrative effort to collect, validate, calculate, and report more and better data, there is proportionately less improvement in accuracy. So the phrase "Is the climb worth the view?" is truly applicable to ABC/M.

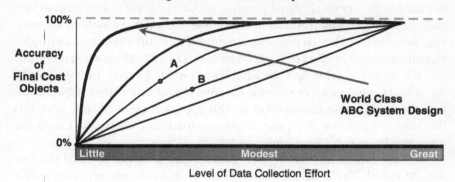

**FIGURE 10.7**    Balancing levels of accuracy with effort. Source: Copyright 2019 www.garycokins.com.

This graphic also draws attention to efficient and inefficient performance levels exhibited by ABC/M project teams in finding the right combination of accuracy and ABC/M administrative effort. There will always be a balanced tradeoff of more data for higher accuracy. But the appropriate questions being raised here are "Which data? And what is the effort to collect those particular data?"

Poorly designed ABC/M systems will yield less accuracy despite greater effort. Even the best-designed systems will yield less increase in accuracy per unit of effort expended as the size of the collection effort increases.

With better design, ABC/M Project Team A is achieving higher accuracy with much less collection effort relative to ABC/M Project Team B.

Unfortunately, most ABC/M project teams perform too far to the right on Figure 10.7 and usually on a much lower "frontier curve." That is, they have put in much greater effort than was needed, and they received less accuracy in costing than they could have achieved if they had been cleverer in two areas of developing their ABC/M model. First, they need to select beforehand what data are most important to collect. Second – and more important – they need to design a good cost assignment structure. The challenge for today's ABC/M teams is to determine how to right-size their ABC/M model – and to right-size it appropriately. Few organizations can afford excesses. In the end, the level of accuracy and detail needed depends on what types of decisions are going to be based on the cost information. And usually the accuracy requirements are not unreasonably harsh.

ABC/M's property of error-dampening means that an ABC/M model does not need to be very detailed and granular and, consequently, very large in size. Unfortunately, because this is counterintuitive, many ABC/M systems are over-engineered in size. They go well beyond diminishing returns in extra accuracy for incremental levels of effort of work. I refer to this as "ABC/M's leveling problem."

What level of detail and precision do you need? Chapter 14 will describe the ABC/M rapid prototyping with iterative remodeling design implementation approach previously mentioned. This approach takes advantage of this thinking to maximize the value of the reported cost information with the minimum effort to create the information.

No one knows in advance how detailed and granular to build the first ABC/M model. The project team, often led by accountants, errs on the side of excess detail. As a result, some ABC/M projects are exposed to a risk of being abandoned because they collapse under their own weight as the system becomes unnecessarily difficult to maintain long before the users comprehend how they can apply the ABC/M information usefully. ABC/M is a solution, but a solution to a problem should not become the next problem. ABC/M rapid prototyping with iterative remodeling accelerates the learning of the properties of ABC/M model design and architecture.

Some of the lessons learned about ABC/M and analysis are:

- Information, even though not precise, can provide an organization with substantially improved support for decision-making and can greatly improve its understanding of cost behavior.
- An organization does not need "excellent" ABC/M analysis to make great improvements.
- No system providing ABC/M information and its analysis is perfect. Good judgment and additional qualitative information are necessary before final decisions are made.
- Excess ABC/M model structure – such as number of activities and drivers – saps the strength of ABC/M in the initial stages.

A simple rule that will be repeated in this book is to constantly ask, "Is the higher climb worth the better view?" That is, by building a more detailed and slightly more accurate ABC/M model, will your questions be better answered? Avoid the creeping elegance syndrome. Larger models introduce maintenance issues.

The next chapter dives deeper to describe the structure of an ABC/M model that ultimately evolves into a permanent, repeatable, and reliable production ABC/M system.

CHAPTER ELEVEN

# Fundamentals: What Is ABC/M?

I N THIS CHAPTER, WE will get into a lot more of the nitty-gritty involved in designing an ABC/M system. Chapter 10 briefly covered some of the basic concepts underlying the ABC/M model and introduced the ABC/M cross in its simplified form as Figure 10.4. Now we will enlarge upon the basic view in Chapter 10 to show the fuller richness and complexity of the ABC/M model as it actually works.

 ## EXPANDING THE TWO-STAGE ABC/M CROSS MODEL

The ABC/M cross in Figure 10.4 depicted the key relationship between ABC/M and the management analysis tools that are needed to bring full realization of benefits to the organization. ABC/M is a methodology that can yield significant information about cost drivers, activities, resources, cost objects, and performance measures. This information gives an organization the opportunity to improve the value of its products and services. The ABC/M data reflect how the organization is consuming its resources, and this image in turn serves as an enabler for inferences and decision support.

The initial focus of early ABC/M applications was the determination of product and service-line costs through better segmentation and assignment of resource expenses consumption. Subsequent applications in larger and more complex organizations revealed that ABC/M information is useful in solving broader problems. For these solutions, the ABC cost calculation usually required more than a simple, so-called "two-stage" cost reassignment, as indicated by the cost assignment view of the ABC/M basic cross model. Figure 11.1 illustrates the expansion of the cost assignment network from two stages to a multistage network.

The expanded ABC/M model includes *intermediate* stages of activities (i.e., activity outputs that are inputs to successive work activities). This expansion recognizes that overhead is complex and escalating in expense. Support departments do work for other support departments that in turn do work for other support departments, ultimately doing work for the front-line primary work activities that produce products or deliver services for end users, service recipients, and customers. Specific usage, not time-based sequence, is the dominant factor for determining this cost assignment structure. These intermediate input/outputs cannot easily be traced directly to final cost objects (i.e., products, service lines, or types of service recipients) since there is no causal relationship. As a result, intermediate activities are two or more stages of cost assignment removed from a final cost object. These support-related activity costs raise the question "How much of this activity is consumed by specific products or service lines?"

ABC/M is more complex than what we have described up to this point. To segment resource expenses consumption to reflect variety and diversity, the

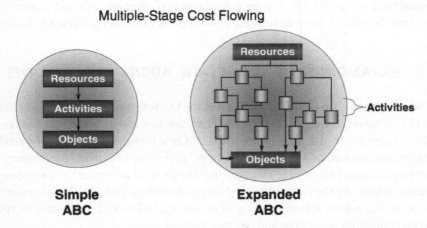

**FIGURE 11.1** Multiple-stage cost flowing. Source: Copyright 2019 www.gary cokins.com.

ABC/M vertical axis expands somewhat. It is virtually impossible to answer this question because the work is simply too indirect and remote from the products or service recipients to detect or sense the relationship. However, these support activities can be traced in proper proportions to other activities that require their input. Such support-related activity costs are eventually burdened into the primary activity costs. These intermediary activities support the work activities that detect the variation and diversity of the products or service lines.

The ABC/M model uses multi-stages to trace all the costs through a network of cost assignments into the final cost objects.

Figure 11.2 diagrams a generic cost assignment network in an expanded ABC/M model. The main difference between this diagram and the basic ABC/M model in Figure 4.1 is the presence of: (1) *intermediate* stages of activity-to-activity cost assignments, and (2) cost object–to–cost object assignments.

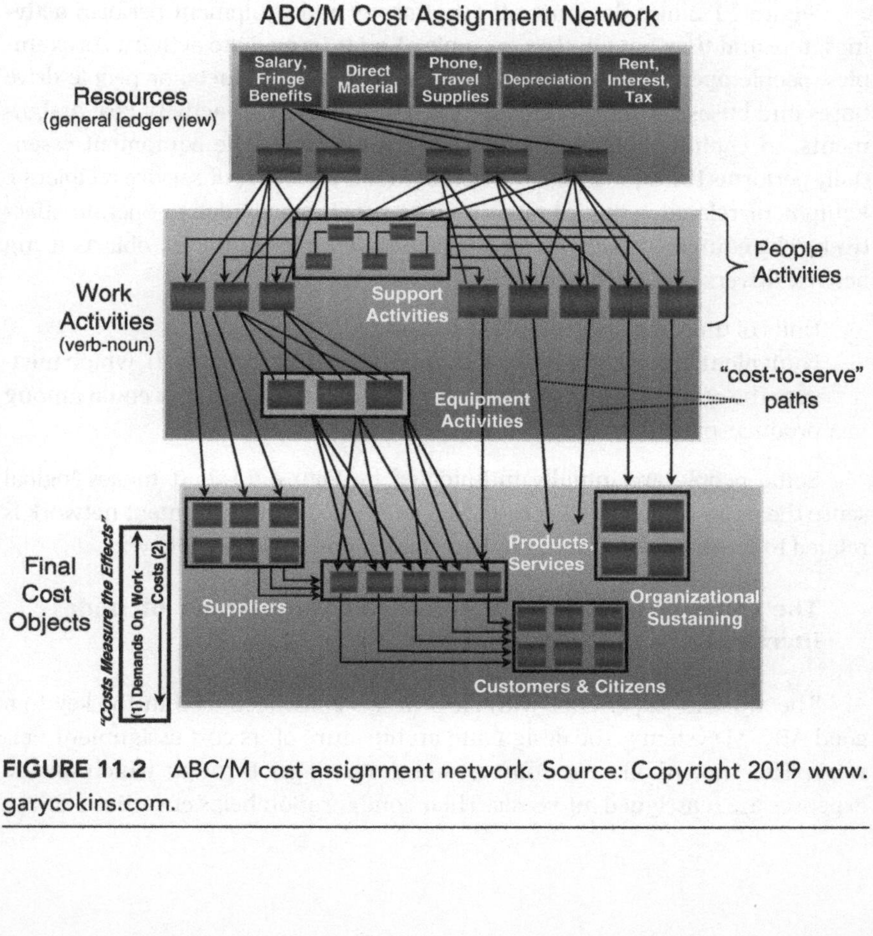

**FIGURE 11.2** ABC/M cost assignment network. Source: Copyright 2019 www.garycokins.com.

It is helpful to visualize the cost assignment paths of the generic expanded ABC/M model of Figure 11.2 as thin straws and wide pipes, where the diameter reflects the amount of cost flowing. The power of the expanded ABC/M model is that the cost assignment paths and destinations provide *traceability* from beginning to end. That is, it is from resource expenditures to each type of (or each specific) product or service recipient, which are the origin for all costs.

It is useful to mentally and visually reverse all the arrowheads in this diagram so that costs flow in the opposite direction. That is what is actually happening in an organization every minute, hour, day, week, month, and year. The citizens, customers, products, service lines, and supplier-related costs are placing demands on work that in turn draws on the resource expenses spending. The calculated costs then measure the effect in the opposite direction. Costs measure effects. This polar switch reveals that all costs originate with a demand-pull from customers and service recipients and that the costs simply measure the effect on resources.

Figure 11.2 also demonstrates that assets and equipment perform activities, too, and they are another example of an intermediate activity. As examples, people operate machines and machines make products, or people drive buses and buses deliver passengers. These are activity-to-activity cost assignments. In capital equipment–intensive organizations, the equipment essentially performs the mainstream work that fulfills the needs of service recipients. Equipment-related activities often require support activities to operate effectively. The equipment activity costs are usually assigned to cost objects using activity drivers that are based on:

- Units of time (e.g., per minute), or
- Equivalent inputs or outputs (e.g., number of units produced), which measure the relative processing time per unit of output, roughly equal among products or service lines

Some people are initially intimidated by Figure 11.2. It makes logical sense the more you work with ABC/M. The ABC/M cost assignment network is related to an observation that has become known as Metcalf's Law:

**The value of a network increases as the number of nodes increases.**

The authors' experience with ABC/M has convinced us that the key to a good ABC/M system is the design and architecture of its cost assignment network. The "nodes" are the sources and destinations through which all the expenses are reassigned into costs. Their configuration helps ensure the utility and value of the data for decision makers. And, although this is counterintuitive, the number-one determinant of the accuracy of the final cost objects is the network itself. By detecting how the diversity and variation of outputs relates to the work, it is linked relationships that influence cost object accuracy more than the quantities in the cost drivers.

 ## IDENTIFICATION AND TREATMENT OF ORGANIZATIONAL SUSTAINING COSTS

The final cost object to the far right in Figure 11.3 is the *organizational sustaining costs*. Many activities in an organization do not directly contribute to value, responsiveness, and quality. That does not mean that those activities can be eliminated, or even reduced, without doing harm to the organization. For example, preparing required regulatory reports for other government agencies certainly does not add to the value of any cost object or to the satisfaction of

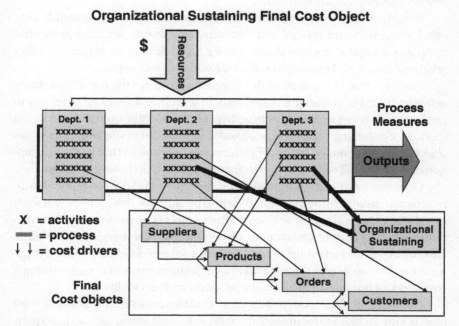

**FIGURE 11.3** Organizational sustaining final cost object. Source: Copyright 2019 www.garycokins.com.

the customer or service recipient. However, this activity does have value to the organization: it permits the organization to function in a legal manner. These types of activity costs are usually traced to a "sustaining cost object" group. Organizational sustaining costs are not involved with directly making or delivering a product or serving a citizen, customer, or service recipient.

*Organizational sustaining costs* are those costs not caused by products or citizen and customer-service needs. The consumption of these costs cannot be logically traced to products, services, citizens, customers, or service recipients. One example is the cost associated with the accounting department closing the books each month. How can one measure which service line or service recipient caused more or less of that work? Another example is the cost of lawn maintenance.

Organizational sustaining costs cannot be directly charged to a service line in any possible fair and equitable way; there is simply no use-based causality originating from the service line or service recipient. (Yet overhead costs are routinely and unfairly "allocated" this way despite the result being misleading costs.) Recovering these costs via pricing or funding may eventually be required, but that is not the issue here; the issue is fairly charging cost objects when no causal relationship exists.

In early ABC/M cost assignment structures, ABC teams conveniently allocated all support and general administrative expenses to activities or directly to final cost objects (e.g., products, service lines) despite no cause-and-effect relationships. This also overstates the true costs of costs objects.

The structure of expanded ABC/M systems leverages the use of sustaining activities traced to sustaining cost objects to segregate activity costs related to products and service recipients from activities that have little to do with delivering services. "Sustaining costs" can be included or excluded in the final cost of cost objects depending on the nature of the decision to be made; that is, the assumption of applying full versus marginal cost absorption is decision-dependent.

Organizational sustaining costs for government and not-for-profit organizations can eventually be fully absorbed into products or service lines, but such a cost allocation is blatantly arbitrary. There simply is no cause-and-effect relationship between an organizational sustaining cost object and the other final cost objects. If and when these costs are assigned into final cost objects, organizations that do so often refer to them as a "management tax" representing a cost of doing business apart from the products and service lines.

Examples of final cost objects that constitute business sustaining cost objects may include senior management (at individual levels, such as headquarters, division, and local) or other government regulatory agencies (such as environmental, occupational safety, or tax authorities). In effect, these organizations

– via their policies and compliance requirements or via their informal desires, such as briefings or forecasts – place demands on work activities not caused by or generally attributable to specific service lines or service recipients.

Other categories of expenses that may be included as organizational sustaining costs could include idle but available capacity costs or research and development (R&D). Remember that ABC is managerial accounting, not regulated financial reporting, so strict rules of generally accepted accounting principles (GAAP) do not need to be followed, but they can be borrowed.

##  THE TWO VIEWS OF COST: COST OBJECT AND PROCESS VIEWS

As government agencies flatten their organizational structures and strengthen their commitment to the interests of their customers, effective business processes become critical to improved performance – if not to survival. An organization's processes are the integrating theme for its work and are the vehicles that ultimately achieve value for customers. Managing business processes, and their outputs, requires understanding what the business processes and their outputs cost, as well as knowing what their value is perceived to be by taxpayers, service recipients, and governing bodies. That brings us to the reason that a more effective measurement of costs is becoming so important.

It is important for ABC/M design teams to correctly design their cost assignment networks and process views at the outset – not later, when the ABC/M system is large and making changes is difficult.

The expanded ABC/M approach calls for two separate cost assignment structures:

1. The horizontal process cost scheme is governed by the time sequence of activities that belong to the various processes.
2. The vertical cost reassignment scheme is governed by the variation and diversity of the cost objects.

In effect, think of the ABC/M cost assignment view as *time-blind*. The ABC/M process costing view, at the activity stage, is output *mix-blind*. The cost assignment and business process costing schemes are two *different* views of the same resource and activity costs. The work activity costs at the intersection of the ABC cross are *shared and common* to both views. These activity costs at the intersection are the starting point of their two alternative route networks for flowing costs – one diversity-based and the other time sequence–based. The activity costs are the *initial* translation of the general ledger or fund accounting expenditures that represent their resource consumption. After the work activities are costed from the resources via resource drivers, the activity costs may then either:

1. Be added across time for the process view, or
2. Be reassigned with their eventual accumulation into the products, service lines, channels, or service recipients for the view of the mix of final cost objects.

Figures 11.4 and 11.5 show these two views of activity costs. After the resource costs are assigned to and translated into activity costs, one may prefer to think of the activity costs at the ABC cross's intersection as being on a pivot. In Figure 11.4, each activity cost is pivoted in the direction of diversity and variation; the activity costs are aimed at the cost object that is the originating

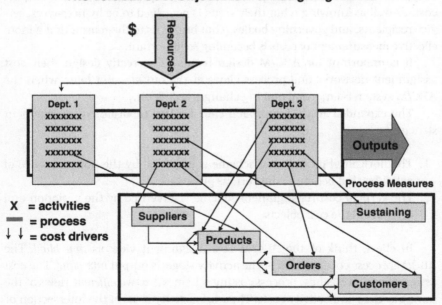

FIGURE 11.4 The vertical cost object view of *assigning* costs. Source: Copyright 2019 www.garycokins.com.

source of that diversity. One way to think of the ABC/M vertical cost assignment view is that end-customers "place demands on work" in one direction, thus consuming the resources. Then the costs flow as a result ("costs measure the effect") in the opposite direction. These relationships preserve the basic tenets of a *full absorption costing* system.

In Figure 11.5 the activity costs are pivoted in the direction of time, the ABC/M horizontal process view. Managers and employees generally find the ABC/M process view easier to understand since it aligns with the *sequence* of their actual activities. Managers are comfortable with a flowchart view of their processes.

In summary, in the ABC cross, the *total* cost of the same activities going horizontally (i.e., total business process costs) and the *total* costs being assigned and causally traced vertically (i.e., total product, customer, receiver, or business infrastructure-sustaining costs) *must equal each other*.

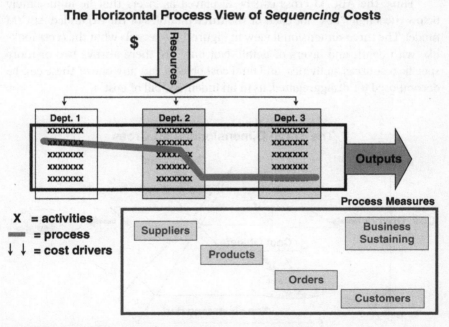

**FIGURE 11.5** The horizontal process view of *sequencing* costs. Source: Copyright 2019 www.garycokins.com.

## LEVELING OR DISAGGREGATION BRINGS ABOUT A THREE-DIMENSIONAL ABC CROSS

One of the questions that organizations implementing ABC most frequently ask is, "How *many* activities should we include in our ABC system?" There is no one correct answer. The number of activities is dependent on the answer to several other questions, such as, "What problem are you trying to solve with the ABC data?" In other words, the size, depth, granularity, and accuracy of an ABC system are *dependent* variables; they are determined by other factors. The level of detail and accuracy of an ABC system depends on what decisions the ABC data will be used for.

Indeed, one of the challenges for ABC/M implementation teams is determining the level of detail to build into the system – specifically, how many activities to use. More refinement usually leads to more activities and greater disaggregation of activities (i.e. levels, or depth), which in turn results in increasingly larger ABC/M systems – despite accounting for the same amount of expenditures. Greater size implies greater administrative effort, but not necessarily more usefulness from the additional data. Greater size can lead to death by details.

Thus, the ABC/M cross can be displayed as layers that lie immediately below the single "box" for each of the three modules of the expanded ABC/M model. The three-dimensional view in Figure 11.6 reveals what the cross looks like with depth and layers of detail. Not only are there always two or more specific resources, activities, and final cost objects, but any one of these can be decomposed (or disaggregated, as in an indented "bill of cost").

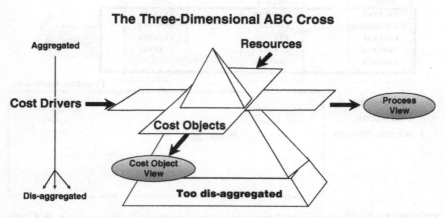

**FIGURE 11.6** The three-dimensional ABC cross. Source: Copyright 2019 www.garycokins.com.

It is now known that the degree of ABC/M data detail – and its accuracy – should depend on its uses (i.e., the types of decisions to be made using the data). High accuracy in the cost of cost objects is not automatically achieved with additional disaggregation (i.e., depth). Moreover, if pursued too far, disaggregation may in fact hamper the effort to sustain an ABC/M system. Controlling the levels (i.e., depth) and size of an ABC system is an important ABC/M system design decision that affects how easily an ABC system can be maintained for updated reporting.

 ## THE IMPACT OF THE REPEATABILITY OF WORK

When work activities are nonrecurring, such as with a law firm's client-billing or when constructing a skyscraper or earth-orbiting satellite, then a more exacting form of direct costing may be needed for higher accuracy. This is where project accounting, work order costing, or job costing is more appropriate. This approach to costing requires that all activity charges be made simultaneously and directly to the ultimate customer account or to a work-step in a project plan.

In Figure 11.7, the horizontal axis represents the repeatability of work, ranging left to right from nonrecurring to recurring. The curve for project accounting, job costing, and work order costing descends in applicability as the

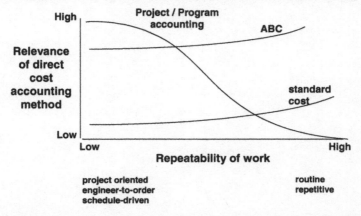

**ABC versus Project / Program Accounting**

In highly non-repeatable project work, project accounting is appropriate, but may only apply to a subset of workers. ABC increases in utility as an organization's continued outputs change slowly.

**FIGURE 11.7** ABC versus project/program accounting. Source: Copyright 2019 www.garycokins.com.

type of work becomes less nonrecurring – that is, more repeatable. With projects, the time schedule, including unplanned delays and their consequences, can severely govern the total costs. Project accounting serves well when the conditions of nonrecurring work and lots of interdependencies are present. However, where work activities are recurring and repetitive, such as with the cashier in the license bureau, project accounting is less applicable.

Since there is broad diversity and variation in services and outputs, even for a cashier, organizations are keenly interested in the unit costs of the output of work. ("What is the cost per license renewal of an individual versus a commercial customer?"). This is where ABC/M provides an economical solution. In Figure 11.7, the curve for ABC/M ascends in applicability as work activities become more recurring, though varying in time duration, even though the work produces or serves a broad variety of diverse products, services, customers, service recipients, and taxpayers.

Next up, Chapter 12 describes how ABC/M information can be used for operational and productivity improvement. This is often referred to as "cost management."

# CHAPTER TWELVE

# Using ABC/M Attributes to Assess Quality and Value-Add

P UBLIC SECTOR ORGANIZATIONS NEED to distinguish among work activities that are:

- Not required at all and can be eliminated (e.g., a duplication of effort)
- Ineffectively accomplished and can be reduced or redesigned (e.g., due to outdated policies or procedures)
- Required to sustain the organization (i.e., work that is not directly caused by making products or delivering services but cannot easily be reduced or eliminated, such as building security
- Discretionary and can be eliminated (e.g., annual employee picnic)
- Directly related to core activities (i.e., making products or delivering services)

ABC/M systems provide for distinguishing these work activities either by incorporating them into a cost assignment structure (i.e., organizational sustaining cost objects) or by tagging their costs as an overlay (i.e., attributes). ABC/M attributes described in this chapter address the third question related to activity analysis.

## ATTRIBUTES ENERGIZE ABC/M COST DATA

Organizations have very few insights about how their individual costs – for products, service recipients, or business processes – vary among themselves aside from the amount of the cost. Traditional cost accounting methods do not provide any way for individual costs to be tagged or highlighted with a *separate dimension* of cost other than the amount that was spent. An example of the range of one tag that can be scored against activities is "very important" versus "required" versus "postponable." Tags are a popular way of measuring how much value-added is contained in the costs and where it is located.

In short, traditional accounting simply provides racked-and-stacked numbers. The problem is that, aside from the cost amount or bolding or italicizing the print font, one cannot differentiate one cost from another. This is true whether one is examining resource expenditures or their calculated costs of activities, processes, and final cost objects (i.e., workflow outputs, service lines, or service recipients). *Attributes* solve this money-level-only limitation of traditional costing. One can think of attributes as offering many other dimensions to segment costs that are different from absorption costing's single dimension, which only reflects variation and diversity consumption of cost objects such as outputs, products, service lines, and service recipients.

Attributes in no way affect the calculation of ABC/M costs. Attributes are user-defined, unlimited in number, and often subjectively assigned. Attributes can be used as a grading method to evaluate the individual activities that contribute to a process output's goods or services. ABC/M attributes allow managers to differentiate activities from one another even if they are equal in the amount of costs.

 ## THE ANALYST'S DREAM

Some practitioners of ABC/M believe that it is the use of attributes that really brings power to ABC/M analysis. This implies that the attributes information may be more important than the traced and assigned cost data that are so fundamental to what ABC/M is doing – calculating the unique costs of work activities and their consuming outputs. In contrast to ABC/M's objective reporting of the facts, attributes take the ABC/M data an additional step by making the data very *suggestive* of what actions to take. Attributes have been referred to as the "air conditioning" for ABC/M.

With attributes one is no longer just tracing or adding up costs as an accounting exercise. They serve an alternative purpose: differentiating among the costs that reside within outputs, such as standard service lines and/or customers, or within business processes. The differentiating is based on something other than the amount of costs.

Monetary information *alone* about the cost amount of an output, product, or service line does not necessarily convey what to do or how to improve. Just knowing the amount of costs may not be sufficient to analyze the results and make judgments. You may want to know more about various types of cost, too; types and attributes are synonymous. Beyond relative magnitude, the activity monetary costs can be *further* differentiated into user-defined categories to facilitate managerial analysis. Without this additional differentiation, the activities will all look the same except for their description and dollar amount.

ABC/M attributes are frequently scored and graded against the work activities. The number of different attributes is unlimited, but many organizations settle in on their favorite half-dozen or so. Key examples include the level of importance and level of organizational performance.

## A POPULAR ATTRIBUTE

Advanced, mature users are masters at employing ABC/M attributes. A popular attribute involves scoring activities along their "high versus low value-adding" scale. The idea is to eliminate low value-adding activities and optimize higher value-adding activities, thus enabling employees and managers to focus on the worth of their organization's work. Employees can see which work really serves customers and which activities may be considered wasteful. Focus and visibility are enhanced because people can more easily see where costs are big or small and also which costs can be changed or managed in the near term. Scoring costs with attributes invokes action beyond just gazing at and analyzing costs.

In the early days of ABC/M, the scoring choices for this specific attribute were limited to either "value-added (VA)" or "non–value-added (NVA)." This simple either/or choice created problems. First, it was a personal insult to employees to tell them that part or all of what they do is non–value-adding – employees are not very happy to hear that. But even more troublesome, the restrictive nature of this scoring method can lead to unresolvable debates. For example, take the activity "expedite orders" to prevent a tardy delivery of a service to an important service recipient. Is this value-added or non–value-added work? A solid argument can support either case. It is better to simply replace the VA versus NVA label with a different set of words that scale along a continuum and better describe levels of importance (e.g., critical, necessary, regulatory, or postponable).

Regardless of what type of scale you use to score or grade value, the objective is to determine the relevance of work or its output to meeting customer and shareholder requirements. The goal is to optimize those activities that add value and minimize or eliminate those that do not. Here are some tips, but by no means hard rules, for classifying value attributes.

High value-adding activities are those that:

■ Are necessary to meet customer requirements
■ Modify or enhance purchased material or product
■ Induce the customer to pay more for the product or service
■ Are critical steps in a business process
■ Are performed to resolve or eliminate quality problems
■ Are required to fulfill customer requests or expectations
■ If time permitted, you would do more of

Low value-adding activities are those that:

■ Can be eliminated without affecting the form, fit, or function of the product
■ Begin with the prefix "re-" (such as rework or returned goods)
■ Result in waste without commensurate value
■ Are performed due to inefficiencies or errors in the process stream
■ Are duplicated in another department or add unnecessary steps to the business process
■ Produce an unnecessary or unwanted output
■ If given the option, you would do less of

Another popular attribute scores how well each activity is performed, such as "exceeds," "meets," or "is below customer expectations." This reveals the level of *performance*. Multiple activities can be simultaneously tagged with grades for two or more different attributes. As an option, activities can be summarized into the processes to which the activities belong. Using two different attributes along the process view allows organizations to see, for example, whether they are very, very good at things they have also judged to be very unimportant – and whether they are also spending a lot of money doing those unimportant tasks!

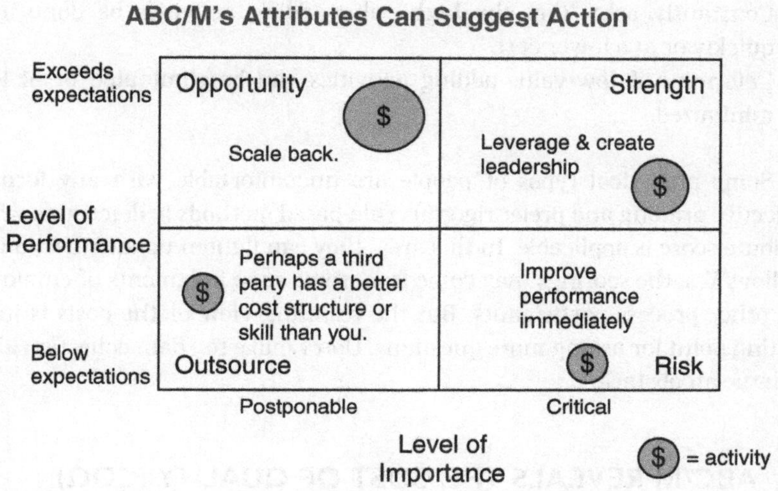

**ABC/M's Attributes Can Suggest Action**

FIGURE 12.1 ABC/M's attributes can be suggestive of action. Source: Copyright 2019 www.garycokins.com.

Note how suggestive attributes are. Figure 12.1 illustrates the four quadrants that result from combining the attributes for performance (vertical axis) and importance (horizontal axis). In the case just described as being good at something unimportant, it is obvious that the organization should scale back and spend less on that kind of work. These activity costs would be in the upper-left quadrant.

Although most attributes are subjectively scored or graded by managers and employees, when the scores are grouped together, the subjectivity begins to become directionally reliable (presuming there was no bias in the scoring of every single attribute). As a result, the attributed costs introduce an emotionally compelling force to consider taking actions, as in the example above.

Here are a few tips related to ABC/M attributes:

■ Keep the definitions concise.
■ Allow employees to develop the classifications – and, more importantly, to classify (or distribute) their own activities with the attributes.
■ Be clear that attributes are tagged to activities – not to the people who perform the work.

- Constantly ask, "Can the high value-adding activities be done more quickly or at a lower cost?"
- Determine if low-value-adding activities can be eliminated or at least minimized.

Some analytical types of people are uncomfortable with any form of subjective grading and prefer rigorous rule-based methods to determine which attribute score is applicable. In this area, they can lighten up and just go with the flow. Yes, the scorings may come from some snap judgments of employees and other process participants. But the resulting view of the costs is just a starting point for asking more questions. Don't make the data collection effort too large an obstacle.

##  ABC/M REVEALS THE COST OF QUALITY (COQ)

Here is another way of thinking about this. When attributes are tagged to activities, each cost object will consume multiple grades of a select attribute. As a result, the cost objects will reflect different blends relative to each other. An analogy would be the different gallonage (cost amount) of different colored paint (an attribute's different score) being poured (activity driver) into an empty paint can (cost object). As each empty can is filled, the color shade of paint will be different, even if the cans are filled to comparable levels (same amount of cost).

In this way, attributes can reveal a different mix of value or performance. For example, there can be a major difference between two products with roughly the same unit cost. That is, one color of paint may cost $50.00 per gallon, with $15.00 of that total coming from a dozen activities scored as "below expectations" performance. Another color may also be $50.00 per gallon, but with only $5.00 of that total coming from two "below expectations" activities. Armed with this information, the product managers of these colors now have more insights to adjust their products' costs by adding or lowering services or price. In this way, the attributes are being used as in benchmarking to compare and contrast – and then to focus.

Attributes make ABC/M data come alive to some people. And when the attributed ABC/M data are exported into on-line analytical processing (OLAP) software and executive information system (EIS) tools, they can have a very stimulating impact on users.

## QUANTIFYING THE MAGNITUDE OF THE COSTS OF QUALITY

Now comes the hard part. Regardless of what the intended purpose for the quality-related data will be and regardless of how precise or accurate the data need to be to meet that purpose, at some point in time you have to come to grips with quantifying the COQ. And that means collecting, validating, and reporting the data.

## COST OF QUALITY CLASSIFICATION SCHEME

The quality management community uses attributes to calculate the cost of quality (COQ). Figure 12.2 illustrates the three popular COQ categories for grading work activities. Categories themselves can be branched into subcategories for more refined reporting.

Category 1 in this graphic means a good and stable process. Category 2 has quality-related costs because the process is not sufficiently stable to trust it, so you must inspect and test. Category 3 has quality-related costs because

**Attributes Can *Score and Tag* COQ Costs**

| Each activity cost gets "tagged" |

Error-Free
Conformance
Non-Conformance

prevention
appraisal
internal failure
external failure

Work activities

stable | ←——— unstable ———→ | ←——— defective ———→

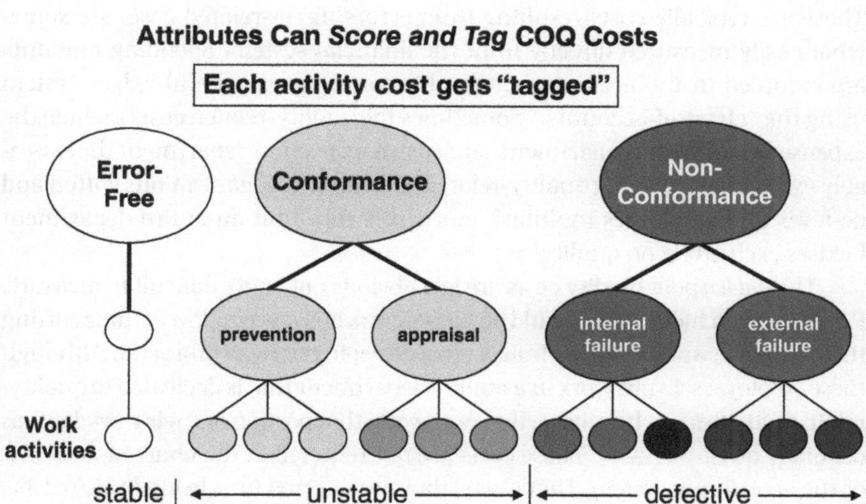

**FIGURE 12.2** Attribute can *score and tag* COQ costs. Source: Copyright 2019 www.garycokins.com.

something is already defective or does not conform to specifications defined for or by the service recipient. With rigor like this, quality teams can pursue stronger improvement programs and shift their time and emphasis away from documentation and reporting to taking corrective actions.

Multiple activities can be simultaneously tagged with these grades. And, of course, the money amount trails along, first at the work activity level and then traced into the cost objects or into the processes to which the activities belong. Attributes can also be directly tagged on resources as well as final cost objects, but tagging activities is the more popular.

 ## HOW DO YOU CATEGORIZE DIFFERENT QUALITY COSTS?

To some, quality costs are very visible and obvious. To others, quality costs are understated. They believe that much of the quality-related costs are hidden and go unreported.

There are *hidden* financial costs beyond those associated with traditional, obvious quality costs. Examples of obvious quality-related costs are rework costs, excess scrap material costs, warranty costs, or field repair expenses. These are typically costs resulting from errors. Error-related costs are somewhat easily measured directly from the financial system. Spending amounts are recorded in the accountant's fund accounting or general ledger system using the "chart-of-accounts." Sometimes the quality-related costs include the expenses of an entire department, such as an inspection department that arguably exists solely as being quality-related. However, as organizations flatten and de-layer and employees multitask more, it is rare that an entire department focuses exclusively on quality.

The *hidden* poor quality costs are less obvious and more difficult to measure. For example, a hidden cost would be those hours of a few employees' time sorting through paperwork resulting from a record-keeping or reporting error. Although these employees do not work in a quality department that is dedicated to quality-related activities, such as inspection or rework, that portion of their workday was definitely quality-related. These costs are not reflected in the chart-of-accounts of the accounting system. That is why they are referred to as being *hidden* costs.

Providing employee teams with visibility of both *obvious* and *hidden* quality-related costs can be valuable for performance improvement. Using the data, employees can gain insights into the causes of problems. The hidden and traditional costs can be broadly categorized as:

- **Error-free costs:** Costs unrelated to planning of, controlling of, correcting of, or improving of quality. These are the do-it-right-the-first-time (nicknamed "dirtfoot") costs.
- **Costs of quality (COQ):** Costs that could disappear if all processes were error-free and if all products and services were defect-free. COQ can be subcategorized as:

  - *Costs of conformance:* Costs related to prevention and predictive appraisal to meet requirements.
  - *Costs of nonconformance:* Costs related to internal or external failure to meet requirements, including defective appraisal work. The distinction between internal and external is that internal failure costs are detected prior to the shipment or receipt of service by the service recipient or customer. In contrast, external failure costs usually result from discovery by the service recipient or customer.

An oversimplified definition of COQ is the costs associated with avoiding, finding, making, and repairing defects and errors (presuming that all defects and errors are detected). COQ represents the difference between the actual costs and what the reduced costs would be if there were no substandard service levels, failures, or defects.

Simple examples of these cost categories for a magazine or book publisher might be as follows:

- *Error-free:* "First time through" work without a flaw
- *Prevention:* Training courses for the proofreaders or preventive maintenance on the printing presses
- *Appraisal:* Proofreading
- *Internal failure:* Unplanned printing press downtime or corrections of typographical errors
- *External failure:* Rework resulting from a complaint by a service recipient or customer.

In principle, as the COQ expenses are reduced, they can be converted into budget surpluses or spent on higher value requirements.

"Attributes" can be tagged or scored into increasingly finer segments of the error-free and COQ subcategories. Attributes are tagged to individual activities for which the activities will have already have been costed using ABC/M. Hence, the subcategory costs can be reported with an audit trail back to which resources they came from. Each of the subattributes can be further subdivided with deeper "indented" classifications.

Since 100 percent of the resource costs can be assigned to activities, then 100 percent of the activities can be tagged with one of the COQ attributes – the activities have already been costed by ABC/M. The attribute groupings and summary roll-ups are automatically costed as well.

Life would be nice in an error-free world, and an organization's overall costs would be substantially lower relative to where they are today. However, they will always experience some level of error. This is human nature. The goal is to manage mistakes and their impact. COQ simply serves to communicate fact-based data – in terms of money – to enable focusing and prioritizing.

As previously mentioned, unless an entire department's existence is fully dedicated to one of the COQ subcategories or coincidentally an isolated chart-of-account expense account fully applies to a COQ category, then most of the COQ spending is hidden. That is, the financial system cannot report those costs.

A danger exists if only a fraction of the quality-related costs is measured and their amount is represented as the total quality costs – this is a significant understating of the actual costs. And, unfortunately, there are as many ways of hiding quality costs as there are people with imagination. Organizations that hide their complete COQ from themselves continue to risk deceiving themselves with an illusion that they have effective management. ABC/M is an obvious approach to make visible the missing COQ amount of spending.

 **DECOMPOSING COQ CATEGORIES**

In effect, the technique for calculating a reasonably accurate COQ is to apply ABC/M and ABC/M's attribute capability. Figure 12.3 reveals a list of categories for work activities that are one additional level below the four major categories of COQ. Each of these subcategories can be tagged against the ABC/M costs. This provides far greater and more reliable visibility of COQ without the great effort required by traditional cost accounting methods.

**Typical Examples of Cost of Quality Categories**

| Conformance | | Nonconformance | |
|---|---|---|---|

| **Prevention** | **Appraisal** | **Internal Failure** | **External Failure** |
|---|---|---|---|
| § Quality education | § Test | § Scrap | § Returned products |
| § Process design | § Measurements | § Rework | § Billing reduction from customer complaint |
| § Defect cause removal | § Evaluations and assessments | § Repairs | § Field repair call |
| § Process change | § Problem analysis | § Unscheduled and unplanned service | § Warranty expenses |
| § Quality audit | § Inspection | § Defect removal | § Legal exposure and costs |
| § Preventive maintenance | § Detection | § Lost process time | § Liability claims |
| | | | § Poor availability |
| | | | § Malfunction |
| | | | § Replacement |
| | | | § Poor safety |
| | | | § Complaint administration |

**FIGURE 12.3** Typical examples of cost of quality categories. Source: Copyright 2019 www.garycokins.com.

## COQ: BOTH GOOD AND POOR QUALITY

Some equate quality-related work activities only with problems and reactionary efforts by employees to fix things. But with COQ, additional quality-related work activities (e.g., inspection) that are not directly associated with poor quality are included as part of the broad COQ category. In short, one can think of COQ's costs of conformance work as good quality COQ and the costs of nonconformance as poor quality COQ. However, both good and poor COQ when combined are costs of quality that may not be incurred at all in a perfect world. In short, prevention and appraisal costs are worth measuring.

This broader picture of COQ provides much greater visibility and thereby ensures that the quality management projects and programs are efficiently run. That is, including the costs that are intended to prevent potential problems can ensure that there is not overspending too far beyond the spending required to satisfy the service recipient or customer. It is natural for organizations to be interested in failure-related costs. These usually attract the most attention. But prevention and appraisal costs are not that difficult to identify and report, and they should not be excluded from the visibility of managers.

When making decisions, the universally popular costs-versus-benefits test can be applied with COQ data. If either subcategory of COQ is excessive, it draws down profits for commercial companies or draws down resources in government agencies that could have been better deployed on higher value-added activities elsewhere.

 **GOALS AND USES FOR THE COQ INFORMATION**

An organization should not invest its time in constructing a COQ measurement system if it is destined to be just another way for some employees to spin numbers. The bottom line message is: Don't start measuring COQ information if you won't use it!

In short, the uses of a COQ measurement system can include (1) favorably influencing employee attitudes toward quality management by quantifying the financial impact of changes, and (2) assisting in prioritizing improvement opportunities. The premise for even bothering to implement COQ is based on the following logic:

- For any failure, there is a root cause.
- Causes for failure are preventable.
- Prevention is cheaper than fixing problems after they occur.

If you accept the premise that it is always less expensive to do the job right the first time than to do it over, then the rationale for quality management and using COQ to give a quality program concrete and fact-based data should be apparent:

- Directly attack failure costs with the goal of driving them to zero.
- Spend time and money in the appropriate prevention activities, not fads, to effect improvements.
- Reduce appraisal costs according to results that are achieved.
- Continuously evaluate and redirect prevention efforts to gain further improvement.

Figure 12.4 illustrates the direction for which quality-related costs can be managed. Ideally, all four COQ cost categories should be reduced, but one may initially need to prudently increase the cost of prevention in order to dramatically decrease the costs of and reduced penalties paid for nonconformance.

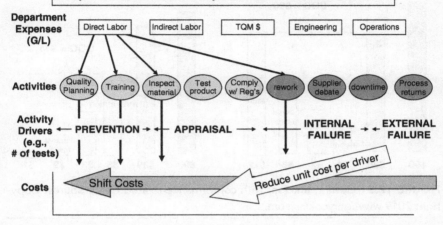

**FIGURE 12.4** Driving cost of quality downward. Source: Copyright 2019 www. garycokins.com.

This makes COQ more than just an accounting scheme; it becomes a financial investment justification tool.

A general set of corrective operating principles is that as failures are revealed – for example, via complaints from service recipients – the root causes should be eliminated with corrective actions. A general rule of thumb is that the nearer the failure is to the end-user, the more expensive it is to correct. The flipside is that it becomes less expensive, overall, to fix problems earlier in the business process. As failure costs are reduced, appraisal efforts can also be reduced in a rational manner.

Figure 12.5 illustrates the midway point of a fictitious manufacturer's COQ as nonconformance-related costs are displaced by conformance-related costs.

The figure illustrates a more desirable end goal for our fictitious manufacturer. Not only are nonconformance costs significantly reduced, but the level of prevention and inspection costs, which some classify as non–value added, are also reduced. The $20,000 of COQ has been reduced by $12,000, to $8,000. The reward for this good work has meant more requests for orders and higher sales without any changes in manpower. The error-free costs have risen by the same $12,000, from $80,000 to $92,000.

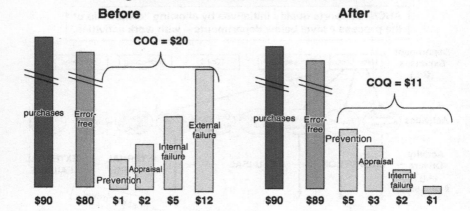

**FIGURE 12.5** Getting efficient with conformance-related COQ. Source: Copyright 2019 www.garycokins.com.

 ## COQ MEASUREMENT SYSTEM

The more formal COQ measurement system provides continuous results. In contrast to a one-time assessment, it requires involvement by employees who participate in the business and administrative processes. More importantly, these employees need to be motivated to spend the energy and time, apart from their regular responsibilities, to submit and use the data.

Commercial ABC/M software products were designed for frequent repeated updating. For such a COQ system to be sustained longer-term, the system requires senior management's support and interest as well as genuinely perceived utility by users of the data to solve problems.

Continuous COQ measurement systems require a greater amount of effort, expertise, and maturity. Many organizations underestimate the maturity requirement. It is advisable that the organization gradually implement its system through a combination of: (1) measuring selected and local areas where relatively higher benefits are more likely to be realized, and (2) starting at more summarized levels of data before decomposing the levels of detail to the more granular work task level. The level of detail should only be relatively greater in the areas where there are anticipated opportunities. The levels of depth and detail can be raised or lowered as problems arise and recede following resolution.

Up to this point ABC/M has been applied to the past historical view of costs. In Chapter 13 we shift to the predictive view – the future is coming at an organization. This involves the planning, forecasting, budgeting, rolling financial forecasts, what-if scenario analysis, and other decision support needs from management accounting information.

# CHAPTER THIRTEEN

# Driver-Based Budgeting and Rolling Financial Forecasts

T HERE IS NOW A better approach to forecasting the location and level of resources and budgeted expenditures. Sometimes called activity-based budgeting (ABB), this approach recognizes that the need for resources originates with a demand-pull triggered by customers, citizens, or any end users of the organization's services and capabilities. In contrast, traditional budgeting tends to extrapolate the level of resource spending for each spending line item for all of the cost centers (e.g., departments) from the spending levels of past periods, and then adds a small percentage increase to allow for monetary inflation. In the traditional approach to budgeting, the budget process starts with the current level of expenses. A problem with budgeting this way is that the past is not a reliable indicator of the future. It is insensitive to changes in demand volume to the organization and any or all of its cost centers.

Increasingly, today's more knowledgeable managers correctly believe that the budget should flow backward in the reverse direction from the outputs to the resources. Activity-based budgeting (ABB) flows backward. ABB assists in logically determining what levels of resources – the types and numbers of employees and spending for supplier or contractors – are required to meet the future demands placed on the organization.

In the 1980s, financial planners – particularly in the US federal government – actually experimented with a precursor to ABB. It was called zero-based budgeting (ZBB). Managers' instincts then were similar to what they are today. Managers suspected it might be better to imagine a budgeting process where each department begins its budget thinking with a clean slate, as if it were just starting up new and staffing the department from scratch. In other words, what resources would a department need next year if it had no idea what it had last year?

However, timing is everything when it comes to major changes in management techniques – and the timing was not right in the 1980s for ZBB to be successful. Cost pressures were not as significant then as they are today. In addition, software modeling tools for ZBB were hard to come by. Those conditions have now changed for the better. Some organizations have implemented ABC/M system that have routinely recalculated with revisions for several years. The more advanced and mature ABC/M users have already constructed models that depict their cost structure and expense behavior reasonably well. The timing and conditions are now suitable for change.

In the first decade of the 2000s, the more mature and advanced ABC users increasingly began using their calculated activity costs, as well as unit-level cost consumption rates for intermediate work outputs and for products and services, as a basis for projecting the resource expense levels and their resulting costs. Popular uses of the ABC information for cost estimating have been for calculating work order quotations and for make-or-buy analysis. The ABC information was also being recognized as a predictive planning tool for ABB. It is now becoming apparent that ABC information has tremendous utility both for examining the "as-is" current condition of the organization and for achieving a desired "to-be" state.

 ## BUDGETING: USER DISCONTENT AND REBELLION

Why is interest in activity-based budgeting (ABB) increasing? Simply put, many managers have problems with the annual budget process, and not just because they are not getting approval for the funding they want. They are disturbed by the budgeting process altogether. There is great cynicism about budgeting as well as an intuitive sense that a better way to budget exists.

Often, a substantial change in management technique is born of a combination of dissatisfaction with current methods and a vision of what a replacement method could look like. For the adoption of ABB, both conditions are present today.

Why are managers and employees cynical about the annual budgeting process? They find that the process takes too long to prepare, is too detailed, and is excessively burdensome. In addition, they view budgeting as a political game that usually results in some departments being overfunded while others labor on as have-nots. Many workers in this latter group toil without relief. Through organizational downsizing, senior management has often removed employees but not taken out the work! Across-the-board cuts in manpower, some of the slash-and-burn variety, are likely to cut into the muscle in some places while still leaving fat as excess capacity in others. Figure 13.1 provides some sarcasm about traditional budgeting in the form of a check-the-box survey.

Thankfully, there is a vision of what a better way of budgeting looks like: ABB. But ABB is better for what purpose and for whom? Fundamentally, we need to understand the purpose of a budget.

Most people think that a budget is a set of predetermined spending limits put in place so that if all departments roughly spend what was allotted to them, then the estimated total approved spending limit for the organization will be reasonably achieved. In this way of thinking, the purpose of a budget is as a control tool rather than as an analytical and resource allocation tool. As an example, don't exceed your spending limit, or you'll get your hand slapped by the accounting police: "You took two more airline flights than planned. Explain why."

## A Quiz. "Our budgeting exercise..."

- [ ] is invasive and time-consuming ... with few benefits.
- [ ] takes 14 months from start-to-end.
- [ ] requires two or more executive "tweaks" at the end.
- [ ] is obsolete in two months due to events and reorganizations.
- [ ] starves the departments with truly valid needs.
- [ ] caves in to the "loudest voice" and "political muscle."
- [ ] rewards veteran sandbaggers who are experts at padding.
- [ ] incorporates last year's inefficiencies into this year's budget.
- [ ] Is overstated from the prior year's "Use-it-or-lose-it" spending.

**FIGURE 13.1** Quiz: "Our budgeting exercise." Source: Copyright 2019 www.garycokins.com.

The broader purpose of budgeting should be to predetermine the level of resource expenses that will be required, such as the types and number of employees, material, supplies, and equipment, to achieve an expected or desired amount of demand for the employees' services – meaning the demands for their work. ABB advocates are interested in the notion of resource requirements as being the result of budgeting, not the starting point. ABB advocates want to be able to first estimate oncoming customer, citizen, and management demands; and second determine the supply of resources, in terms of expenses, that will be needed to match the supply with the work demands. In short, ABB advocates want to reverse the traditional budget equation and start with the expected outcomes, not with the existing situation.

With hindsight, we now realize that the fund accounting and general ledger systems, as well as their budgets derived from them, are a mirror of the organization chart, not of the end-to-end business processes that traverse the department "boxes" in the organization chart. But the processes are what actually deliver value to customers, citizens, and service recipients. And worse, the budget has no visibility into the "content of work" – the time and effort of work activities. Moreover, it has no provisions for logically determining how external or internal cost drivers govern the levels of spending caused by demands on work from those cost drivers. Traditional budgeting is done more by push than pull.

Here are further observations about traditional budgeting, some of which appeared in the survey quiz in Figure 13.1:

■ Today's budget preparation process takes an extraordinarily long time, sometimes months, during which the organization often reshuffles and resizes. In addition, customers and citizens often change their behavior, for which a prudent reaction often cannot be accommodated in the budget.
■ The annual budget is steeped in tradition in some organizations, yet the effort of producing it heavily outweighs the benefits it supposedly yields.
■ Budgets are useful for organizations that are stable and in which senior managers do not trust their organization to spend money intelligently or with discipline. Both of those conditions are invalid today.
■ Many companies confuse budgeting (i.e., spending control) with financial planning (i.e., forecasting). Computer models today can forecast the expected outcomes of all sorts of assumption-based scenarios without the need for a formal budget exercise.
■ The budget should reflect and support the executive team's strategy. Strategies should be formulated at two levels. First, the diversification

strategy level answers, "What should we be doing?" Second, the operational strategy level asks, "How should we do it?" Unfortunately, most of the effort is on the latter question, and organizations get preoccupied with simply finishing the budget – which by that time the budget may be disconnected from the executive's strategy.

■ "Use it or lose it" is a standard practice for managers during the last fiscal quarter because their next year's budget will be pegged to what they projected to spend this year. Budgets can be an invitation to some managers to spend needlessly.

In response to the rising awareness that current methods of budgeting are flawed and deficient, leaders should move away from siloed cost center planning to process-based thinking with demand volume planning. Many commercial companies spend months preparing their budget prior to the fiscal year being budgeted. Public sector organizations likely devote a similar amount of time to creating a budget. And the budget is typically obsolete within a few months after it is published. A better way to budget will consolidate what is today an extremely fragmented and disjointed exercise, as will be described in this chapter.

 ## WHAT'S BROKEN ABOUT BUDGETING?

How many people in your organization love the annual budgeting process? Probably few or even none. The mere mention of the word "budget" raises eyebrows and evokes cynicism. It should.

What is broken about the annual budgeting process? Here are some of the issues related to budgeting:

■ **Obsolete budgeting.** As listed in the quiz in Figure 13.1, the budget data is out of date within weeks after it is published, which took months to prepare it.

■ **Bean-counter budgeting.** The budget is considered a fiscal exercise produced by the accountants that is disconnected from the strategy of the executive team – and from the mission-critical spending needed to implement the strategy.

■ **Political budgeting.** The loudest voice, the strongest political muscle, and the prior year's budget levels should not be valid ways to award resources for next year's spending.

- **Overscrutinized budgeting.** Often the budget is revised midyear or, more frequently, with new forecasted spending. Then an excess amount of attention focuses on analyzing the differences between the actual and new projected expenses. These include budget-to-forecast, last-forecast-to-current-forecast, actual-to-budget, actual-to-forecast, and so on. This reporting provides lifetime job security for the budget analysts in the accounting department.
- **Sandbagging budgeting.** The budget numbers that roll up from lower- and mid-level managers often mislead senior executives because of sandbagging (i.e., padding) by the veteran managers who know how to play the game.
- **Wasteful budgeting.** Budgets do not identify waste. In fact, inefficiencies in the current business processes are often "baked into" next year's budget. Budgets do not support continuous improvement.
- **Blow-it-all budgeting.** Reckless "use it or lose it" is a standard practice for managers during the last fiscal quarter. This is because their next year's budget will be pegged to what they projected to spend this year. Budgets can be an invitation to some managers to spend needlessly.

As earlier mentioned, the annual budget is steeped in tradition, yet the effort of producing it heavily outweighs the benefits it supposedly yields. How can budgeting be reformed? Or should the budget process be abandoned altogether because its inflexible fixed social contract incentives to managers drives behavior counter to the organization's changing goals and its unwritten "contract" with executives? And, if the budget is abandoned, then what should replace its underlying purpose?

The accountants do not help matters. When they develop the annual budget, they equate the functional silos to the responsibility cost center view that they capture expense transactions in their general ledger and fund accounting system. When they request each cost center manager to submit the next year's budget, ultimately it is an "incremental or decremental" game. That is, each manager begins with their best estimate of their current year's expected total spending – line-item by line-item – and they incrementally increase it with a percentage. Budgeting software reinforces this bad habit by making it easy to make these calculations. At the extreme, next year's spending for each line is computed as shown in Figure 13.2. Using spreadsheet software, you multiply the first line-item expense by the increment, in this example by 5%, and simply copy and paste that formula for every line-item below it. Isn't it laughable? But the truth hurts. This is what leads to that use-it-or-lose-it unnecessary blow-it-all spending earlier described.

## Spreadsheet Budgeting – It is Incremental!

| | a | b | c |
|---|---|---|---|
| 1 | | **Current Year** | Budget Year |
| 2 | **Wages** | $ 400,000.00 | Formula = Column B * 1.05 |
| 3 | **Supplies** | $ 50,000.00 | |
| 4 | **Rent** | $ 20,000.00 | Copy down |
| 5 | **Computer** | $ 40,000.00 | |
| 6 | **Travel** | $ 30,000.00 | |
| 7 | **Phone** | $ 20,000.00 | |
| 8 | **Total** | $ 560,000.00 | |

Sheet 1

**FIGURE 13.2** Spreadsheet budgeting: it's incremental! Source: Copyright 2019 www.garycokins.com.

As described in Chapter 8, "By this evolution point in budgeting, there is poor end-to-end visibility about what exactly drives what inside the organization. Some organizations eventually evolve into intransigent bureaucracies. Some functions become so embedded inside the broader organization that their work level is insensitive to changes in the number and types of external requests. Fulfilling these requests was the origin of why their function was created in the first place. They become insulated from the outside world." This is not a pleasant story, but it is pervasive.

 ## THE FINANCIAL MANAGEMENT INTEGRATED INFORMATION DELIVERY PORTAL

Today's solution to solve the budgeting conundrum and the organization's backward-looking focus is to begin with a single integrated data platform – popularly called a business intelligence (BI) platform – and its Web-based reporting and analysis capabilities. Speed to knowledge is now a key to improving performance.

The emphasis for improving an organization and driving higher value must shift from hand-slap punishment controlling toward automated forward-looking planning. With a common platform replacing disparate data sources, enhanced with input data integrity cleansing features and data mining capabilities, an organization can create a flexible and collaborative planning environment. Part Six describes information technology as enabler to VBM.

**A RADICAL IDEA: STOP BUDGETING!**

Some commercial companies have become sufficiently frustrated with the annual budgeting process that they have abandoned creating an annual budget. An international research and membership collaborative called the Beyond Budgeting Round Table (BBRT)[1] advocates that rather than attempt to tightly control managers' spending on a line-by-line basis, it is better to step back and question what the purposes of budgeting are. Their conclusion is that organizations would be better off moving away from long-term financial projections at a detailed level and replacing this form of monitoring by empowering managers with more freedom to make local spending decisions, including hiring employees.

BBRT believes in removing second-guess approvals from higher-level managers and granting managers more decision rights. BBRT views fiscal year-end budget figures as if they are a fixed contract that managers will strive for rather than react to changes not assumed when the budget was created. In place of budget spending variance controls, BBRT advocates a shift in reporting emphasis and also accountability with consequences on outcomes – performance reporting with KPIs and their targets – not on the inputs. BBRT believes that secondary purposes for budgeting, such as cash flow projections for the treasury function, can be attained with modeling techniques performed by business analysts.

Regardless of how an organization approaches its own reforms to budgeting, VBM provides confidence in the numbers, which improves trust among managers. What today will accelerate the adoption of reforms to the budgeting process and a VBM culture – senior management's attitude and willpower or the information technology that can realize the vision described here? This book's authors would choose both.

 **PREDICTIVE ACCOUNTING AND BUDGETING WITH MARGINAL EXPENSE ANALYSIS[2]**

Managers are increasingly shifting from reacting to after-the-fact outcomes to anticipating the future with predictive analysis. They are proactively making adjustments with better decisions. Despite some advances in the application of new costing techniques, are management accountants adequately satisfying the need for better cost planning information? Or is the gap widening?

---

[1] www.bbrt.org.

[2] The ideas in this chapter on activity-based resource planning (ABRP) are based on research from a professional society, the Activity Based Budgeting Project Team of the Consortium for Advanced Manufacturing International's (CAM-I) Cost Management Systems (CMS) group. More is at www.cam-i.org.

There is a widening gap between what management accountants provide and report and what managers and employee teams want and need. This does not mean that information produced by management accountants is of little value. In the last few decades, accountants have made significant strides in improving the utility and accuracy of the historical costs they calculate and report as described in prior chapters of this book. The gap is caused by a shift in managers' needs, from needing to know what things cost (such as a cost of a service or task) and what happened to a need for reliable information about what their future costs will be and why.

Despite the accountants advancing a step to catch up with the increasing needs of managers for insights and cost information to make better decisions, the managers have advanced beyond their accountants. The accountants need to catch up. The rest of this chapter will help us understand this widening gap, and more importantly how accountants can narrow and ideally close the gap.

## WHAT IS THE PURPOSE OF MANAGEMENT ACCOUNTING?

Contrary to beliefs that the only purpose of managerial accounting is to collect, transform, and report data, its primary purpose is first and foremost to influence behavior at all levels – from the desk of the CEO down to each employee – and it should do so by supporting decisions. A secondary purpose is to stimulate investigation and discovery by surfacing relevant information (and consequently bringing focus) and generating questions.

The widening gap between what accountants report and what decision makers need involves the shift from analyzing descriptive past period historical information to analyzing predictive information, such as budgets and what-if scenarios. Obviously, all decisions can only impact the future because the past is already history. However, there is much that can be learned and leveraged from historical information. Although accountants are gradually improving the quality of reported history, decision makers are shifting their view toward better understanding the future.

This shift is a response to a more overarching shift in executive management styles, from a command-and-control emphasis that is reactive (such as scrutinizing cost variance analysis of actual versus planned outcomes) to an anticipatory, proactive style where organizational changes and adjustments, such as staffing levels, can be made before things happen and before minor problems become big ones.

Figure 13.3 illustrates the large domain of accounting as a taxonomy with three components: tax accounting, financial accounting, and managerial

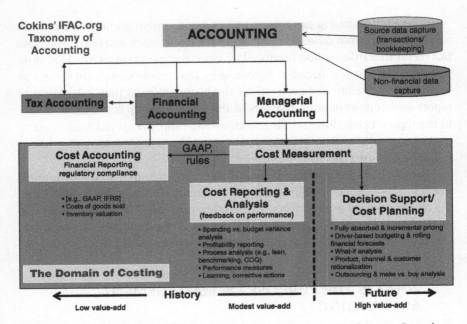

**FIGURE 13.3** Cokins's IFAC.org taxonomy of accounting. Source: Based on data from PABC IGPG "Evaluating and Improving Costing in Organizations" published by the International Federation of Accountants, 2009. Copyright 2019 www.garycokins.com.

accounting. (This figure was created by this book's author, Gary Cokins, for the International Federation of Accountants [IFAC], an organization with global accounting institutes as its members.) Two types of data sources are displayed at the upper right. The upper source is from financial transactions and book-keeping, such as purchases and payroll. The lower source is nonfinancial measures such as payroll hours worked or number of services delivered. Many are the activity drivers used with ABC. These same metrics can be forecasted.

The financial accounting component in the figure is intended for external statutory reporting, such as for regulatory agencies, banks, stockholders, and the investment community. Financial accounting follows compliance rules aimed at economic valuation, and as such is typically not adequate or sufficient for decision making. And the tax accounting component is its own world of legislated rules.

Our area of concern – the management accounting component – is segmented into three categories: cost accounting, the cost reporting and analysis, and decision support with cost planning. To oversimplify a distinction between financial and managerial accounting, financial accounting is about valuation and managerial accounting is about value creation through good decision making.

The message at the bottom of the figure is the value, utility, and usefulness of the accounting information increases, arguably at an exponential rate, from the left side to the right side of the figure.

 ## DESCRIPTIVE VERSUS PREDICTIVE ACCOUNTING

Figure 13.4 illustrates how a firm's view of its expense structure changes as analysis shifts from the historical *cost reporting* view to the predictive *cost planning* view. The latter is the context from which decisions are considered and evaluated.

In the figure's left-hand side during the historical time period, the resource expenses were incurred. The capacity these expenses were incurred for was *supplied*, and then they were either (1) *unused* as idle or protective buffer capacity; or (2) they were *used* to make products, to deliver services, or to sustain the organization internally. This is the *cost reporting and analysis* component

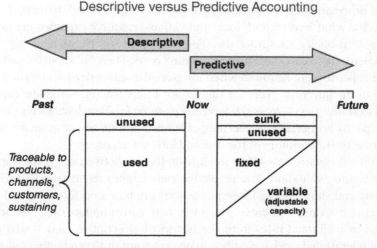

**FIGURE 13.4** Descriptive versus predictive accounting. Source: Copyright 2019 www.garycokins.com.

from Figure 13.3 that calculates output costs. The money was spent, and costing answers where it was used. This is the *descriptive* view of costs. Accountants refer to this as full absorption costing when all the expenses for a past time period are totally traced to outputs. It traces expenses (and hopefully does not allocate expenses on causal-insensitive broad averages by using ABC) to measure which outputs (e.g., services) uniquely consumed the resources. Full absorption costing uses direct costing methods, which are relatively easy to apply, and ideally supplements the reporting with ABC for the indirect and shared expenses, which are trickier to model, calculate, and report.

In contrast, the figure's right-hand side is the *predictive* view of costs – the *decision support with cost planning* component from Figure 13.3. In the future, the capacity levels and types of resources can be adjusted. Capacity only exists as a resource, not as a process or work activity. The classification of a resource's expense as sunk, fixed, semi-fixed, or variable depends on the planning time horizon. The diagonal line reveals that in the very short term, most capacity and its expenses are not easily changed; hence, they are classified as fixed. As the time horizon extends into the future, then capacity becomes adjustable. For example, assets can be leased, not purchased; and future workers can be contracted from a temporary employment agency, not hired as full-time employees. Therefore, these expenses are classified as variable.

In the predictive view of Figure 13.3 changes in demand – such as the forecasted volume and mix of services or work orders – will drive the consumption of processes (and the work activities that belong to them). In turn, this will determine what level of both fixed and variable resource expenses are needed to supply capacity for future use. For purchased assets, such as expensive equipment, these costs are classified as sunk costs. Their full capacity and associated expense were acquired when an executive authorized and signed their name to the purchase order for the vendor or contractor. Some idle capacity (such as staffing a call center) is typically planned for. This deliberately planned idle capacity is intended to meet temporary demand surges, or as an insurance buffer for the uncertainty of the demand forecast accuracy.

Since decisions only affect the future, the predictive view is the basis for analysis and evaluation. The predictive view applies techniques like what-if analysis and simulations. These projections are based on forecasts and unit-level cost consumption rates. However, cost consumption rates are ideally derived as calibrated rates from the historical, descriptive view – where the rate of operational work typically remains constant until productivity and process improvements affect them. These rates are for both direct expenses and rates that can be calibrated from an ABC system. And when improvements or process changes occur, the calibrated historical cost consumption rates can be adjusted up or down from the valid baseline measure that is already being experienced. Accountants refer to these projections as marginal or incremental expense analysis. For example, as future incremental demands change from the existing, near-term baseline operations, how is the supply for needed capacity affected? Marginal and incremental costing will be discussed later in this chapter.

##  WHAT TYPES OF DECISIONS ARE MADE WITH MANAGERIAL ACCOUNTING INFORMATION?

There are hundreds of pages on managerial and cost accounting in university textbooks. Let's try to distill all those pages to a few paragraphs. The broad decision-making categories for applying managerial accounting are:

**Rationalization.** Which products, services, channels, routes, citizens, customers, and others are best to retain or improve? And, which are not and should potentially be abandoned or terminated (if possible)?

Historical and descriptive costing can be adequate to answer these questions. In part, this explains the growing popularity in applying ABC principles to supplement traditional direct costing. There is much diversity and variation in routes, channels, citizens, customers, and so on that cause a relative increase in an organization's indirect and shared expenses to manage the resulting complexity. IT expenses are a growing one. Having the direct and indirect costs become a relevant starting point allows you to know what the variations cost. This answers a "What?" question. It is difficult, arguably impossible, to answer the subsequent "So what?" question without having the facts. Otherwise, conclusions are based on gut feel, intuition, misleading information, or politics.

**Planning and budgeting.** Based on forecasts of future demand volume and mix for types of services or products, combined with assumptions of other proposed changes, how much will it cost to match demand with supplied resources (e.g., workforce staffing levels)?

This is a "Then what?" question. When questions like these and many more like them are asked, one needs more than a crystal ball to answer them. This is where the *predictive* view of costing (the right side of Figure 13.3) fits in. This is arguably the sweet spot of costing. On an annual cycle, this is the budgeting process. However, executives are increasingly demanding rolling financial forecasts at shorter time intervals. This demand is partially due to the fact that, as previously mentioned, the annual budget can quickly become obsolete and future period assumptions, especially continuously revised demand volume forecasts, become more certain. At its core, this costing sweet spot is about resource capacity planning – the ability to convert and reflect physical operational events into the language of money – expenses and costs.

**Capital expense justification.** Is the return on investment (ROI) of a proposed asset purchase, such as equipment or an information system, justified?

If we purchase equipment, technology, or a system, will the financial benefits justify the investment? A question like this involves what microeconomics refers to as "capital budgeting." Capital budgeting analysis typically involves comparing a baseline, reflecting business as usual, with an alternative scenario that includes spending on (i.e., investing in) an asset where the expected benefits will continue well beyond a year's duration. An example would be investing in an automated warehouse to replace manual, pick-and-pack labor. Some refer to the associated investment justification analysis as "same as, except for" or comparing the "as-is" state with the "to-be" state. A distinction of capital budgeting is that it involves discounted cash flow (DCF) equations. DCF equations reflect the net present value (NPV) of money, incorporating the time that it would take for that same money to earn income at some rate if it were applied elsewhere (e.g., a bank certificate of deposit). The rate is often called the organization's cost of capital.

**Make-versus-buy and general outsourcing decisions.** Should we continue to do work ourselves or contract with a third party?

If we choose to have a third party make our product or deliver our service instead of ourselves – basically outsourcing, or vice versa by bringing a supplier's work in-house – then afterward, how much of our expenses remain and how much will we remove (or add)? This type of decision is similar to the logic and math of capital budgeting. The same description of the capital budgeting method applies – measuring "same as, except for" incremental changes. Ideally, activity-based costing techniques should be applied because the primary variable is the work activities that the third-party contractor will now perform, which replace the current in-house work. Since cost is not the only variable that shifts, a service-level agreement with the contactor should be a standard practice.

**Process and productivity improvement.** What can be changed? How to identify opportunities? How to compare and differentiate high-impact opportunities from nominal ones?

Some organizations' operations functions are focusing on reducing costs and future cost avoidance. (Strategic profitable revenue enhancement is addressed with managerial accounting for *rationalization*.) These operational functions are tasked with productivity improvement challenges, and they are less interested in understanding strategic analysis and more on streamlining processes, reducing waste and low-value-added work activities, and increasing asset utilization. This is the area of Six Sigma quality initiatives, lean management principles, and just-in-time (JIT) scheduling techniques. Examples of these types of costs are:

- Unit costs of outputs and benchmarking
- Target costing
- Cost of quality (COQ)
- Value-adding attributes (such as non-value added vs. value-added)
- Resource consumption accounting (RCA)
- German cost accounting (*Grenzplankostenrechnung* [GPK])
- Accounting for a lean management environment (also Kaizen costing)
- Theory of constraint's throughput accounting

The term "cost estimating" is a general one. It applies in all of the decision-making categories above. One might conclude that the first category, rationalization, focuses only on historical costs and thus does not require cost estimates. However, the impact on resource expenses from adding or dropping various work-consuming outputs (i.e., products, services, citizens, customers) also requires cost estimates to validate the merit of a proposed rationalization decision.

 ## ACTIVITY-BASED COST MANAGEMENT AS A FOUNDATION FOR PREDICTIVE ACCOUNTING

ABC/M information is now also being recognized as a predictive planning tool. It is now apparent that the information has a tremendous amount of utility for both examining the "as-is" current condition of the organization and achieving a desired "to-be" state.

Cost estimating is often involved with what-if scenarios. The reality is that decisions are being made about the future, and managers want to evaluate the consequences of those decisions. In these situations, the future is basically coming at the organization, and in some way the quantity and mix of activity drivers will be placing demands on the work that the organization will need to do. The resources required to do the work are the expenses. Assumptions are made about the outputs that are expected. Assumptions should also be made about the intermediate outputs and the labyrinth of interorganizational relationships that will be called upon to generate the expected final outcomes.

##  MAJOR CLUE: CAPACITY ONLY EXISTS AS A RESOURCE

As most organizations plan for their next month, quarter, or year, the level of resources supplied is routinely replanned to roughly match the demand volume and expected future demand volume. In reality, the level of planned resources must always exceed demand volume to allow for some protective buffer, surge, and sprint capacity. This also helps improve service performance levels. However, management accountants will be constantly disturbed if they cannot answer the question "How much unused and spare capacity do I have?" because in their minds this excess capacity equates to non-value-added costs.

The broad topic of unused and idle capacity will likely be a thorny issue for absorption costing. As management accountants better understand operations, they will be constantly improving their ability to segment and isolate the unused capacity (and the nature of its cost) by individual resource. Managerial accountants will be increasingly able to measure unused capacity either empirically or by deductive logic based on projected standard cost rates. Furthermore, accountants will be able to segment and assign this unused capacity expense to various processes, managers, or senior management. This will eliminate overcharging (and overstating) service costs resulting from including unused capacity costs that the product did not cause.

Figure 13.5 illustrates that the effort level to adjust capacity becomes easier farther out in time. It takes a while to convert in-case resources into as-needed ones. However, committed expenses (in-case) today can be more easily converted into contractual (as-needed) arrangements in a shorter time period than was possible ten years ago. Fixed expenses can become variable expenses. The rapid growth in the temporary staffing industry is evidence. Organizations can replace full-time employees who are paid regardless of the demand level with contractors who are staffed and paid at the demand level, which may be measured in hours.

Understanding the cost of the resource workload used to make a product or deliver a service is relevant to making these resource reallocation decisions. Ignoring incremental changes in the actual resources (i.e., expense

### Capacity Only Exists as Resources

**In the very short term, you would not fire employees on Tuesday due to low work load, but hire them back on Wednesday. But in the future you may replace full-time employees with contractors, or lease assets you might have purchased. In this way, so-called fixed costs behave variably.**

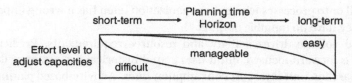

**FIGURE 13.5** Capacity only exists as resources. Source: Copyright 2019 www. garycokins.com.

spending) when making decisions can eventually lead to a cost structure that may become inefficient and ineffective for the organization. There will always be a need to adjust the capacity based on changes in future demand volume and mix. This in turn equates to raising or lowering specific expenses on resources.

 ## PREDICTIVE ACCOUNTING INVOLVES MARGINAL EXPENSE CALCULATIONS

In forecasting, the demand volume and mix of the outputs are estimated, and one then solves for the unknown level of resource expenditures that will be required to produce and deliver the volume and mix. One is basically determining the capacity requirements of the resources. Estimating future levels of resource expense cash outflows becomes complex because resources come in discrete discontinuous amounts. For example, you cannot hire one-third of an employee. That is, resource expenses do not immediately vary with each incremental increase or decrease in end-unit volume. Traditional accountants address this with what they refer to as a "step-fixed" category of expenses.

As previously mentioned, the predictive accounting method involves extrapolations that use baseline physical and unit-level cost consumption rates that are calibrated from prior-period ABC/M calculations.

Figure 13.6 illustrates how capacity planning is the key to the solution. It is a closed loop flow. Planners and budgeters initially focus on the direct and recurring resource expenses, not the indirect and overhead support expenses. They almost always begin with estimates of future demand in terms of volumes and mix. Then, by relying on standards and averages (such as the product routings and bills-of-material used in manufacturing systems), planners and budgeters calculate the future required levels of manpower headcount and spending with suppliers and contractors. The predictive accounting method suggests that this same approach can be applied to the indirect and overhead areas as well or to processes where the organization often has a wrong impression that they have no tangible outputs.

Demand volume drives activity and resource requirements. Predictive accounting is forward-focused, but it uses actual historical performance data to develop baseline unit-level cost consumption rates. Activity-based planning and budgeting assesses the quantities of workload demands that are ultimately placed on resources. In step 1 in the figure, predictive accounting first asks, "How much activity workload is required for each output of cost object?" These

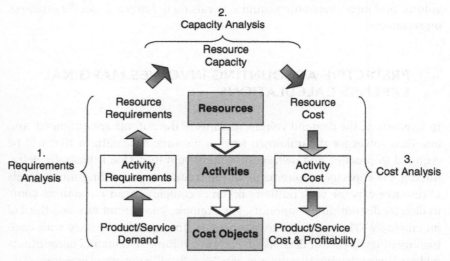

**FIGURE 13.6** Predictive accounting closed-loop information flow. Source: Copyright 2019 www.garycokins.com.

are the work activity requirements. Then predictive accounting asks, "How much resources are needed to meet that activity workload?" In other words, a workload can be measured as the number of units of an activity required to produce a quantity of cost objects.

The determination of expense does not occur until after the activity volume has been translated into resource capacity using the physical resource driver rates from the direct costing and ABC/M model. These rates are regularly expressed in hours, full-time-equivalents (FTEs), square feet, pounds, gallons, and so forth.

As a result of step 1 there will be a difference between the existing resources available and the resources that will be required to satisfy the plan – the resource requirements. That is, at this stage organizations usually discover they may have too much of what they do not need and not enough of what they do need to meet the customers' expected service levels (e.g., to deliver on time). The consequence of having too much implies a cost of unused capacity. The consequence of having too little is a limiting constraint that if not addressed implies there will be a decline in customer service levels.

In step 2 a reasonable balance must be achieved between the operational and financial measures. Now capacity must be analyzed. One option is for the budgeters, planners, or management accountants to evaluate how much to adjust the shortage and excess of actual resources to respond to the future demand load. Senior management may or may not allow the changes. There is a maximum expense impact that near-term financial targets (and executive compensation plan bonuses) will tolerate. These capacity adjustments represent real resources with real changes in cash outlay expenses if they were to be enacted.

Assume that management agrees to the new level of resources without further analysis or debate. In step 3 of the flow in the figure, the new level of resource expensed can be determined and then translated into the expenses of the work centers and eventually into the costs of the products, service lines, channels, citizens, and customers. Step 3 is classic cost accounting – but for a future period. Some call this a *pro forma* calculation. The quantities of the projected resource and activity drivers are applied; and new budgeted or planned costs can be calculated for products, service lines, outputs, citizens, customers, and service recipients.

At this point, however, the financial impact may not be acceptable to the executive team. When the financial result is unacceptable, management has options other than to continue to keep readjusting resource capacity levels. For example, they can limit demand volume.

## PREDICTIVE COSTING IS MODELING

By leveraging ABC/M with predictive accounting, an organization can produce a fully integrated plan including budgets and rolling financial forecasts. It can be assured that its plan is more feasible, determine the level of resources and their expenses to execute that plan, then view and compare the projected results of that plan against its current performance to manage its various profit margins.

All this may seem like revisiting an Economics 101 textbook. In some ways it is, but here is the difference: in the textbooks, marginal expense analysis was something easily described but extremely difficult to compute due to all of the complexities and interdependencies of resources and their costs. In the past, computing technology was the impediment. Now things have reversed. Technology is no longer the impediment – the thinking is. How one configures the predictive accounting model and what assumptions one makes become critical to calculating the appropriate required expenses and their pro forma calculated costs.

 ## PUT YOUR MONEY WHERE YOUR STRATEGY IS

An easy way for executive teams to attempt to reduce their organization's expenses is to lay off employees. But this is merely a short-term fix. An organization cannot continue to endlessly reduce its expenses to achieve long-term sustained prosperity.

Belt-tightening an organization's spending can be haphazard. Rather than evaluating where the company can cut costs, it is more prudent to switch views and ask where and how the organization should spend money to increase long-term sustained value. This involves budgeting for future expenses, but as described here the budgeting process has deficiencies.

 ## A SEA CHANGE IN ACCOUNTING AND FINANCE

How can budgeting be reformed? Let's step back and ask broader questions. What are the impacts of the changing role of the chief financial officer (CFO)? How many times have you seen the obligatory diagram with the organization shown in a central circle and a dozen inward-pointing arrows representing the menacing forces and pressures the organization faces – such as outsourcing, globalization, governance, and so on? Well, it's all true and real. But if the CFO's function is evolving from a bean counter and reporter of history into a strategic business adviser and an enterprise risk and regulatory compliance manager, what should CFOs be doing about the archaic budget process?

Progressive CFOs now view budgeting as consisting of three river streams of spending that converge to yield the total enterprise spending for the next fiscal year:

▪ **Recurring expenses.** Budgeting becomes an ongoing resource capacity planning exercise similar to a 1970s factory manager who must project the operation's manpower planning and material purchasing requirements. These are repeatable processes that are driven by demand volume.

▪ **Nonrecurring expenses.** The budget includes the one-time investments or project cash outlays to implement projects and initiatives. These are project driven.

▪ **Discretionary expenses.** The budget includes optional spending that is nonstrategic.

Of the broad portfolio of interdependent methodologies that make up today's VBM framework, two methods deliver the capability to accurately project the recurring and nonrecurring spending streams:

1. **Demand-driven operational expense projections.** As previously described in this book, activity-based costing (ABC) solves the structural deficiencies of myopic general-ledger cost-center reporting for calculating accurate costs of outputs (such as products, channels, and customers). The general ledger does not recognize cross-functional business processes that deliver the results, and its broad-brush cost allocations of the now-substantial indirect expenses introduce grotesque cost distortions. ABC corrects those deficiencies. Advances with applying ABC/M enables that "backward calculation mentioned. It is based on forecasts of demand item volume multiplied times calibrated unit-level cost consumption rates to determine the needed capacity and thus the needed recurring expenses. Without that spending, service levels will deteriorate.

2. **Project-driven expenses.** Later in this chapter, three types of projects will be described: strategy goals execution, risk mitigation, and capital investments.

**A PROBLEM WITH BUDGETING**

Companies cannot succeed by standing still. If you are not improving, then you are falling behind. This is one reason why Professor Michael E. Porter, author of the seminal 1970 book on competitive edge strategies, *Competitive Strategy: Techniques for Analyzing Industries and Competitors,* asserted that an important strategic approach is continuous differentiation and improvement of products and services. However, some organizations believed so firmly in their past successes that they were shut down or outsourced (e.g., government agencies) or went bankrupt (e.g., companies) because they had become risk-adverse to changing what they perceived to be effective strategies.

As described in Chapters 3 and 4 of this book, strategy execution is considered one of the major failures of executive teams. One of the obstacles preventing successful strategy achievement is the annual budgeting process. In the worst situations, the budgeting process is limited to a fiscal exercise administered by the accountants, which is typically disconnected from the executive team's strategic intentions. A less poor situation, but still not a solution, is one in which the accountants do consider the executive team's strategic objectives, but the initiatives required to achieve the strategy are not adequately funded in the budget. Remember, you have to spend money to make money. This introduces the question "Can your organization *afford* its strategy?"

In addition, the budgeting process tends to be insensitive to changes in future volumes and mix of forecast products and services. As described in the prior chapter, the next year's budgeted spending is typically incremented or decremented for each cost center from the prior year's spending by a few percentage points.

Components of the VBM framework can be drawn on to resolve these limitations. The big arrow at right side of Figure 13.7 illustrates that the correct and valid amount of spending for capacity and consumed expenses should be derived from two broad streams of workload that cause the need for spending: demand driven and project driven. Demand-driven expenses are operational and recurring from day to day. In contrast, project-driven spending is nonrecurring and can be from days to years in time duration.

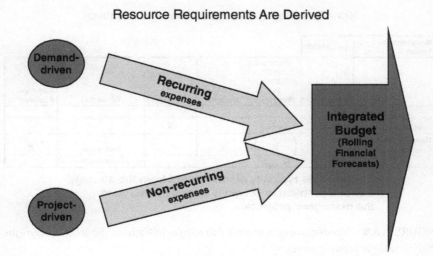

**FIGURE 13.7** Resource requirements are derived. Source: Copyright 2019 www.garycokins.com.

## VALUE IS CREATED FROM PROJECTS AND INITIATIVES, NOT THE STRATEGIC OBJECTIVES

As described in Chapter 4, a popular solution for failed strategy execution is the evolving methodology of a strategy map with its companion, the balanced scorecard with KPIs and their targets. Their combined purpose is to link operations to strategy. By using these methods like a strategy map, alignment of the work and priorities of employees can be attained without any disruption from restructuring the organizational chart. A strategy map and its balanced scorecard directly connect the executive team's strategy to individuals, regardless of their departments or matrix-management arrangements.

In Chapter 4 the authors also argued that projects and initiatives should be defined from the strategy map. What matters is that the projects and initiatives be financially funded regardless of how they are identified. Figure 13.8 revisits Figure 4.6. It illustrates who ideally should be responsible for one of the five elements of each strategic objective in a strategy map: the executive team or the managers and employees.

## Non-Recurring Expenses // Strategic Initiatives

| Measurement Period | 1st Quarter | | | | | |
|---|---|---|---|---|---|---|
| | Strategic Objective | Identify Projects, Initiatives, or Processes | KPI Measure | KPI Target | KPI Actual | Comments/ Explanation |
| Executive Team | X | | | X | | |
| Managers and Employees | | X | X | | *their score* | X |
| | | | | | *<----- period results ------->* | |

**Budgeting is typically disconnected from the strategy. But this problem is solved if management funds the managers' projects.**

**FIGURE 13.8** Nonrecurring expenses/strategic initiatives. Source: Copyright 2019 www.garycokins.com.

In Figure 13.8, the second column of X choices, what if the managers and employee teams that identified the projects are not granted spending approval by the executives for those initiatives? Presuming that KPIs with targets were established for those projects, these managers will score poorly and unfavorably. But worse yet, the strategic objectives the projects are intended to achieve will not be accomplished. By isolating this spending as strategy expenses, the organization protects these; otherwise it is like destroying the seeds for future success and growth. Capital budgeting is a more mature practice and not the issue that budgeting for strategic projects and initiatives is.

Value creation does not directly come from defining mission, vision, and strategy maps. It is the alignment of employees' priorities, work, projects, and initiatives with the executive team's objectives that directly creates value. Strategy is executed from the bottom to the top. David Norton (co-creator of the balanced scorecard with Robert S. Kaplan) uses a fisherman's analogy to explain this: strategy maps tell you where the fish are, but the projects, initiatives, and core business processes are what *catch* the fish.

## DRIVER-BASED RESOURCE CAPACITY AND SPENDING PLANNING

For daily operations where the normal recurring work within business processes occurs, a future period's amount of product- and service-line volume and mix will never be identical to the past. In future periods, some customer-demand quantities will rise and others decline. This means that unless the existing capacity and dedicated skills are adjusted, you will have too much unnecessary capacity and not enough capacity that is needed. These are dual problems. The former results in unused capacity expenses. The latter results in missed sales opportunities, or customer-infuriating delays due to capacity shortages. Both drag down profits.

Figure 13.9 illustrates advances in applying activity-based costing (ABC/M) to minimize this planning problem. ABC/M principles solve operational budgeting by leveraging historical consumption rates to be used for calculating *future-period* levels of capacity and spending.

As an oversimplification, future spending is derived by calculating the ABC/M cost assignment network backward. This was described in Figure 13.6 closed loop activity-based planning and budgeting (ABP/B). The organization starts by forecasting its activity-driver quantities (those were the actual driver quantities for past-period costing). Then it uses the calibrated activity driver unit-level consumption rates from its historical costing to compute the amount of required work activities in the operational processes. Next, it equates these workloads into the number and types of employees and the needed non-labor-related spending.

This technique provides the correct, valid resource capacity and spending requirements. With this knowledge, management can intelligently intervene and approve adjustments by adding or removing capacity. It is a logical way of

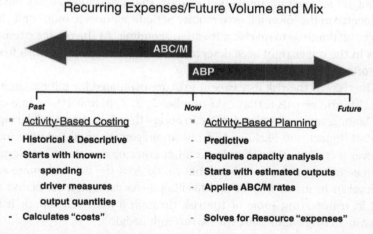

**Recurring Expenses/Future Volume and Mix**

| Past | Now | Future |
|---|---|---|
| ■ <u>Activity-Based Costing</u> | | ■ <u>Activity-Based Planning</u> |
| - **Historical & Descriptive** | | - **Predictive** |
| - **Starts with known:** | | - **Requires capacity analysis** |
| **spending** | | - **Starts with estimated outputs** |
| **driver measures** | | - **Applies ABC/M rates** |
| **output quantities** | | |
| - **Calculates "costs"** | | - **Solves for Resource "expenses"** |

**FIGURE 13.9** Recurring expenses/future volume and mix. Source: Copyright 2019 www.garycokins.com.

matching supply with demand. Once the capacity interventions (e.g., employee headcount) and planned spending are approved, then a true and valid driver-based budget can be derived – not an incremental or decremental percent change from last year – for each cost center.

## INCLUDING RISK MITIGATION WITH A RISK ASSESSMENT GRID

Measuring and managing risk possibilities identified in step 3 is now transitioning from an intuitive art to more of a craft and science. (Risk management was discussed in Chapter 6.)

To introduce quantification of risk to this area that involves qualitative and subjectivity, at some stage each identified risk requires some form of ranking, such as by level of severity from the impact if the risk even were to occur – high, medium, and low. Since the severity of a risk event includes not just its impact but also its probability of occurrence, developing a *risk assessment grid* has become an accepted method to quantify the risks and then collectively associate and rationalize all of them with a reasoned level of spending for risk mitigation. A risk map helps an organization visualize all risks on a single page.

Figure 13.10 displays a risk assessment grid with the vertical axis reflecting the magnitude of impact of the risk event occurring on the strategy execution and the horizontal axis reflecting the probability of each risk event's occurrence. Individual risk events located as circles in the map are inherent risks and not yet selected for mitigation actions; that evaluation comes next. The risks located in the lower left area require periodic glances to monitor if the risk is growing: nominal to no risk mitigation spending. At the other extreme, risk events in the upper right area deserve risk mitigation spending with frequent monitoring.

The risks in the risk assessment grid are evaluated for mitigation action. What this grid reveals is that risks number 2, 3, 7, 8, and 10 are in a critical zone. Management must decide if it can accept these five risks considering their potential impact and likelihood. If not, management might choose to avoid whatever is creating the risk as for example entering a new market. Some mitigation action might be considered that would drive the risks to a more acceptable level in terms of impact and likelihood. As examples, an action might result in transferring some of the risk through a joint venture, or it might involve incurring additional expense through hedging.

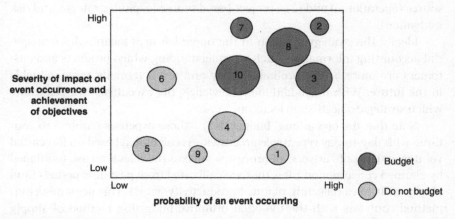

**Risk Assessment Grid**
... ERM is not just contingency planning

**FIGURE 13.10** Risk assessment grid. Source: Copyright 2019 www.gary cokins.com.

Management must decide on the cost versus benefits of the mitigation actions. Will the mitigation action, if pursued, move a risk event within the predefined risk appetite guidelines? Is the residual risk remaining after mitigation action acceptable? If not, what additional action can be taken? How much will that additional action cost, and what will be the potential benefits in terms of reducing impact and likelihood? After these decisions are made, then similar to the projects and initiatives derived from the strategy map, risk mitigation actions can be budgeted.

 **FOUR TYPES OF BUDGET SPENDING: OPERATIONAL, CAPITAL, STRATEGIC, AND RISK**

Figure 13.11 illustrates a broad framework that begins with strategy formulation in the upper left and ends with financial budgeting and rolling forecasts in the bottom right. The elements involving accounting are shaded darker. Some budgets and rolling financial forecasts may distinguish the *capital budget* spending (#2 in the figure) from *operational budget* spending (#1), but rarely do organizations segregate the important *strategic budget* spending (#3) and *risk budget* spending (#4).

The main purpose of the figure is to illustrate that the budget depends on and is derived from two separate sources: (1) a future demand-driven source (operational) and (2) a project-based source (capital, strategic, and risk mitigation).

Ideally, the strategy creation in the upper left uses meaningful managerial accounting information, such as understanding which products and customers are more or less profitable today and are potentially more valuable in the future. With this additional knowledge, the executives can determine which strategic objectives to focus on.

Note that the operational budget (#1) – those expenses required to continue with day-to-day repeatable processes – is calculated based on forecasted volume and mix of "drivers" of processes, such as the sales forecast, multiplied by planned consumption rates that are calibrated from past time periods (and ideally with rates reflecting planned productivity gains). This demand-driven method contrasts with the too-often primitive budgeting method of simply incrementally increasing the prior year's spending level by a few percentage points to allow for inflation, as was illustrated in Figure 13.2. The operational budget spending level is a dependent variable based on demand volume, so it should be calculated that way.

Regardless of whether an organization defines the strategic initiatives before or after setting the balanced scorecard's KPI targets, it is important to set aside strategy spending (#3) not much differently than budgeting for capital expenditures (#2). Too often, the strategy funding is not cleanly segregated anywhere in the budget or rolling financial forecasts. It is typically buried in an accounting ledger expense account. As a result, when financial performance inevitably falls short of expectations, it is the strategy projects' "seed money" that gets deferred or eliminated. The priority must be reversed. Organizations must protect strategy spending and allow it to go forward as it is to successfully accomplish the executive team's strategy.

The same goes for the risk mitigation expenses (#4). Enterprise risk management should be included in spending projections.

Note the question in the bottom right corner of Figure 13.11. Since the first pass at the "derived" budget or rolling forecast will likely be unacceptably too high and rejected by the executive team, the result is to adjust the plan. Hopefully, the project-based, strategy budget spending will be protected, similarly with the risk mitigation spending. Once the strategy and risk management spending are protected, the only other lever is to plan for productivity improvements in the cost consumption rates. This is where process-focused improvement programs like lean management and Six Sigma quality management are

## Linking Strategy and Risk to the Budget

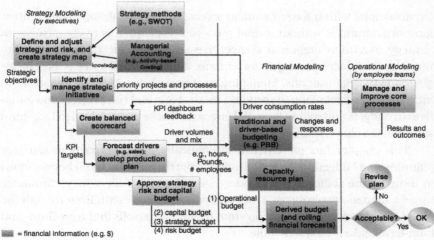

 = financial information (e.g. $)

**FIGURE 13.11** Linking strategy and risk to the budget. Source: Copyright 2019 www.garycokins.com.

leveraged. It is in this way that focused cost reductions (or future cost avoidance) become part of the VBM framework.

Put your money where your strategy is!

## FROM A STATIC ANNUAL BUDGET TO ROLLING FINANCIAL FORECASTS

Most executive teams request frequent updates and revisions of the financial budget. These are referred to as rolling financial forecasts because the projection's planning horizon is usually well beyond the fiscal year-end date, such as out 18 months to 2 years. Imagine if you're a chief financial officer (CFO) or financial controller required to reprocess the budget as a rolling forecast quarterly (or even monthly). There are not enough cost center spreadsheets to do it! Only with computer automation that integrates several of the methods of the VBM framework, including good predictive analytics with forecasts of demand volume, can an organization produce valid derived rolling financial forecasts.

**MANAGING STRATEGY IS LEARNABLE**

Organizations with a formal strategy execution process dramatically outperform organizations without formal processes. Building a core competency in strategy execution creates a competitive advantage for commercial organizations and increases value for citizens and stakeholders of public sector government organizations. Managing strategy is learnable. It is important to include and protect planned spending for strategic and risk projects and initiatives in budgets and rolling financial forecasts. Those projects lead to long-term sustainable value creation.

This chapter has presented a dramatically new approach to resource planning and budgeting. The value added from this approach can be enormous in terms of the ability to secure adequate funding to deliver on performance targets, to manage resources, and to report to management. Even though the initial implementation effort is far from trivial, the payoffs in the medium- and long-term make it all worthwhile.

Chapter 14 will conclude the discussion on a practical way to implement a progressive management accounting system. It involves rapid prototyping with iterative remodeling to arrive at that permanent, reliable, and repeatable production system (referenced in Chapter 10) in just a few weeks, not months.

# CHAPTER FOURTEEN

# Implementing ABC/M with Rapid Prototyping

ABC/M RAPID PROTOTYPING FOLLOWED by iterative remodeling of each of ABC/M's prior model's results has been proven as a superior approach to successfully implementing and sustaining ABC/M systems. It is a way to overcome the temptation (and habit by accountants or consultants) to construct an ABC/M system that is too large, too complex, and too detailed prior to the organization's ability to absorb what ABC/M is all about and how it can work for the organization. ABC/M rapid prototyping is accomplished in just a few days as a workshop facilitated by a skilled ABC/M practitioner. It is also an effective way to drive out the natural fear and resistance to ABC/M through training and participation.

ABC/M rapid prototyping is effective because the organization is modeling their own organization's expenses and calculated costs, and not a fictitious one. Employees, managers, and executives relate to it because they recognize the people, processes, work, and outputs (e.g., services). People learn better through doing.

ABC/M rapid prototyping accelerates the organization's use of ABC/M information by relying on only a few key employees first to rapidly construct a high-level ABC/M model. The initial model is deliberately called Model 0 so as not to give the impression that its information is to be used for decisions. The purpose of Model 0 is to accelerate learning by the organization, gain buy-in, and begin considering what types of uses and decisions they will draw on the information from the eventual permanent and repeatable ABC/M system. View this as "start small but think big."

ABC/M rapid prototyping is an implementation approach where the initial ABC/M Model 0 is immediately followed with iterative remodeling of the same expenses and calculated costs included in the prior model, but deeper and with more resolution and visibility.

 **AFTER MODEL 0**

Once the initial ABC/M Model 0 has been constructed and the participants have a good grasp of what ABC/M is and does, then with the help of co-workers they all can selectively adjust the model to lower levels of detail and higher accuracy.

With the subsequent model iterations, additional employees from the local areas highlighted in the initial ABC/M model can revise and modify the initial effort. These employees are in a much better position to improve the prior iterative version of the ABC/M model because they are more knowledgeable about the work in their respective areas and their outputs.

The intent of ABC/M rapid prototyping is to make your mistakes quickly, up-front, and early in the process when it is easier to change the ABC/M model, not later when it is far more difficult. Through prototyping, organizations can build a working and useful ABC/M model in days as opposed to trying to build a Rolls-Royce ABC/M model in months. With this sped-up approach, the benefits from improvements gleaned from the ABC/M information can be reaped almost immediately. The initial ABC/M models can then graduate into a repeatable, reliable ABC/M system. This implementation approach is more practical and sensible than ABC/M pilots or one-shot, big bang ABC/M implementations where the implementers cross their fingers and pray that it will all work at the end.

Think of ABC/M rapid prototyping as "crawl, walk, run, and fly." Model 0 is the crawl. The subsequent iterations (Model 1, 2, etc.) are the walk. The eventual ABC/M "system" is the run. The "fly" is exploiting the possible uses of the ABC/M information as described earlier in prior chapters.

In the field of photography, you cannot presume that handing a camera to someone means that person knows how to take pictures. ABC/M rapid prototyping is similar to giving an organization a chance to snap some photos to see how they turn out.

**ABC/M IS PERFECTLY OBVIOUS – AFTER THE FACT!**

At first glance, the idea of implementing ABC/M can be overwhelming, and this perception might prevent an organization from even proceeding with implementing its system. Those unfamiliar with ABC/M share a general misconception that it involves a massive enterprise-wide involvement of people with a mudslide of data that must address activities in great detail from all parts of the organization.

Another misconception is that all employees will be tasked and required to complete daily or weekly timesheets reporting the time they worked on activities. Employees do not like timesheets. Some are fearful that managers and co-workers will know what they actually do and for how long. With ABC/M rapid prototyping, only a knowledgeable few managers are tasked with estimating the time for all of their co-workers.

Another misconception is that there will be no results until the ABC/M system is completely constructed and operating like a production information system. These people are unaware that ABC/M is an analytical tool that is best designed as a layer of reporting that sits on top of and apart from the transaction-intensive accounting and operations information systems.

An additional misconception about ABC/M is that it will take forever to implement and perhaps may not be worth the effort. With ABC/M rapid prototyping, an ABC/M system can be launched quickly and cheaply. By reducing the administrative effort but still raising awareness of the benefits, ABC/M rapid prototyping shifts the cost-versus-benefits evaluation from reluctance to higher levels of interest. These include a desire to move ahead with haste and a genuine motivation to finish the ABC/M model iterations so that a permanent and repeatable ABC/M reporting system can be installed and used.

 **ITERATIVE ABC/M MODELING**

Any issues related to source input data can be quickly flushed out. Figure 14.1 gives a sense for a succession of models plus some key benefits. Iterative ABC/M prototyping with expanding granularity and more detail (but same scope) accelerates learning about model design and cost behavior. The figure illustrates how the ABC/M models can eventually become the ABC/M system within a few weeks, not months as is often perceived.

### Rapid Prototyping with Iterative Remodeling
*(crawl, walk, run, fly)*

Each iteration enhances the use of the ABC system.

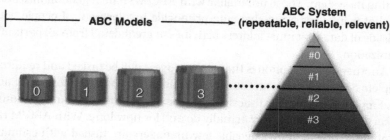

Make your mistakes early and often, not later when the system is too hard to change.

**FIGURE 14.1** Rapid prototyping with iterative remodeling. Source: Copyright 2019 www.garycokins.com.

---

ABC/M rapid prototyping is a valuable accelerated learning technique for a small but important number of employees and managers. Not only can these key participants, referred to as "functional representatives," get a solid vision of what their ABC/M system will look like, but they also start thinking about what they will do with the more robust ABC/M information when they get it.

Once an ABC/M model is designed, it becomes more obvious to the employees who constructed it, and there is agreement that the resulting costs are logical and defensible.

ABC/M rapid prototyping is effective because it starts where people already are – they know what their organization is doing. They also recognize that they do not understand their costs and that they mistrust their current cost information. ABC/M rapid prototyping gives them a chance to model their expense and cost structure. The enthusiasm for implementing ABC/M comes more easily after initial ABC/M models are completed, regardless of their size or scale. After the first ABC/M Model 0 is quickly completed, the participants can then see multiple views of their organization's costs – its resources, activities, processes, and outputs. They also realize how ABC/M information can collectively provide answers to questions they just could not fathom with the limited information provided by their existing cost accounting system.

## RAPID PROTOTYPING: EIGHTEEN HOLES OF GOLF ON A POLO HORSE

ABC/M rapid prototyping is a much faster way to get phased-learning, buy-in, and results compared with the traditional approach to designing an ABC/M system. Traditionally, full-fledged ABC/M system implementations have been accomplished through intensive interviewing of many employees. With ABC/M rapid prototyping, those few "functionable representatives" who are knowledgeable about the majority of what the organization does are brought together. They construct the first ABC/M Model 0 in just a couple of days with a trained facilitator and an ABC/M software specialist. The focus is far less on achieving accuracy or results and much more on learning and getting a vision.

The workshop begins the same way as a traditional proof-of-concept ABC/M pilot, by forming a cross-functional team of "functional representatives." After that, however, the similarities to a pilot end. All too often, ABC/M teams improperly build an ABC/M pilot too deep and too detailed, and they don't even realize it. They overengineer the ABC/M system design and resulting costing system, and then don't get the results they expected. It is death by details.

An ABC/M pilot takes a long time even though it is supposed to be brief. As a result, the organization can develop skepticism or lose interest since they conclude that no payback will be coming any time soon. The ABC/M effort may then go dormant. ABC/M projects never die. It is inevitable that ABC/M will be implemented. It may take a future catastrophe that jars an organization that stopped its earlier ABC/M project to admit that the current cost accounting system has either mislead them or left them clueless about their costs. When a major decision in hindsight is deemed a big mistake because the traditional costs were misleading, then the ABC/M system implementation gets restarted.

In contrast to pilots, which often are formally announced to employees with a loudly broadcast "banners-and-bugles" procession, ABC/M rapid prototype modeling is stealthier and less invasive. When senior management makes a major announcement that an ABC/M system will be installed, some employees only hear the "C" in ABC/M for the costing, and their defensive shields of fear and resistance go up. Employees may interpret the project as a cost-cutting exercise, perhaps terminating their jobs, rather than as a way to provide for better decision-making.

The purpose of the ABC/M rapid prototype is not to be secretive but rather for a select few employees – the "functional representatives" – within the organization to quickly gain some understanding. A key lesson learned is how to balance the tradeoff between higher accuracy and a greater effort to maintain the ABC/M system. Review Figure 10.7 that illustrated that there is a point of diminishing returns of higher cost accuracy for the extra administrative effort to collect, validate, calculate, and report the information.

The "functional representatives" learn a lot about the properties of ABC/M They also learn about some of the behavioral implications of how people might react when they see the ABC/M information. With ABC/M information, many employees will see things they have never seen before. It is important early on to learn how to treat the ABC/M information responsibly. ABC/M is not an accounting police tool to punish or embarrass people. It is more like a managerial information database and enabler for organizational improvement.

In contrast to ABC/M pilots that begin with collecting vast amounts of data through extensive interviews and questionnaires from many people, the initial ABC/M rapid prototyping is, as noted, conducted in a burst of a few of days.

Many adults learn better and more quickly through doing as opposed to listening to lectures about the concepts. So, the ABC/M model construction begins almost immediately. A key insight the team learns – and will share with their co-workers – is that incremental improvement is preferable to postponed perfection.

The "functional representatives" are always intellectually engaged in constructing the ABC/M prototype Model 0 since they are not modeling some fictitious case study organization; it is their own organization. The modeling also deals with and represents the people they know and work with, the things these co-workers do, and the outputs they provide to others. The participants are never bored during this fast-paced workshop. Simple rules are used to speed things up. For example, no one is allowed to bring in any data with them; the model is entirely constructed with what they already know. The only exception to this rule is for the financial data. Total expenses for the period being modeled, usually the current or past year, are a good starting point. Senior managers who will eventually see the ABC/M models will be able to relate to these total costs since they are already familiar with them. This also ensures that the initial ABC/M Model 0 will be complete and not mistakenly omit a function. No stones are left unturned.

 ## BUILDING THE FIRST ABC/M MODEL 0: TAP DANCE NOW, WALTZ LATER

The first step in building the initial ABC/M model is quite simple. The organization chart of employees and contractors, if applicable, is divided into groups of people who do similar things. These groups are often (but not always) the functional departments. This may result in 10 to15 groups. The key is to count and sum the number of employees from each group to ensure that no portion of the cost structure to be analyzed is inadvertently left out. When the entire organization is initially modeled, validating this completeness is no problem since the total number of employees tends to be a well-known number and can be reconciled to. Each functional representative takes responsibility for the groups of people he or she is most familiar with. Next, the functional representatives define three significant activities for each group they have selected to represent. Figure 14.2 shows an example of a time-effort worksheet that has been successfully used to collect the ABC/M information.

Within 20 minutes, each form for each group is completed. Simple rules can be applied when defining the activities. As examples, the work activities should follow a "verb-adjective-noun" grammar convention. Assume that people are productive only five hours of an eight-hour day and ignore the other three hours for work breaks and social time. (The three hours will later get baked into the five productive hours. Treatment of those hours is more of a work culture issue.) Instruct the "functional representatives" that the three activities should account for more than 90 percent of what the group does throughout the year. This rule

## Work Activity Input Form

**Example for sales function with 45 license processors**

Natural Work Group Name (e.g., sellers)          No. of employees

| Work Activity Description | % | Ideal Activity Cost Driver | Code | Example |
|---|---|---|---|---|
| 1. process license application | 45 | no. of license applic | C | |
| 2. resolve customer disputes | 35 | no. of customer disputes | C | |
| 3. create strategies | 20 | no. of planning sessions | D | |
| 4. | | no. of | | |

**100%**

Codes:
A = Suppliers
B = Products, Services
C = Customer Prospects
D = Business Infrastructure
E = Intermediate Assignments (to other activities)

**FIGURE 14.2** Work activity input form. Source: Copyright 2019 www.gary cokins.com.

forces each activity definition to be worded in what may appear to some as being too summarized for each group. But about 40 to 60 activities will likely result from all the input forms, which is more than adequate to trace the activity costs to cost objects with higher accuracy than their organization's traditional method can.

Use estimates for the employees' time-effort in increments of 5 percent. Discourage allocation of 80 percent or more to any one of the three activities; if the participant struggles with that, allow only that activity to be subdivided into two components, thus yielding four activities for that group but still summing to 100 percent. Do not allow these two specific activities: "supervise and mentor employees" and "attend meetings" (even though these activities occur). Excluding them will ensure that all the work activities will lend themselves to being traceable to cost objects.

Ignore salary and wage differentials. Simply use an average salary for every employee. In effect, the mail clerk earns the same salary as the executives in this first Model 0. In most cases, this assumption won't make a significant difference to the costs of outputs, service lines, and customers for purposes of this first model. ABC/M's property of error dampening will help bring about that result. In future model iterations, salary differentials for different departments can be considered.

Additional rules to speed up the process involve not allowing consensus among the "functional representatives" when it comes to defining the activity dictionary, the activity drivers, or the activity driver assignments, nor for estimating the quantities that flow through the activity drivers. Each functional representative knows his or her own area sufficiently and does not need any help from the others. Functional representatives "own" their area of coverage. Any estimating error on their part cannot have any grave consequence. The consequence of error is simultaneous overcosting and undercosting, but these minor errors offset and wash out anyway when the costs reassign to the cost objects. Regardless, the intent of this first ABC/M prototype model is not precision costing. It is stimulating for the participants and the ABC/M project team. What they will have at the end is an economical and low-risk technique to get to their eventual repeatable and reliable ABC/M production system.

 ## COST OBJECT PROFILING: A KEY TO GETTING DESIRED RESULTS

The use of preliminary estimates works well with ABC/M, as just described, because any estimating errors in the activity costs will offset when they are further traced (combined) into the outputs, service lines, customers, and service recipients. (The concept of offsetting error may be counterintuitive, particularly to accountants who are trained for high precision and perfection, but the properties of an ABC/M assignment network as a "closed" system make offsetting errors possible.) Error dampening works even better when no activity cost is too large relative to the other activity costs. This way any estimating error of any single activity cost cannot materially affect the cost of all the outputs. Error dampening also works better when the cost objects are deliberately predefined into look-alike groupings that already reflect the diversity and variation that ABC/M is so good at tracing into. The facilitator can ensure that well-segmented costs are easily accomplished by predefining the groupings to achieve this effect.

Like a caricature sketch artist at an amusement park, the facilitator leading the workshop is skilled at selecting just enough activities and cost objects to reasonably represent the organization without choosing so many that the ABC/M model goes too far past those diminishing returns in extra accuracy for the extra effort. The technique of predefining the groupings of final cost objects is accomplished through "profiling." In most cases the organization has already been referring to families of its products and service lines. The functional representatives realize that there may be dozens or hundreds of specific products and service lines within each family. Those subdivisions are already known and likely codified by their organization.

Cost object profiling is much more needed for the citizens, customers, and service recipients because the standard groupings that organizations use do not usually work well for ABC/M. For example, some organizations may segment their service recipients by demographic traits or geographic locations. But large differences in how service recipients consume the workload may have little to do with where these service recipients are physically located. Segmenting customers by demographic groups or by the levels of special attention required may be a much better segmentation to reflect more dominant ways in which workloads are disproportionately consumed. Some ABC/M teams refer to these customer groups as "clusters" or "centroids."

Figure 14.3 shows a worksheet that the facilitator uses to define multiple and various types of customer or service-recipient groupings. At a minimum, by selecting only three bases of difference, with only two extremes, the eight unique combinations (i.e., 2x2x2=8) are ensured to preset the diversity of any costs into these eight cost objects.

With profiled final cost objects and 30 or more work activities, no one activity being too large, the functional representatives are assured that they will trace to and calculate fairly reasonable costs in their first effort.

# Final Cost Object Customer Segmentation Profiling

**A key to initial ABC Rapid Prototyping to identify major sources of diversity.**

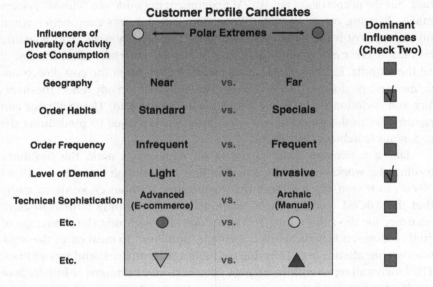

**FIGURE 14.3** Final cost object customer segmentation profiling. Source: Copyright 2019 www.garycokins.com.

---

 **TEACH THEM TO FISH, AND THEY CAN FISH ON THEIR OWN**

The construction of the ABC/M Model 0 is fairly straightforward. Each activity is traced to the cost objects that cause the activity levels to fluctuate up or down. This link ensures that a causal relationship exists, complying with costing's causality principle. Next, measurable activity drivers are identified for each activity, and finally activity driver quantities are estimated in total and for each cost object in relative proportions. Commercial ABC/M software does the rest by reassigning the costs through the linked cost assignment network into the final cost objects (refer back to Figure 11.2).

After the costs related to salary and fringe benefits have been totally assigned to the cost objects, distribution of the remaining resource expenditures goes quickly. The financial controller provides the top ten nonwage expense items in a way that they account for roughly 90 percent of the nonwage resource expenses. Nonwage expenses almost always follow the work, and each expense item usually traces into less than four of the many defined work activities. Sometimes the expense type is dedicated to only one activity. Since the ABC/M cost assignment network was already completed an hour before this workshop, all that needs to be done after these last resources are connected to activities is to recalculate the model. The nonwage-related costs trace all the way through into the final cost objects. The ABC/M model is then complete and ready for analysis.

The combination of using informed estimates by knowledgeable workers and the error-dampening property of the ABC/M assignment network has very significant implications. Together, these mean that using estimates in place of facts will have a minimal adverse impact on the accuracy of an ABC/M system's final cost objects. This also means that only a few key employees are initially needed to provide the data. Everyone is somewhat surprised that their organization can achieve ABC/M results without having to have all the data available from a subsystem to get started and see reasonable results. This revelation also ensures that ABC/M will get some traction as a way to improve the organization's performance rather than potentially stall out as a complicated information technology (IT) and systems project. The IT aspects of ABC/M come much later, well after a few users are already relying on the ABC/M information for making better decisions.

The ABC/M rapid prototyping experience is like a practice round in a sport without keeping score. By having those few "functional representatives" construct the initial ABC/m Model 0 from scratch, they much better understand what they have created. There is ownership. The results are sufficiently credible to them, despite the resulting calculated costs usually being quite different from their beliefs and from the standard costs provided by their existing accounting system. These traditional accounting costs will likely have been calculated based on flawed allocations and misguided thinking. ABC/M is very logical. Allocating costs using factors without any causal relationships is not.

 ## CONSTRUCTING AND POPULATING ABC/M MODEL 0: THE STARTING POINT

As previously mentioned, the initial ABC/M rapid prototype is named Model 0 to reinforce an understanding that Models 1, 2, and so on will be used as further refinements. An ABC/M cost assignment network is scalable. Revisit Figure 11.6, which illustrates how the ABC/M cross has scalable depth and can always be further disaggregated into lower levels of detail.

Groupings of resource expenses, work activities, types of outputs, and types of customers or service recipients should be subdivided (i.e., disaggregated) only if more segmentation achieves needed visibility or additional accuracy. The participants learn the ABC/M rule to always ask, "Is the higher climb worth the better view?" After ABC/M Model 0, the ABC/M project team can gather additional specific data when it becomes apparent that the accuracy of outputs is more sensitive to those specific data. They can then substitute the higher-grade data for the estimates. The project teams can also substitute a few different activity drivers as better drivers than the ones they initially and spontaneously selected and used.

Instead of presuming that detail is needed everywhere, ABC/M rapid prototyping deliberately starts at high levels and adds more detail selectively and only where it is justified. Sensitivity to error can always be tested by adding more detail to the existing ABC/M model. The team learns the properties of estimating error in an ABC/M cost assignment network. To some, particularly to accountants, the result is counterintuitive. The impact of estimating error for the activity costs means some are slightly overcosted while the others must be undercosted; there must be zero-sum error. But as the activity costs combine further down the network into the final cost objects, any error begins to offset. In ABC/M, error does not compound; it dampens out. As a result, higher levels of accuracy can be quickly achieved with minimal effort. Then much less additional accuracy comes from more effort.

In a few weeks the ABC/M iterative models graduate into the repeatable and reliable ABC/M production system that can be refreshed. With iterative remodeling, the ABC/M team learns to identify and include activity drivers as they are needed rather than to assume they are required.

Refreshing the ABC/M rapid prototype models or the ABC/M production system is done with a blend of updated measured data and estimates for the remaining and less vital areas of the ABC/M model. Of course, the financial ledger expenditure data, with its 100 percent resource data, should be a source. (Some organizations, however, have simply begun with the total expenses from their most recent run of their payroll.) The purpose of the initial rapidly prototyped models is not to pin down all the details right away, but rather to stimulate the participants. It gets them thinking, exchanging ideas, realizing how their current data are limiting or misleading, and most importantly envisioning how their organization may use the output data to address problems and make decisions.

ABC/M is basically a self-discovery experience. Even when a much larger ABC/M system is up and running, the ABC/M information does not necessarily provide final answers. It tells people where to look and what additional questions to ask. These early participants begin experiencing what ABC/M is and what it is not. They will likely become a much more effective means of informing their organization about ABC/M's benefits than the designated ABC/M project team or hired consultants (whom other employees may suspect have self-serving motives).

ABC/M rapid prototyping helps prevent "death by details." ABC/M project teams often have a problem determining the right level of detail, work activities, products, channels, and customers to focus on. There are pitfalls if an ABC/M system is designed using traditional IT development methodologies to solve this problem – the "ABC/M leveling problem." With IT methods, one of the work steps in the traditional schedule for the first few weeks is usually to perform the "data requirements definition." But this step is not appropriate for designing the ABC architecture. This is because there are too many interdependencies among ABC/M's resources, activities, and cost objects. There is interplay among the levels of detail, each affecting the ultimate accuracy of outputs to be costed.

The intent of the ABC/M rapid prototype is to get reasonably right results in a workable and timely fashion. Drilling too deep too soon is a trap that should be avoided. The extra benefits of a little more accuracy aren't worth the extra effort. Ironically, after Model 2 or so, the data requirements are a derivative of the ABC/M rapid prototyping workshop. Ideally Model 0 should be completed in two days so that the third and last day of the experience can be dedicated to playing with the model, analyzing the ABC/M information, and learning the principles and properties of ABC/M.

Perhaps the most important thing the ABC/M team can do on the last day of their workshop is to add a few attributes to the model. Two effective attributes are the level of importance and the level of performance. This lets the participants appreciate that their ABC/M system delivers much more visibility than just calculated cost amounts. They realize that attributes begin to suggest what general directions they should investigate. Where should they scale back on spending? Where should they invest more energy? What processes might they consider outsourcing? What activities, products, or customers should be promoted more?

 ## ANALYZING MODEL 0 TO GET BUY-IN

Finally, the ABC/M team can begin analyzing their model with the intent of evaluating the impact of specific changes. By adding volume and quantity data, the model quickly computes the unit costs for each product, service line, and any intermediate output such as the cost per equipment hour if that is relevant. As part of the unit cost calculation, ABC/M also reveals the per-unit cost of each contributing element, such as for each activity cost. Since unit-of-work output costs can substantially vary even for outputs with comparable total unit costs, the team can begin their own form of internal benchmarking to explore best practices.

Through this mock analysis, the team inevitably begins to test the feasibility of using the ABC/M information for some of the pressing issues their organization may be struggling with, such as estimating the costs of taking on certain types of orders from specific types of customers or service recipients. They can learn what options are available by examining the assumptions they initially made related to fixed and variable costs that they now have displayed. They can play with alternative ways to assign depreciation costs to equipment other than the traditional way the existing accounting system is assigning depreciation. And they can see costs without any depreciation, since depreciation is a sunk cost (not just a fixed cost), if they want to consider using a marginal cost rather than a fully absorbed cost in their analysis.

The "functional representatives" and the ABC/M team can get a glimpse of how much of their cost structure is organizationally sustaining relative to costs that make and deliver products or serve their customers and service recipients. That ratio may be shocking. The total sustaining costs may be greater than 30 percent of their cost structure, excluding purchased material costs. Is that good or bad? It probably depends on other factors. But at least they can see the amount and consider whether they want to maintain those same levels of spending on nonproduct, nonservice, and non-customer-related costs. The "functional representatives" can also discuss the concept of unused capacity management now that the cost information is structured in a format that makes more sense to them.

The point here is not to overanalyze anything. It is to get the participants to connect the data to uses of the information – and to connect some of those uses to some of the burning high-priority issues of the organization. This creates the needed buy-in to proceed with building the next ABC/M Model 1 and ABC/M in general.

 ## SECURING AND PROPAGATING THE LEARNING: A COMMUNICATION PLAN

A useful way to expand learning and simultaneously gain further buy-in is to immediately have the Model 0 participants make a brief unrehearsed presentation to specially selected peers, and perhaps an executive or two, covering the following points about their few days building Model 0:

- What did we do?
- What did we learn?
  - About our organization's expense and cost structure?
  - About the ABC/M methodology and ABC/M model properties?
- What are our options for next steps?

It is important that these invited guests also have their expectations well managed, just as the functional representatives' expectations were. The peer group needs to know that the ABC/M Model 0 structure they are observing is a miniature-scale model, and that the calculated costs were derived entirely from estimates (except for the starting annual financial expense totals). Fortunately, even in first ABC/M rapid prototype Model 0, the ABC/M properties begin to "pile up" the output costs in directionally accurate and roughly with the same relative amounts as will the subsequent larger-scale ABC/M Models 1, 2, and so on.

An important reason to conclude the first ABC/M rapid prototyping workshop by presenting to peers and some senior executives is for the ABC/M project team to much better appreciate that they really need two ABC/M plans: (1) an implementation plan, and (2) a communication plan. The second plan may well be more important than the first. These two types of plans will be further discussed in Chapter 16, "Organizational Change Management." ABC/M is about organizational and behavioral change management. Who is initially exposed to ABC/M and subsequently the sequence of who else is exposed are very relevant to successfully implement ABC/M. If naysayers or threatened managers who have clout are introduced too soon into the process, they can stop the project before ABC/M has a chance to take hold.

By generating some visible benefits with an initial group of positive-attitude employees, enthusiasm builds. Invariably, everyone will learn that costs are abstract and intangible. Costs measure the effects of the things that are placing demands on work. So, measuring and calculating costs is actually modeling to get a representation of how resource expenses are consumed and used. Resources are where the capacity to do work resides. By working with and iteratively refining ABC/M models, managers and employee teams find their knowledge growing. They begin to appreciate the ABC/M adage (which we previously referenced in Chapter 10) that "it is better to be approximately correct than precisely inaccurate!"

## TIME-PHASING ABC INTO ABM

With ABC/M rapid prototyping, after an organization understands how the diversity and variation of its outputs create its cost structure, it can much better understand how the same activity costs can be oriented to the time-based horizontal process view. This facilitates "process analysis."

Figure 14.4 indicates that organizations should first perform cost assignments vertically to discover how diversity and variation in outputs, products, service lines, citizens, and customers relate to complexity and thus to higher indirect support expenses. ABC/M rapid prototyping reinforces this lesson. (This was displayed in Figure 11.4.)

With ABC/M's vertical cost assignment view, the functional representatives can first examine the work activity costs on a per-unit cost of output basis. Comparisons can be made between and among identical work activities and their costs, on a per-unit-of-work basis, as well as for different kinds of outputs.

Some costing approaches, practiced when the business process reengineering (BPR) movement was at its high point of interest in the 1990s,

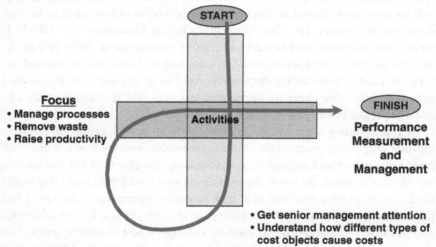

FIGURE 14.4   Time-phasing ABC into ABM. Source: Copyright 2019 www.gary cokins.com.

simply calculated a one-step cost allocation of the general ledger into activity costs – and stopped there. (This was displayed in Figure 11.5.) The activity costs were immediately applied as costs sequenced in time across the end-to-end processes. They lacked the emotional charge from also seeing the per-unit costs of the variety and mix of the outputs from those same business processes.

Some organizations have business process flowcharts on their conference room walls but have not committed to significantly changing their processes. When ABC/M information reveals the true per-unit cost of each output, including intermediate outputs, "organizational shock" often sets in. Then genuine "root-cause analysis" problem-solving begins. Fortunately, ABC/M provides reliable and fact-based information at an early point to assist the ABC/M project team and functional representatives. In short, the lesson is do ABC vertical assignment first, and perform process analysis afterwards.

Some organizations initially design highly disaggregated activity models with intent to reduce cost. By first reporting on the costs of outputs, senior management will be engaged and know where to focus.

##  HOW ABOUT THE FUTURE OF ABC/M?

It is an understatement to say that business, government, and commerce are swiftly changing. Why are incumbents losing ground to reinventors (i.e., those who can transform themselves)? Today one cannot move at the pace of evolution; this is disruptive revolution. One cannot just continue to follow the existing way of doing things but a little better. It must be much, much better.

Unfortunately, an overarching issue with ABC/M involves its perception as just another way to spin financial data rather than its use as mission-critical managerial information. The information age we find ourselves in can be mind-boggling. As technology advances, so will the demand to access massive amounts of relevant information. The organizations that survive will be those that can answer these questions:

- How do we access all these data?
- What do we do with the information?
- How do we shape the data and put them in a form with which we can work?
- What will happen when we apply technologies developed during the information age for the information age?

Clearly, as information technology evolves, governments will increase their levels of service and their effectiveness. Furthermore, as the needs of citizens and service recipients change, governments will run into global competitors, perhaps even other governments, that increasingly look to information and information technology for competitive advantage. ABC/M is involved in this broad arena of "outsmartmanship."

ABC/M puts the "management" back in management reporting. For those people who are involved with ABC/M projects, the key is to create and orchestrate change rather than merely react to it and attempt to make the best of a poor situation. It will be fun watching government move from the learning stages into mastery of building and using ABC/M systems.

This chapter concludes Part Five. We now move on to the final three chapters where the discussion is on information technology as an enabler to VBM, organizational and behavioral change management, and the authors' aspirations for the future of VBM.

# PART SIX

## VI

# How Information Technology Impacts VBM

# CHAPTER FIFTEEN

# Information Technology as an Enabler

N CHAPTER 2, WE DISCUSSED the "House of VBM," as described in Figure 2.6:

> The "Technology Enablers" involve information technology (IT) that supports the modeling and calculations used by ERM and the EPM methods (including resources and cost management).

## INFORMATION TECHNOLOGY TO ACHIEVE RESULTS

For the VBM framework with its EPM methods to work effectively, an organization must have information technology (IT) systems that can support them. Furthermore, in the context of performance, risk management, and resource and cost management, IT systems serve as enablers.

The EPM methods (the ellipse in "The Mechanism" in the "House of VBM" in Figure 2.6), contribute to the balancing of the three scales in Figure 2.1. As described in Chapter 5, the EPM methods are continuously interacting to balance and improve the three scales: the three Rs of results, resources, and risks. This is where decision-making occurs.

From a decision-making perspective, starting with accurate, reliable, and valid source data is key. An IT issue often involves low-quality input data, nick-named "dirty data." There are tools to clean data called "extraction, transform, and load (ETL)" that filter source data. For effective decision-making, remember this: in the absence of facts, anybody's opinion is a good one! And usually the biggest opinion wins, which is the opinion of one's supervisor or one's supervisor's supervisor. So, to the degree these senior managers are making decisions based on intuition, gut feel, flawed and misleading data, or office politics, their organization is at risk.

 ## DATA MANAGEMENT

Data is trustworthy and useful only if it is reliable and can be validated. Reliability implies consistency. For example, if one takes an action five times, one should get roughly the same results every time. Validity implies quality. A test is valid if it measures what it is supposed to measure. IT can provide reliable data, but its data also needs to be valid if one is to have any confidence in the resulting decision. IT systems provide such capabilities. A centralized system with data extraction, data cleansing, and data management capabilities appropriate to the decision at hand provides the type of reliability necessary for that confident decision-making.

Some organizations that have progressed down the VBM framework road find themselves in a laborious process of having to manually collect data, cal-culate measures, and refresh reports with new information. This can be very time-consuming and a poor use of resources. However, by automating these manual processes, work hours can be freed up so that employees can better use their time to focus on more strategic performance improvement activities.

Organizational leaders and management are empowered when they are armed with information relevant to a decision to be made. Pair a process for handling and managing the data with VBM enabled with EPM methods, and the result is information that is more accurate, reliable, valid, and current than ever before. Only when these methods are employed can performance measures – inputs, outputs, and outcomes – be calculated and automatically updated on a reliable and repeatable basis.

It is true that most agencies and their programs have many systems con-taining useful data that support their needs. However, for VBM to be success-ful, the ability to extract data from a variety of disparate operational systems, all while managing the process, is paramount. That leads to a need for data integration, ideally on a single integrated information platform.

Automated data extraction and data management are needed to effectively provide data-driven information. The automation capability allows reliable and valid information to be surfaced. Ultimately, this enables users to proactively manage their areas of responsibility. Performance reports, applications, dashboards, and balanced scorecards can show users at a glance where performance is today, not yesterday. This feedback provides information to inform managers on how well they are performing on what is relatively most important.

 ## BUSINESS INTELLIGENCE AND ANALYTICS

Once data is integrated, business intelligence (BI) and analytics are of critical value to assess and report on performance and cost. Analytics allows a manager to peel back the layers and get to the heart of the performance matter. A dashboard is "thin" if it provides only metrics and performance against targets; this just tells you where you are at a glance. When you ask, "*Why* are we performing at that level?" analytics and business intelligence come into play. A dashboard or scorecard is "deep" if it can provide:

- Business intelligence (BI) to drill down into data and reports to reveal causes of trends
- The ability not just to *look* at summarized data and records of information, but to *analyze* it as well

An example of drilling down with financial transactions is viewing line items of a purchase order.

Most business intelligence software offerings allow one to ascertain performance only historically, by using queries and reporting. This is shortsighted, especially in the context of performance management. The objective is not to just *monitor* the dials but to *move* the dials. Many in the IT community refer to BI, which is a term coined over a decade ago, to be about reporting. The higher stage of maturity is with analytics. A popular continuum for analytics comprises these four stages:

Descriptive → Diagnostic → Predictive → Prescriptive

The prescriptive stage is synonymous with optimization. For example, of all the what-if scenario options from the predictive stage, what is the *best* option, choice, or decision?

Today, performance, risk management, and cost management applications are easier to use and bring more value to the table than their rudimentary predecessors. Executives do not need to be technology-savvy, because the systems are intuitive and provide a wealth of information with a few clicks of the mouse (and eventually verbal speech recognition commands). In fact, information can also be within reach for the masses, because many applications are Web-enabled and allow access not just for a few key personnel, but for rather hundreds or thousands of people to access the system and use the information in their jobs. Imagine having access to information that gets everyone on the same page. Information technology supporting the VBM framework can enable communication, alignment, and focus because the supporting technology is scalable and available to the appropriate individuals in the organization.

Applying business intelligence (BI) and analytics software can be extremely valuable with improving performance, managing risk, and reducing expenses, or alternatively, getting more results with the same level of spending and level of risk exposure. Analytical techniques such as operational analytics, logistics, and predictive modeling can be used to enhance processes to make them as efficient and effective as possible.

Since analytics are based on algorithms, statistical models, and other types of modeling already developed by skilled and capable people, it can be helpful in recognizing substantial productivity improvements and potential cost savings if the proper data is available. For instance, analytics can predict future resource needs for planning and budgeting purposes. By using predictive analytic techniques such as "what-if" scenario analyses – which can calculate the mix of the level and types of resources, costs, and risks needed to realize results – then analytics can be used to develop models that predict likely outcomes given certain influencing factors, including resources and environmental conditions. Overall, the ability to understand and determine the various levels and types of resources required in relation to expected results enables organizations to prepare accordingly.

In Chapter 16 we will discuss the need to consider organizational change management issues required to pursue the full vision of the VBM framework. There are barriers that slow the adoption rate of VBM. Few of them involve information technology. Software tools are proven. The barriers are predominantly social ones, including resistance to change, which is human nature.

# Influencing Behavior for VBM

CHAPTER SIXTEEN

# Organizational Change Management

## CULTURAL RESISTANCE TO CHANGE

Chapter 2 stated:

> A major obstacle to adopting or successfully implementing
> performance improvement initiatives is cultural resistance to change.
> Another significant obstacle is that internal departments do not share
> information or collaborate. Combined, these two obstacles imply fear
> of being held accountable for results. A third obstacle is the executive
> team's policies and strategy are insufficiently communicated to their
> managers and employees.

**GREAT LEADERSHIP VERSUS GOOD MANAGEMENT**

As was described in Chapter 15, VBM requires information technology to deliver timely, valid, and reliable data on performance, costs, and risks to decision makers balancing considerations of results sought, resources allocated, and risks accepted. Data, technology, and the resulting management decision process thus all work together to deliver maximum stakeholder value. These methods and systems also enable good managers to become world-class leaders by ensuring that their organizations are focusing on the right things. As author Peter Drucker said, "Management is doing things right; leadership is doing the right things."

A result of not understanding the distinction between management and leadership is that most organizations are overmanaged and underled. Distinguishing between leadership and management is essential to successfully implementing VBM. What is the distinction? Management's role is to cope with the *complexity* of a government environment, so they become experts in mastering "red tape," organization charts, tools, and planning exercises. In contrast, leadership copes with constantly accelerating *change*. The leadership role is to set direction and answer: "Where do we want to go?" After this is answered, the leaders' skills are used to provide a vision, inspire employees, and empower. This facilitates the subordinate managers to answer the follow-up: "How will we get there?" Without leadership, especially in government, the full vision of VBM will not be realized.

Leaders should not be risk-adverse but rather must be risk managers. Leaders do not view organizational power and influence of change as being hierarchical in the organization chart but rather more on who can get things done. Leaders rely on vision and inspiring people. Both leaders and their subordinate managers are necessary for any government organization.

The role of a leader in the private sector is to define the organization's mission and strategy. In the public sector, the mission may be clear but the strategy and measurements of achievement often are not. The problem is that even when leaders have the ability to formulate a good strategy and policies, they are often frustrated by the failure to implement them successfully. In fact, for all the strategic plans written that promise to modernize government and make it more efficient, the majority of strategies are rarely realized. One reason may be the lack of a clear linkage between strategy and goal attainment. Another reason may be in communicating that strategy downward into the organization for execution by management. (This was discussed in Chapters 3 and 4.)

VBM is about organizational value management – strategically managing and improving an organization to accomplish its goals and objectives. The purpose of VBM is to make attaining the leadership team's strategy and policies everyone's job. As previously described earlier in this book, VBM balances the three scales in Figure 2.1: results (performance), resources (costs and capacity), and risk.

A driving force behind the value in VBM is that managers and employees are stymied in their decision-making. They are asked to increase service levels, improve process efficiencies, and achieve performance targets – all in an environment of flat or shrinking budgets and uncertain risks. Internal tension and conflict are natural in any organization because there will always be competing goals, but managers need the capabilities to evaluate trade-offs and analyze more deeply. VBM provides these capabilities.

VBM encompasses the processes, metrics, software tools, and systems that help manage and improve an organization's delivery of stakeholder value. As it relates to government, VBM involves improving the performance of an entire agency or unit within an agency. By leveraging EPM methods VBM then increases value, including managing the performance of contractors, programs, and functional areas such as IT, finance/budget, personnel, supply chain, and procurement.

 ## HOW TO ACCELERATE THE ADOPTION RATE OF VBM

Technology is not an impediment to adopting VBM, as software capabilities are proven. The barriers involve resistance to change and unfamiliarity. These are social, behavioral, and cultural issues, and few managers are trained in behavioral change management. What is involved with these barriers, and how can managers overcome resistance and get organizational buy-in? Organizations that achieve competency with VBM are able to sustain their long-term viability.

What the authors have learned through observation during their careers is that passion along with curiosity drives discovery. Passion is the mysterious force behind nearly every step-change in a process or introduction of a new idea.

## THE QUEST TO GET BUY-IN FOR IDEAS

It is not sufficient for this book to explain only the "how-to" for implementing VBM. What is needed beyond explaining the "how-to" is to also explain the "why" of VBM implementation, including the benefits from VBM.

Numerous studies have consistently shown that the majority of major change initiatives fail to fully achieve their intended objectives. There is nothing to suggest an implementation of VBM will be any more likely to succeed if the challenges of organizational behavioral change are not considered and addressed.

 ## WHAT ARE BARRIERS THAT SLOW THE ADOPTION OF NEW IDEAS LIKE VBM?

Barriers that impede the adoption rate of new ideas, like VBM, are removable. As mentioned in Chapter 15, *technical barriers* such as disparate data sources or "dirty" data now have software solutions like extraction, transform, and load (ETL). With a little effort, problems like insufficient data are also not insurmountable. We also now realize that *modeling design deficiency barriers*, such as not selecting good key performance indicators (KPIs), can be knocked down with experienced consultants or better training courses. Other barriers are misperceptions that VBM is too complex or initial failures with prior pilot projects. But these are not showstoppers, and they, too, can be overcome.

What type of barrier continues to primarily obstruct the adoption rate of VBM? That barrier category is *social, behavioral, and cultural*. These obstacles include people's natural resistance to change; fear of knowing the truth (or others knowing the truth); reluctance to share data or information; and "we don't do that here." Never underestimate the magnitude of resistance to change. Only babies like change – of their diapers! It is natural for people to love the *status quo*.

An example of this social and arguably political barrier is a conflict between the IT function and managers – a brick wall. There will need to be a shift from face-to-face adversarial confrontation to a side-by-side collaborative relationship to remove this wall. Part of the problem is how IT and managers view each other.

Managers often view IT as an obstructionist and uncooperative gatekeeper of data without the skills to convert that data into useful information. Experienced managers want easy and flexible access to the data and the ability to manipulate it. They want a set of capabilities for investigation and discovery. IT typically tries to prevent this. Managers view IT as bureaucrats who manage a set of technologies and whose main goal is to keep the lights on.

In contrast, IT increasingly views managers as competitors who may solve problems but don't have to operate and maintain the IT systems. And IT sees managers as a risky group that has low regard for data governance and security.

Managers need speed and agility to be reactive and proactive, which requires them to be closer to the data for analysis and better decision-making. Both IT and the managers that they support will need to collaborate and compromise by better understanding and appreciating each other's changing roles.

## REMOVAL OF THE BARRIERS

A problem with removing behavioral barriers to deploy VBM is that few managers have training or experience as organizational change management specialists. They are not sociologists or psychologists. However, effective managers are learning to become like them. The need for the "why-to" and its motivating effects on organizations should ideally be an obsession for advocates of VBM. The challenge is how to alter people's attitudes.

## EARLY ADOPTERS AND LAGGARDS

Another barrier involves organizations that are too distracted with problems and prefer to search for quick fixes. The urgent crowds out the important. They do not take the time to solve problems with a better way. In our personal lives, many of us have no problem making everyday decisions, such as whether to purchase a smart phone or join a social network. How can we as individuals make decisions so quickly while organizations often struggle and are slow to react?

The field of marketing scientifically examines influences on the rate of adoption of products, services, and technology. Everett Rogers, a business researcher, developed his diffusion of innovations model with five categories of adoption: innovators, early adopters, early majority, late majority, and laggards. Which category best describes many organizations with respect to implementing VBM? This book's authors believe that most fall in the laggards' category.

Innovators and early adopters quickly move forward because either they are having financial difficulties needing new solutions or they are very progressive and driven to continuously seek a competitive edge. On the other hand, the late majority and laggard organizations are either risk averse with the resistance to change previously mentioned, or they have weak leadership with little vision.

This book's authors believe there is another possible explanation for the laggards: they are too distracted. There is no doubt that increasing volatility is part of the problem. Examples include changes in political ideologies, geo-politics, the internet, global communications, and social networks. VBM can be adopted by late majority and laggard organizations, regardless of volatility with proven methods and techniques, such as with pilot projects and rapid pro-totyping models for a proof of concept.

Organizations that want to move beyond the laggard category must take on the mentality of the early adopters, who understand the importance of VBM to enhance decision-making and align employee behavior and priorities to execute the executive team's strategy. They must be proactive, not just reactive. Most importantly, remember that it's never too late to go from being in the middle of the pack to taking a commanding lead.

 ## WHERE TO BEGIN?

In 2000, a *Harvard Business Review* article titled "Cracking the Code of Change"[1] by Nitin Nohria and Michael Beer proposed two theories of change, which they named Theory E and Theory O. Theory E was change based on economic value, which they defined as focused on providing greatest shareholder value. Theory O was focused on increasing organizational capability. They asserted that both theories were valid models for achieving at least some of management's goals, but they imposed costs that were often unrecognized. They went on to state:

> Theory E change strategies are the ones that make all the headlines. In this "hard" approach to change, shareholder value is the only legitimate measure of corporate success. Change usually involves heavy use of economic incentives, drastic layoffs, downsizing, and restructuring.

In contrast, Theory O change revolves around the capability of the organi-zation to learn and change the organizational culture, both as individuals and as

---

[1] Nitin Nohria and Michael Beer, "Creating the Code of Change," *Harvard Business Review*, May–June 2000.

a group. This contrasts with Theory E in which the human aspect is not greatly considered. It was noted that "E change strategies are more common than O change strategies among companies in the United States, where financial markets push corporate boards for rapid turnarounds." They similarly noted that O change strategies are more common in European and Asian companies. As the authors previously proposed in Chapter 2, the goal of any organization should not be exclusively focused on achieving intended results while ignoring growth in capabilities, or focused on growing capabilities while ignoring end results. Both are required for ultimate success in maximizing opportunities for increased value, and alignment of organizational capability with maximizing overall stakeholder value is a core tenant of VBM. This is why in Chapter 3 we discussed the need to interactively engage between organizational levels during the planning process so that stakeholder requirements could inform organizational capability requirements, and organizational capabilities could help establish reasonable stakeholder expectation. As a result, an approach to organization change management that incorporates this top-down, bottom-up alignment process is essential.

 ## HOW TO MOVE FORWARD?

In 1997, one of the authors – Doug Webster – created a model for change management, referred to as UMTI, that was based on the following four steps:

**Step 1. Understanding.** Seeking to change an organization – and the individuals that make up that organization – begins with developing understanding of the need for change. This is a logical, problem-based analysis of why the current mode of operations or actions is not adequately meeting the needs of the current or future organization.

**Step 2. Motivation.** Once individuals intellectually understand the organization's need for change, they must be motivated to engage in the change. This begins to get to the proverbial challenge of "What's in it for me?" (WIIFM). Besides understanding why the overall organization may need to change, successful change always requires a critical mass of individuals who are motivated to support the needed change.

**Step 3. Tools.** This refers to enabling a motivated individual to actively support the change. This could, for example, include training or other actions or activities to enable a motivated individual actually to participate in and contribute to the needed change.

**Step 4. Incentives.** If the change is to be sustained, new desired behaviors must be rewarded, and old undesired behaviors must be discouraged. Without changing organizational incentives, continued acceptance of old practices may well lead to the organization as a whole defaulting back to old, undesired practices.

As a means of more easily remembering these four critical steps of organizational change management, the creator began referring to them as the "Head" (understanding), "Heart" (motivation), "Hands" (tools), and "Feet" (incentives to sustain the journey) of organization behavioral change.

In 2003, Jeff Hiatt – founder of Prosci – introduced an almost identical change management model known by the acronym ADKAR. The similarity to the author's change management model is evident from this table.

| Webster | Hiatt |
|---|---|
| Understanding (Head) | Awareness |
| Motivation (Heart) | Desire |
| Tools (Hands) | Knowledge |
| Tools (Hands) | Abilities |
| Incentives (Feet) | Reinforcement |

Regardless whether you use one of these or another model of change management – and many exist in the literature – it is important that you carefully consider your organizational behavioral change management program.

In 2009 the book *Chasing Change*,[2] co-authored by Doug Webster, offered the process flow roadmap shown in Figure 16.1 to illustrate a high-level project plan for the organizational behavioral change process. It is important to understand that, while this process flow is depicted as linear, it does not necessarily have to be. Depending upon the demands put on the organization by internal and external environmental factors, some of the activities may need to be revisited, or executed in parallel. The overriding characteristic of this process flow should be its dynamic flexibility, and it should not be viewed purely as a set of prescriptive steps to follow. It should be customized and viewed in light of the needs of the organization.

It should be noted that the organizational areas and behaviors most in need of cultural change can vary from organization to organization, and from

---

[2] Bob Thames and Douglas Webster, *Chasing Change: Building Organizational Capacity in a Turbulent Environment* (John Wiley & Sons, 2008).

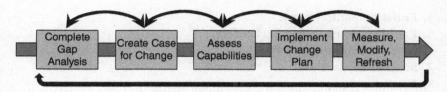

**FIGURE 16.1** The closed loop change process. Source: Bob Thames and Douglas Webster, *Chasing Change: Building Organizational Capacity in a Turbulent Environment* (John Wiley & Sons, 2009). Used with permission.

change initiative to change initiative. It is thus important to understand the nature of the change needed. To understand where the organization needs to change to be successful in the future is the purpose of the "Complete Gap Analysis" step in the preceding flow diagram. Once the organization understands where it needs to head for future success and the implications for organizational behavioral change that may be required, change initiators need to "create a case for change." While this need for change may be obvious to those who initiated the proposal, that need may not be so obvious to those on whom success for the change will depend. Establishing such a need for change is thus critical for Doug Webster's "Understanding" and "Motivation" steps, or for Jeff Hiatt's "Awareness" and "Understanding" steps.

The book *Chasing Change* also made the case for targeting organizational behavioral change efforts to where they will make the most important contributions. This is the purpose of the "Assess Capabilities" step. The authors of *Chasing Change* argued that organizations should tailor their change initiatives to their particular organization by understanding the gaps between existing behavior and needed behavior. While that book offered a framework with 13 different dimensions of change, the point for the reader is that careful thought should be given to the specific types of behavioral change required for success. Is there greater need for collaboration, transparency, accountability, trust, forward thinking, and so on? All organizations seek not to face the same gaps in required organizational behavior, so thought must be given to where such change should be specifically targeted.

One of the best-known experts in organizational change management is John Kotter, who offers a somewhat different perspective on change management. That perspective is not incompatible with the above, but is simply another way of considering the challenge of change. His eight-step model is:

1. **Create** a sense of urgency.
2. **Build** a guiding coalition.
3. **Form** a strategic vision and initiatives.

4. **Enlist** a volunteer army.
5. **Enable** action by removing barriers.
6. **Generate** short-term wins.
7. **Sustain** acceleration.
8. **Institute** change.

Both the Kotter and Webster/Hiatt models are valid and valuable, and should not be viewed as replacements for one another. Whichever model or models are used, the important point is that organizational change management is a critical element for success. Numerous studies have shown that up to 70 percent of change initiatives fail to meet expectations, and the single most important contributor to such failure is a lack of adequate organizational change management. The technical aspects of understanding and implementing value-based management are much more straightforward than the organizational change challenges that are likely to result. An organization that is prepared to recognize and overcome these challenges as they arise will be far more likely to achieve success with VBM.

 **MOVING FORWARD**

The authors have sought to make the case for a broader perspective on what defines a successful organization, and how to achieve and maximize that success. Success as envisioned in this book is not about simply improving performance, reducing cost, minimizing risk, or even having the happiest workforce. It is instead about how to integrate these and other considerations in a manner that maximizes overall value in the eyes of the various stakeholders. Recognizing that different stakeholders can seek different outcomes from the same organization, such a statement is on its face challenging. However, considering the variety of stakeholder interests as a portfolio of interests, and seeking to maximize the overall value of that portfolio, is the intent of VBM.

This chapter has sought to introduce the role of the "soft side" of that change in terms of the organizational culture. Let us now literally turn the page to consider what the future may hold in VBM, particularly for the public sector, in the next and final chapter.

# PART EIGHT

## VIII

# The Future

# CHAPTER SEVENTEEN

# The Future of Public Sector VBM

A S YOU NEAR THE end of this book, the authors hope that you have seen potential value for your organization in what has been presented. However, a question that likely comes to mind is what might be the future of the VBM concept as applied to the public sector in general? Answering such a question of course requires forecasting the future – always a challenging process. However, two factors to consider in such prognostication are: (1) What has been the progress of related concepts in recent history, and (2) to what extent can we expect the future environment to place further demands on organizations for VBM and associated concepts? In other words, does past progress in management practices point to a future for the application of VBM concepts, and does the foreseeable future of public sector needs increase or decrease the need for a concept like VBM?

 **A POTENTIAL FUTURE FOR VBM**

To consider the first question, it is obvious that there has been a steady stream of advancing thought focused on making organizational management processes more effective and efficient since at least the time of Frederick Winslow Taylor, the "father of scientific management," in the late 1800s. Concepts and practices such as strategic planning, quality management, organizational change management, cost-benefit analysis, activity-based costing, value-chain analysis, benchmarking, and countless others are the products of twentieth-century management thinkers.

The specific management challenges for the public sector were also recognized in the twentieth century, resulting in many commissions and studies over the years. However, a major contribution to the government management literature was the book *Reinventing Government: How the Entrepreneurial Spirit Is Transforming the Public Sector* by Rancho Cordova, California, city manager Ted Gaebler and journalist David Osborne, in 1992. The book clearly had an impact: President Bill Clinton, less than two months after taking office in 1993, announced his intent to "reinvent government," stating, "Our goal is to make the entire federal government less expensive and more efficient, and to change the culture of our national bureaucracy away from complacency and entitlement toward initiative and empowerment."

The National Partnership for Reinventing Government was created on March 3, 1993, and placed under the leadership of Vice President Al Gore. Reform efforts did not end with the Clinton administration, as President George W. Bush announced the President's Management Agenda (PMA) initiative in 2001. Every US administration since has carried on with its own version of the PMA.

It certainly does not appear that efforts to advance management practices in the public sector have in any way slowed. Value-based management is one potential step forward in the ongoing march to more effective management practices.

If value-based management can be viewed as filling a void in existing management practices in general, then the second question is, Will there be a demand for such a capability, particularly in the public sector? To provide a meaningful response to this question, we need to consider current and projected changes to demands being placed on the public sector.

A starting observation may be that the level of trust in government is not static. It is dynamic and constantly shifting in response to current events. However, the annual Edelman Trust Barometer Global Report[1] indicated that citizens place little trust in many of the world's governments. In a 2017 report by the Pew Center, public trust in the US government was near an all-time low.[2]

---

[1] https://www.edelman.com/sites/g/files/aatuss191/files/2019-03/2019_Edelman_Trust_Barometer_Global_Report.pdf?utm_source=website&utm_medium=global_report&utm_campaign=downloads

[2] https://www.people-press.org/2017/12/14/public-trust-in-government-1958-2017/

The authors suggest that VBM can contribute to increased trust and improved use of limited taxpayer funds in two ways. First, VBM can optimize the use of limited public funding by identifying and delivering most cost effectively what is considered of greatest value by the relevant set of stakeholders. Second, VBM can contribute to the transparency needed to build and retain trust by citizens and taxpayers. While management practices alone are certainly not a solution to regaining such trust, an improved understanding of what stakeholders value, along with an improved ability to deliver that value, cannot help but contribute to improved public satisfaction and trust.

##  MOVING FORWARD

VBM represents a logical next step in the evolution of modern management practices, and a strong case for the usefulness of VBM in meeting citizen needs can be made. However, one important question remains: Will public sector organizations implement the necessary changes? A meaningful answer to this question requires consideration of the change management implications. Let's use the change management model introduced in the prior chapter to do so.

The change management model represented by the "head, heart, hands, and feet" of change proposed that organizations need to: (1) understand the need for change, (2) be motivated to implement the change, (3) acquire the knowledge and skills needed to implement the change, and (4) provide the incentives needed to maintain the change and not regress to former behaviors.

The authors have sought to make the case for change in this book. Evidence on the need for change surrounds us on a daily basis given the challenges facing the public sector. However, evidence – and the importance and relevance of that evidence – is often "in the eye of the beholder." By this we mean that indisputable evidence of certain conditions or observations can be presented to different individuals, who in turn arrive at differing and conflicting interpretations and decisions. Consider any decision made by a senior public official, for example, and one can quickly identify individuals or groups who find the decision flawed. Such disagreements can of course be traced to inadequate consideration of the needed steps for change, or the consequences of change. However, in many cases, the problem is not that a decision was inadequately considered and/or communicated. Instead, it is that the personal values held by the individuals evaluating the decision or proposed action differ.

For example, any controversial proposal has supporters and detractors. Consider the debates between environmentalists and commercial for-profit businesses. In some cases, the differences in opinions may be a disagreement about the underlying facts. However, even when agreement is reached on the set of relevant facts, different individuals and groups will apply differing value systems to the decision process. There is thus constant debate between political parties in any government, whether at the national, state, or local level. This debate often comes down to how different groups and individuals differently value the tradeoffs involved in proposed actions, even when the underlying facts are in agreement. This means that, as related to VBM, gaining acceptance of the need to maximize value may be readily achieved, but defining what constitutes such value may be much more challenging.

Implementation of VBM will thus not eliminate disagreement on proposed courses of action. It will, however, allow the proponent of an action to: (1) better make the case of how a proposal offers value to various stakeholders, and (2) deliver that value once the course of action is selected. VBM can make the case that governments are limited by resources and that choices for optimizing value must be made. As we wrote earlier in this book, governments have enough money to do anything but not to do everything. Citizens can relate to this message because it reflects tradeoff decisions they need to make in daily life. Once a decision is made on the set of products and services that deliver maximum combined stakeholder value, VBM lays out the road map to deliver on that value proposition. In summary, VBM allows identification of that set of current and proposed products and services that offer overall maximum portfolio value, and then management of the actions needed to deliver that value.

 ## A FINAL THOUGHT

Few of us were alive when governments were truly tested to make difficult choices, such as during World War II. Citizens may have understood that sacrifices needed to be made. How willing will citizens be to make sacrifices today? Imagine at the extreme an immense earthquake taking a major metropolitan city down to near rubble or an asteroid hitting a heavily populated area. Choices will need to be made. Should they be knee-jerk reactions with minimal thought, or choices based on near real-time but systematic decision-making methods? VBM facilitates making decisions, whether this involves extreme catastrophic conditions or simply trade-off analysis that prioritizes the best ways forward for stakeholders.

The public sector is a particularly challenging environment, because there is seldom an approach or set of actions that will satisfy all stakeholders. Balance and prioritization are key to understanding the optimal set of strategic policies, goals, and objectives to be pursued by any public sector organization. However, once that direction is set, understanding the needed balance of results sought, resources and budget allocated, and risks accepted across the portfolio of products and services to be delivered is key to maximizing the delivery of value to stakeholders. VBM will help guide such challenging but critical efforts as leaders and their organizations move forward on behalf of public interests. The authors wish you well on this journey!

# Index

Page references followed by f and t indicate an illustrated figures and tables.